African American Genealogy

African American Genealogy

A Bibliography and Guide to Sources

Curt Bryan Witcher

ROUND
TOWER
BOOKS

FORT WAYNE INDIANA 2000

HALF HOLLOW HILLS
COMMUNITY LIBRARY

Published by: ROUND TOWER BOOKS
P.O. Box 12407
Fort Wayne IN 46863-2407

© 2000 Curt Bryan Witcher

Cover photograph: Ben Berry (born 1868) and his sister Lucy Jane Berry Minisee (born 1871) with her children. Isaac Berry, their father, was a runaway slave who fled to Canada and later settled in Michigan. *(courtesy State Archives of Michigan)*

Publisher's Cataloging in Publication Data

Witcher, Curt Bryan.
    African American genealogy : a bibliography and guide to sources / Curt Bryan Witcher.

ISBN: 0-9643925-3-4

    1. Afro-Americans - Genealogy - Bibliography.
2. Afro-Americans - Genealogy - Handbooks, manuals, etc.
I. Title.
Z1361.N39 W771 2000   973.0496 073

Printed in the United States of America
by Sheridan Books

... for my family,

those who came before, those present, and those yet to come,

always ...

. . . to Dancing Eyes . . .

CONTENTS

Preface	9
Introduction	13
General Sources	31
Alabama	68
Arizona	73
Arkansas	73
California	75
Colorado	77
Connecticut	78
Delaware	78
District of Columbia	79
Florida	81
Georgia	85
Illinois	92
Indiana	94
Iowa	99
Kansas	99
Kentucky	100
Louisiana	103
Maine	114
Maryland	115
Massachusetts	120
Michigan	122
Minnesota	123
Mississippi	123
Missouri	130
Nebraska	132
Nevada	133
New Hampshire	133
New Jersey	133
New Mexico	134
New York	135
North Carolina	138
North Dakota	156

Ohio	156
Oklahoma	159
Oregon	160
Pennsylvania	161
Rhode Island	164
South Carolina	166
Tennessee	180
Texas	184
Vermont	187
Virginia	188
Washington	211
West Virginia	211
Wisconsin	212
Bahama Islands	212
Canada	213
Caribbean	216
Cuba	216
Grenada	216
Jamaica	216
Liberia	217

PREFACE

This publication is based on the extensive collections of the Allen County Public Library's Historical Genealogy Department. For forty years, this family history research center has been committed to service excellence in the genealogical field. A special credit is due the department's librarians, whose continuing efforts as conscientious bibliographers and extremely knowledgeable information professionals ensure both the growth and accessibility of these collections.

The introductory material in this work is intended to provide the beginning African American family historian with a basic guide to conducting this exciting and rewarding work. Research strategies and methodologies are outlined, and particularly significant record groups are highlighted. Reproductions of documents typically encountered are used to illustrate this introductory guide to sources.

The lengthy bibliography which comprises the bulk of this book is arranged in a standard format. Following the author, title, and publication information for each item is additional descriptive data intended to assist the researcher in appraising the utility of the work for further investigation. Each entry is concluded with an Allen County Public Library call number or location identifier. As the Historical Genealogy Department uses a modified Dewey Decimal numbering scheme, these call numbers will typically have limited applicability outside the research collection in Fort Wayne.

The bibliography's first section, called "General Sources," cites works that do not have a specific geographic focus. Many outstanding resources useful for exploring the historical context of African American life in North America can be found here. This general section is followed by lists of sources for each state, and then by citations pertaining to Canada, several Caribbean countries, and Liberia. In each section, entries are arranged alphabetically by author, or by title when no author is given.

Under many states, there is a source entitled *Records of Ante-Bellum Southern Plantations from the Revolution through the Civil War*. This publication consists of microfilmed copies of numerous plantation records found in the special collections of universities and southern archives. Because so much valuable data is contained on this microfilm, the citations under each state are arranged to assist the researcher in more quickly identifying pertinent information. The journals, diaries, and other plantation manuscripts that deal in a general way with the entire state are listed first, followed by the county specific records. Each entry lists the individual, family, business, or government entity that created the records followed by the inclusive dates and the series, part, and roll numbers.

Periodical articles are not generally cited; rather, the periodicals themselves are listed in the appropriate geographic section. The exceptions to this are articles that I found particularly worthy of note. Web sites are not included aside from those few mentioned in the introduction.

What I hope the researcher will find are many valuable and previously undiscovered items among the sources listed here. It would be worthwhile to study the many items in the "General Sources" section as well as all the materials under the specific geographic area of interest. It is the aspiration of this author that the work in hand will provide both the sources and the ideas to promote your own research success.

Martin Luther King, Jr.'s father is listed on this 1900 federal census record of Clayton Co., Georgia (Enumeration District 10, sheet 20) as Jim King's two year old son, Mike. Through family sources we learn that Mike vowed at his father's deathbed to change his name legally to Martin Luther in honor of his father's two brothers.

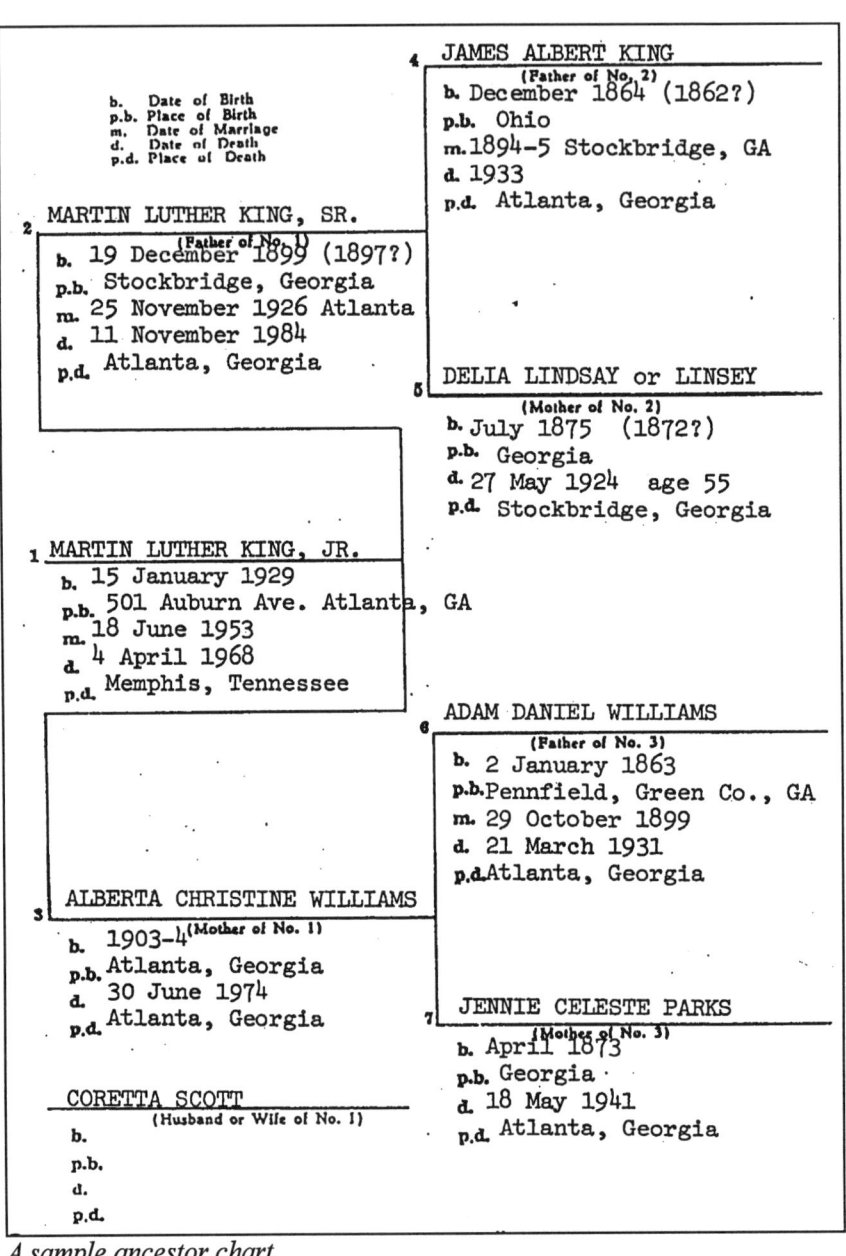

A sample ancestor chart.

INTRODUCTION

African Americans continue to explore the histories of their families in great numbers. The quest to identify by name and to know something of the lives of your ancestors may be the most challenging and rewarding work you will ever do. The following brief research guide and extensive bibliography of sources should help you succeed in your quest.

Family Sources

In the beginning stages of any genealogical endeavor, it is important to contact *all* living relatives for any information they might be able to provide about the family. Parents, grandparents, aunts, uncles, and cousins can all provide useful details about previous generations. In addition to the personal names, dates, and places of birth, marriage, and death you will want to collect, ask them about occupations, religious affiliations, military service and educational background. Remember to check for family Bibles, scrapbooks, baby books, diaries, memorial cards, certificates and photographs they may have available at home. Care should also be taken to collect and preserve the stories and anecdotal information that will add interest to your family history and provide vital clues for future genealogical investigations.

In the process of gathering all this family data and oral history, you will likely discover a number of contradictory "facts." For example, you may discover two slightly different death dates for a great-grandparent, or find two different small towns given as the birth place for a grandmother. Don't let these discrepancies hinder the data gathering process or lead you to pre-judge the accuracy of a particular item. Instead, be sure to note the source of each piece of information you gather so that more informed decisions about what is correct and accurate may be made further along in the research process.

Once your beginning information has been gleaned from family sources, arrange the basic data on ancestor charts and family group sheets in generational or chronological order. This organizational step is key in

MISS MURRAY B. ATKINS.
Assistant Epistoleus, Alpha Kappa Alpha Sorority.
Butler College, A. B. 1920.
Kappa Chapter.

Miss Atkins received her college training at Butler College. She was playground instructor during the summer of 1919 and is now teaching in the public schools of Indianapolis.

Miss Nelie M. Quander, a charter member of the A. K. A. Sorority, first president of the Boule, and at the present time Eastern Organizer received her A. B. degree from Howard University, and her M. A. degree from Columbia University.

In 1916 she was sent by the Children's Bureau to Delaware to make a study of the economic an social conditions affecting feebleminded children in that state. During the summer of 1918, she was sent by the Woman's War Work Council to Detroit to make a survey of social and economic conditions affecting women in industry.

Miss Quander is now a teacher in the Shaw Junior High School in Washington, D. C. and she stands for the highest in American womanhood.

MISS NELLIE M. QUANDER.
Founder and Incorporator,
Eastern Organizer, Alpha Kappa Alpha Sorority.
M. A. Columbia University.

MRS. PAULINE KIGH REED.
Central and Western Organizer,
Alpha Kappa Alpha Sorority.
Wilberforce University, B. S., 1917.
Zeta Chapter.

Mrs. Reed was previously a teacher in the Lincoln High School of Sedalia, Missouri, and was recently Registrar at Wilberforce University. She became Mrs. Chester A. Reed on April 18, 1921.

Significant biographical data fills this page from the first issue of the sorority publication, **Ivy Leaf,** *in December of 1921.*

preparing to use the wide variety of historical records available in libraries and archives. How well you organize and document information gleaned from family sources will directly impact how successful you will be in initially using basic records.

Basic Sources and Methods

Tracing an African American family history involves many of the same sources and methods used in tracing any other family histories in the post-Civil War period. Vital records of birth, marriage, and death, census records, county histories, military records, church records, and various other sources can all be used to extend family lines from the present back to 1865. As in other genealogical research, success requires careful attention to detail as well as the identification and thorough evaluation of *all* evidence related to the family being studied.

In addition, the genealogist must understand that racial discrimination impacted record keeping so that much information pertaining to African Americans was segregated from the main body of official records both north and south of the Mason-Dixon line. Certain age-old myths and assumptions must also be discarded to avoid hampering your research efforts. All African Americans were *not* enslaved prior to the Civil War; most slaves did *not* live on large plantations; and all African Americans did *not* take the surnames of their owners.

Historical Context

A worthwhile exercise in investigating any family history is to explore in some depth the history of the area in which the family lived. Knowing who settled in which neighborhoods and being able to identify local churches, schools, businesses, and other organizations will not only help you understand your ancestors but may also lead you to specific records.

Town, county, and state histories can all assist you in conducting a thorough area study. One exemplary state publication is entitled ***Peopling Indiana: The Ethnic Experience*** (Indianapolis, IN:

Coretta Scott King's ancestors appear on this 1900 federal census record of Perry County, Alabama (Enumeration District 75, sheet 7). The entries demonstrate the fact that extended families often lived in close proximity to each other, making it critical for the thorough researcher to explore an entire township or precinct in the census once a known ancestor has been located. Some important clues revealed in the document include: the female Scott head of household is a widow and mother to ten children, though only eight of those children are still living; a grandson is living with the female Scott head of household; and a female "Clemons" cousin is living in the Jefferson Scott household.

Indiana Historical Society, 1996). For the African American genealogist, there are twenty-five pages of data in this book, including one hundred and seven footnotes. Among the numerous topics covered, these pages describe the major black settlements in the state, the causes and results of African American migration to the state, and the various laws and codes which affected both the movement and life of Hoosier African Americans. Similar publications should be examined for each state in which you plan to do research.

Community, church, and organizational histories are other valuable tools for placing your family in proper historical context. More importantly, they can also provide specific biographical details on members of your own ancestral family.

Census Records and City Directories

Census records are an important staple for all genealogists. In most instances, the U.S. federal census provides a "snapshot" of the ancestral family every decade, listing (in more recent years) names, ages, birth places, occupations, and a variety of other details. At an early stage in your research, you should locate your family in each federal census from 1920 backwards in time to at least 1870. Indexes for each state and year are available in many libraries and will assist you in this effort. Careful examination of all census data will help you to document your ancestors and discover avenues for further research.

Since people in the same extended family or ethnic group often settled together, it is a good idea to explore nearby census households. Thorough researchers typically investigate the entire township, or other minor jurisdiction, in which particular ancestors are found in hopes of discovering other related individuals.

For the years 1850 and 1860, slave schedules were taken in conjunction with the federal population schedules for the southern states. These schedules list the name of the slave owner and describe each slave by age, sex, and color. Rarely will any slave be named. Though not named, these schedules can still be valuable in identifying the families to which particular African Americans belonged before emancipation.

A List of Slaves.

INDENTURE made 22 June 1796, between Thomas John Parker of Vere, co. Middlesex, Jamaica, now residing at Canbury House, co. Surrey, of the 1st part, James Craggs of Vere, esquire, Sarah Mackenzie of Canbury House, spinster, and James Hobbes of New Bond Street, co. Middlesex, banker, of the 2nd part, and James Bowes of St. Pancras, co. Middlesex, gent, of the 3rd part; by which Thomas John Parker grants transfer to James Bowes his plantations called "Hillside Plantation," "Brazaletto Plantation," and "Chesterfield Plantation" in Vere, in the Island of Jamaica, in trust to raise 40,000^l for Henry Parker, John Stevens Parker, George Mackenzie Parker and James Craggs Parker, the sons of Thomas John Parker and his wife Rachel Stevens.
    Signature on fold T. J. Parker. Witness: Charles Killet.
    Schedules annexed containing lists of negroe slaves.

Schedule A.

Drivers
Hector
Dorindas Hector
Harry William
Rachel
5 Phillis

Carpenters
Dago
Robin
Peter
Abbas Tom
10 Tom Fin
William
Hurricane
Philip
Robert
15 Becks Bob

Coopers
Andrew Jameson
Becks James
Adam
Plato
20 Quamina
Blackmore
Anthony
John Cuffie
Lid Adam

Bricklayers
25 James Lewin
Duke
Tom Drake
Ned
Richard
30 Robert
Dago

Blacksmiths
Toney
Quashie

ffield Men
Roger
35 Johnny
Quaco
Cudjoe
Bat
Bossue
40 Nickie
Dor^d Quamina
Windsor
Joe Mingo
B. S. Quashie
45 Neptune
Phibbas Quashie
Judys Harry
C. P. Tom
Jack

50 Scipio
Tony
Dyer
Dickey
Toby
55 Charles
C° Dorrick
Plass's Quaco
Benn° Tom
Plass Dorrick
60 Flo^s Jemmy
Ned
New Negroe James
Simon
Cubina
65 John
Johnny
Cuffie
Quashie
Cudjoe
70 Richard
Cretins Quashie
Dago
N° Codjoe
Michael
75 Joe
James
Oxford
Charles Noble
Jennys John

86

A typical periodical treasure found in **Fragmenta Genealogica** *(London: Private Press of Frederick Arthur Crisp, 1904), p. 86.*

In addition to widely available federal census records, it is important to know that state and local enumerations may have been taken for the particular areas in which you are conducting research. These enumerations are a wonderful complement to the federal schedules. Typically taken in the years between the federal censuses, state and local census records tend to mirror their closest federal counterparts in the type of data provided. They also often have an "extra" for the researcher–such as religious belief and Civil War military service indicated on the Iowa 1895 schedules.

City directories are valuable as another type of enumeration or census, and typically provide an individual's name, occupation, place of employment, and street address. They are especially useful in identifying individuals between censuses. African Americans are often, though not always, denoted with a "B" or similar mark. In some of the larger cities, African Americans may have their own directory. These specialized ethnic directories can be a gold-mine of information, providing the names of African American churches, schools, businesses, and organizations.

Periodical Literature

The importance of using periodical literature in any genealogical project cannot be overstated. Easily one quarter to one third of the secondary source material available for any geographic area can be found in the pages of the newsletters and journals of the local, county, and state historical, genealogical, and ethnic societies.

Besides indexes, abstracts, and transcriptions of original records, the researcher will find articles providing important historical background. The articles on African Americans and the institution of slavery in these journals cover a wide range of subjects including black history in nearly every locale in the country, slave rebellions and social conflicts, runaway slaves and slave communities, and schools for African Americans during slavery and reconstruction.

These periodical publications can also be used to identify records of interest through citation analysis. Citation analysis is the process of

FIVE POUNDS Reward,
And all reasonable charges.

RUN away from the House of Major Prevost, in Bergen County, on the 29th of September last, a Negro Man and his Wife: The Fellow is serious, civil, slow of Speech, rather low in Stature, reads well, is a Negro Preacher, about 40 Years of Age, he is called MARK. The Wench is smart, active and handy, rather lusty, has bad Teeth, and a cast in one Eye; she is likely to look upon, was brought up in New-London, is called Jenny; as she had a Note to look for a Master, its likely she may make a travelling Pass of it.— Whoever takes up said Negroes, and brings them to the Subscribers, or secures them in any of his Majesty's Gaols, or gives such Information of them as they may be had again, shall be entitled to the above Reward, and all reasonable Charges paid, either by Major Prevost, Archibald Campbell, in Hackinsack; or Thomas Clarke, near New-York.

6s—

This notice of runaway slaves appeared in the *New-York Journal; or, The General Advertiser*, January 12, 1775.

studying the footnotes, endnotes and bibliographies of articles to uncover additional sources of information that might provide genealogical data about a particular family or place. Carefully reading well documented articles for the area and time period in which you are conducting research will also often uncover unique and seldom used records.

One of the best sources for accessing the genealogical data in family and local history periodicals is the *Periodical Source Index* on CD-ROM or online at Ancestry.com. This index provides nearly one and one half million subject references to articles in more than five thousand periodical titles. You can search this database by geographic area and surname, or use keywords such as slave(s), slavery, manumission(s), blacks, Negro(es), African American(s), Afro-American(s), and the like. Boolean operators can also be used to limit result pools that are too large to browse and evaluate effectively.

Many journals will also have their own detailed subject and every name indexes. These should be used once you have identified significant journals covering the area where your family lived.

Newspapers

Newspapers of yesteryear offer an unparalleled chronicle of the people, organizations, institutions, and movements within a particular community. Accessing those papers and studying their contents is essential in gathering the maximum amount of information about African Americans, the areas where they lived, and the important events in their lives. Obituaries, community announcements, estate proceedings, bills of sale, notices of auctions, and notices of runaways as well as the general news stories of the day are all potentially useful for your research.

Local public libraries and state libraries are the best sources to contact when seeking collections of historic newspapers. Local public libraries tend to collect and preserve copies of the papers from their cities, towns, and counties. State libraries, particularly with the help of federal grants through the national newspaper microfilming projects, have attempted to obtain microfilm copies of every newspaper published in their respective states. In many states, it is the state library which makes its microfilmed newspapers available through interlibrary loan.

Many communities also have Black or African American newspapers. These publications can be especially valuable by providing a different point of view on the major news stories of the day and by covering those items which the general papers may overlook.

As interest in genealogy and local history continues to climb, you can expect the publication of more newspaper indexes. These indexes provide the researcher with quicker, more direct access to data contained in the thousands of pages of newsprint you would otherwise have to study. An example of one such index is *The ESCN (Early South Carolina Newspapers) Database Reports* which contain many useful 18th century references.

Internet Sources

The Internet offers increasing amounts of data as well as research aids and guides for the African American family historian. Besides searching under the surnames of interest in the numerous "surname finder files" on the web (for example, those at Ancestry.com, FamilyTreeMaker.com, and FamilySearch.org), there are several strategies you can employ to efficiently access the many resources available on the world wide web.

First, you should utilize the important gateway site for African American family history and genealogy, *AfriGeneas: African Ancestored Genealogy* <www.afrigeneas.com>. Among the offerings at this site are searchable data files, a beginners guide, an online newsletter, research guides and tips, an online library of African American research materials, collections of state and world resources, important links to other web pages, and a chat room and mailing list.

Second, you should regularly visit web sites that collect and organize large numbers of genealogical and historical links. This will help you keep up to date with the rapid growth of resources available on the Internet. *Cyndi's List* <www.CyndisList.com> is one such frequently updated and well maintained site. It loads quickly and organizes more than sixty-five thousand links in easy to understand categories. More than one hundred and fifty links can be found under the "African-American" subject heading.

Cyndi's List is also beneficial in reminding the researcher, through its layout and organization, that accessing data under the phrase African American is only one avenue through which a genealogist can explore the web. Looking under the surname, geographical, occupational, and religious sections organized in *Cyndi's List* will also typically net relevant information and links.

A third strategy in identifying useful data for African American research is to explore the USGenWeb pages <www.USGenWeb.org> for the states and counties in which research is being conducted. While you will find inconsistency from site to site, county GenWeb pages typically list the major repositories of records and published materials, and increasingly offer searchable data files and digitized copies of documents. They are definitely sites worth exploring.

A final strategy to employ is to visit the web sites of state libraries, state archives, and state historical societies, where you will find a growing number of online databases. These institutions collect a wide variety of historical materials useful for genealogical research. There are links to all fifty state libraries at <www.lib.de.us/libraries/otherlibs/statelib.shtml> and all fifty state archives at <www.sos.state.ga.us/archives/sarl.htm>. These would be two good sites to bookmark on your Internet browser.

Sources for "Free People of Color"

There were free African Americans living in both the North and the South in the pre-Civil War era. An excellent work detailing the struggles free African Americans faced in the south, particularly if they were successful, is entitled ***Black Masters: A Free Family of Color in the Old South*** by Michael P. Johnson and James L. Roark.

In many areas, there were special laws and codes which governed what free African Americans could do, where they could live, and how they needed to interact with white society. It is interesting to note that

INDIANA TERRITORY. *A Law concerning Servants.*

(L. S.) Adopted from the Virginia code, and published at Vincennes, the twenty-second day of September one thousand eight hundred and three, by William Henry Harrison, governor, and Thomas T. Davis, and Henry Vander Burgh, judges in and over said Territory.

§ 1st. ALL negroes and mulattoes (and other persons not being citizens of the United States of America,) who shall come into this territory under contract to serve another in any trade or occupation, shall be compelled to perform such contract specifically during the term thereof.

§ 2nd. The said servants shall be provided by the master with wholesome and sufficient food, cloathing and lodging, and at the end of their service if they shall not have contracted for any reward, food, cloathing and lodging, shall receive from him one new and complete suit of cloathing, suited to the season of the year, to wit: a coat, waistcoat, pair of breeches and shoes, two pair of stockings, two shirts, a hat and blanket.

§ 3rd. The benefit of the said contract of service, shall be assignable by the master to any person being a citizen of this territory, to whom the servant shall in the presence of a justice of the peace freely consent that it shall be assigned, the said justice attesting such free consent in writing, and shall also pass to the executors, administrators and legatees of the master.

*Excerpt from **The Laws of Indiana Territory, 1801-1809**, (Springfield, IL: Illinois State Historical Library, 1930), p.42.*

while the northern states were against the institution of slavery, many northern communities had laws which prohibited African Americans from living within their boundaries.

Careful study of the laws and codes involved can assist you in determining where a particular African American family may have been living and lead you to additional records. As an example, "free people of color" often had to register in the communities where they intended to live, offering documents to local officials to support their claims of freedom. The lists made of such individuals can be found in special "Negro Registers." Many libraries have some published lists of these free African Americans.

Considerable attention should also be paid to the workings of religious groups and abolition societies. Their proceedings and papers, though often unindexed, can provide historical background on African Americans in a particular area and also identify specific free blacks. For example, several individuals belonging to the Society of Friends (commonly known as Quakers) petitioned Congress in the early 1800s. They were concerned that the "emancipated blacks" whose freedom they had purchased were being taken or sold back into slavery by unscrupulous slave dealers and slave hunters. In their petition, they mentioned the African Americans who were freed and the Quakers who purchased their freedom. Entries such as "Esther and child, Rebekah and children, Joab and Penny, by Aaron Morris, Jun" can be found in this petition.

Slave Records

Research in the pre-Civil War South becomes more difficult for the descendant of African American slaves, but there are still a variety of sources available for the family historian. A significant number of slave owners, plantation owners, and overseers kept detailed records of the slaves they owned and nearly every other aspect of plantation life.

Tracing those slaves means examining the wills, estate inventories, deeds, and tax records related to the owners' families because these items often document individual slaves and record their transfer to new owners or their manumission. Slaves might be listed in the records

NAMES OF SLAVE OWNERS.	Number of Slaves	Age	Sex	Color	Fugitives from the State
1 W E F Shelton	1	60	M	B	
2	1	59	M	B	
3	1	55	F	B	
4	1	60	F	B	
5	1	35	F	B	
6	1	9	F	B	
7 Jane Boggs	1	28	F	B	
8	1	25	F	M	
9	1	20	M	M	
10	1	6	M	B	
11 Franklin Barton	1	33	F	B	
12	1	8	F	B	

Slave Schedules for 1860–Georgia (NARA Microcopy No. 432, Roll 153), Whitfield County.

under their given names or under their given names and surnames. It should be remembered that a slave's surname could change when he or she changed owners, but that a name change did not necessarily or automatically occur.

The plantation was a business and slaves were viewed as an important part of the plantation's assets. Indeed, how successfully the enslaved African Americans were "managed" in a large degree determined the profitability of the plantation. This business context is vital for the researcher to understand when viewing plantation records. Statements may appear unkind, and many were. They are made in the context of the African American as property, not as a person. Careful evaluation of these business records, though, can uncover meaningful genealogical data that is unavailable in any other source.

Although many plantation records were destroyed during the course of the War Between the States, a large number have survived. To find and use these records it is helpful to know the name of the slaveowner and the location of the plantation.

If local libraries and archives do not have the needed plantation records, the holdings of the Library of Congress should be searched as its collections contain many plantation journals, family accounts, and diaries of the Old South. Through its ***American Memory Project***, the Library of Congress is also digitizing hundreds of thousands of pages of documents for use on the Internet. Another essential means of accessing plantation records is through the microfilm publication ***Records of Ante-Bellum Southern Plantations from the Revolution through the Civil War***, available at the Allen County Public Library and other major research facilities.

Church records can prove to be another important source since much of a slave's free time was centered around religious and church related activities. Church records can give an admission date, discharge date, and sometimes a death date for the slave.

Several case studies have been published that provide excellent insights on how to use and evaluate source materials in putting together slave genealogies. Perhaps one of the best and most well known is an article which appeared in the ***National Genealogical Society Quarterly*** (volume 75, number 1, March 1978, page 5-14) entitled, "From Maria to Bill Cosby: A Case Study in Tracing Black Slave Ancestry." Also worthy of note is ***Slave Genealogy: A Research Guide with Case Studies*** published by Heritage Books, Inc.

One final note. In working with plantation records and the records of the Freedmen's Bureau, which assisted emancipated slaves after the Civil War, you will encounter groups of related documents that tell an individual's story. Many such stories can be found in the ***Records of the Assistant Commissioner for the State of Virginia, Bureau of Refugees, Freedmen, and Abandoned Lands, 1865-1869*** (NARA Microcopy M1048, Roll 11). I conclude this guide with the example of William Brown.

Freedmen's Bureau files typically contain a cover sheet indicating what issues are being addressed. In the document below you see that "Brown, Wm. (Col'd) makes a statement in regard to himself and children." On the following two pages you will find part of his petition and the Bureau's response. In this case, William Brown discusses the details of his final years in slavery and how he was separated from his children. The Bureau claims that it "cannot interfere in this matter."

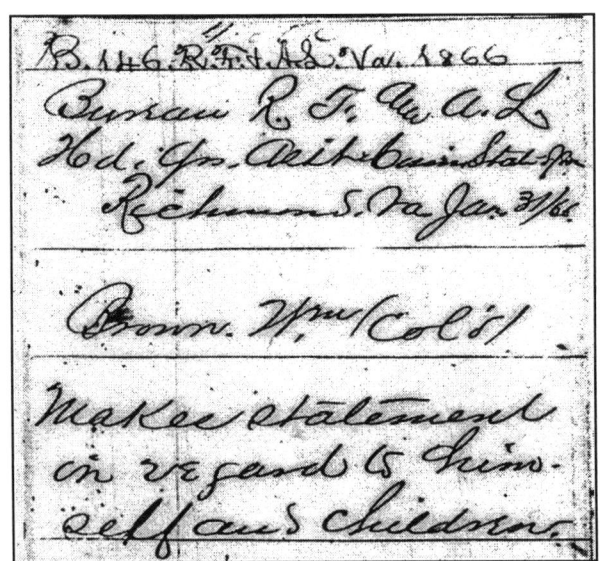

Bureau of Refugees, Freedmen & Abandoned Lands.

Head Quarters, Asst. Commissioner, State of Virginia.

Richmond, Va., January 31st, 1866.

Statement of
William Brown (Colored) Hanover County, Va.

Was sold from Middlesex County, Va, three years ago, last September, and left five children at Mortimore Evins, or Evans, near Jamaica Post Office in said County. The mother of these children was given to another man, soon after he was sold —

Brown was there in November, Evins wanted the children bound to him, Brown would not give his consent, (as the children did not want to stay at Evins) — He promised to call for them on the 1st Jany, and take them away; — bad weather prevented him from going for them. Brown found out that after he left, Evins went to Tappahannock and had the children bound to the mother & then bound to him until they were 21 years old, "by the Clerk of the Court"

J. 42. 1. Vol. 67

Bureau of R. F. and A. L.
Office Supt. 3rd Dist.
Richmond, Va., March 23rd 67.

Respectfully returned to Bvt. Brig. Genl. O. Brown, Asst. Comr.
State of Virginia. William Brown (cold) recognises the within named
children to be his and refuses to allow them to return to Mr. Evans,
whom he alleges, treated the children so cruelly that they ran away
and came to Richmond Va, to seek the protection of their father. Brown
also states Evans compelled the mother of the children, through fear,
to indenture them. These children are now well provided for by Brown
who is abundantly able to care for them.

(Signed) James M. Baker
Capt. 43. Infy. a. Supt.

Bureau of R. F. and A. L.
Hd. Qrs. Asst. Comr. Sts. of Va.
Richmond Va, Mch. 25th 67.

Respectfully returned to Maj. Jas. Johnson. The Bureau cannot
interfere in this matter.

(Signed) O. Brown
Bvt. Brig. Genl. Vols.
Asst. Comr.

GENERAL SOURCES

The A. M. E. Church Review. Philadelphia: Publishing House of the African M. E. Church. V. 1, 1884 - V. 2, 1910. /Microfilm/

Abajian, James de T. *Blacks in Selected Newspapers, Censuses and Other Sources: An Index to Names and Subjects*. Boston, MA: G. K. Hall and Company, 1977. Bibliographies. /Microfilm Rolls 1-6/

Abajian, James de T. *Blacks in Selected Newspapers, Censuses and Other Sources: An Index to Names and Subjects*. Boston, MA: G. K. Hall and Company, 1985. First Supplement. /GC 016.929 B56 V. 1-2 Oversize/

Adams, Nehemiah. *South-side View of Slavery; Or, Three Months at the South in 1854*. Boston, MA: T. R. Marvin, 1854. 214p. /GC 975 Ad1s/

African American Family History Association, Inc. Newsletter. Atlanta, GA: The Association, v.15-, 1992-. /Periodical/

The African American Odyssey. Washington, DC: Library of Congress, 199-. 24p. Illustrations. /GC 973 Af832/

African Roots Explore New Worlds: Pre-Columbus to the Space Age. S.l.: s.n., 1992. 11p. /GC 973 Af838/

Afro-American Historical and Genealogical Society Journal. Washington, DC: Afro-American Historical and Genealogical Society, v.1-, 1980-. /Periodical/

Afro-American Life, History and Culture. Washington, DC: United States Information Agency, 1985. 779p. Indices. An extensive, annotated bibliography. (SUDOC: IA 1.27 Af8) /GC 929 Af8a/

Allen, William Francis, Charles Pickard Ware & Lucy McKim Garrison. *Slave Songs of the United States*. New York: Books for Libraries Press, 1971. 115p. /GC 973 Al54s/

America's Top Black Graduating Engineers, Class of 1985. Kansas City, MO: Minority Resource Network, Inc., 1985. 151p. /GC 929.11 Am35/

American Convention for Promoting the Abolition of Slavery and Improving the Conditions of the African Race. New York: Bergman Publishers, 1969. /GC 929.11 Am3435m V. 1 & 2/

American Negro Historical Society Collection, 1790-1905. Wilmington, DE: Scholarly Resources, Inc., 19--. /Microfilm Rolls 1-12/

American Negro Historical Society Collection, 1790-1905. Wilmington, DE: Scholarly Resources, Inc., 19--. A reel list of the twelve roll microfilm collection. /GC 973 Am35595/

Angell, Stephen Ward. *Bishop Henry McNeal Turner and African-American Religion in the South*. Knoxville, TX: The University of Tennessee Press, 1992. 340p. Bibliography. Index. Notes. Photographs. /GC 929.102 M56an/

Aptheker, Herbert. *American Negro Slave Revolts*. New York: International Publishers, 1993. 415p. Bibliography. Index. Notes. /GC 975 Ap84a/

Arnold, Thomas St. John. *Buffalo Soldiers: The 92nd Infantry Division and Reinforcements in World War II, 1942-1945*. Manhattan, KS: Sunflower University Press, 1990. 245p. Appendices. Index. Maps. Photographs. /GC 940.5410 Aa1arn/

Asante, Molefi K. and Mark R. Matteson. *The Historical and Cultural Atlas of African Americans*. New York: Macmillan Publishing Company, Inc., 1992. 198p. Bibliography. Index. Maps. Photographs. /GC 973.003 As1h/

Ashe, Arthur R., Jr. *A Hard Road to Glory: A History of the African-American Athlete, 1619-1918*. New York: Warner Books, 1988. 194p. Bibliography. Index. Photographs. /GC 973 As35h 1619-1918/

Ashe, Arthur R., Jr. *A Hard Road to Glory: A History of the African-American Athlete Since 1946*. New York: Warner Books, 1988. 571p. Bibliography. Index. Photographs. /GC 973 As35h 1946/

Ashyk, Dan, Fred L. Gardaphe, and Anthony Julian Tamburri. *Shades of Black and White: Conflict and Collaboration between Two Communities*. Staten Island, NY: American Italian Historical Association, 1999. 378p. Selected essays from the 30th Annual Conference. Index. /GC 929.15 Am35c/

Astor, Gerald. *The Right to Fight: A History of African Americans in the Military*. Novato, CA: Presidio Press, 1998. 529p. Bibliography. Index. Photographs. /GC 973.001 Aa1ast/

Bancroft, Frederic. *Slave Trading in the Old South*. New York: Frederick Ungar Publishing Company, 1959. 415p. Index. /GC 975 B221s/

Barbeau, Arthur E. *Black American Soldiers in World War I*. Pittsburgh, PA: University of Pittsburgh, 1970. 662p. Bibliography. /GC 940.410 Aalbar/

Barber, Lucy. *African American History Sources: A Bibliography*. Alexandria, VA: The Alexandria Library, 1992. 58p. Index. /GC 975.5 B22a/

Barrow, Charles Kelley, J. H. Segars, & R. B. Rosenburg. *Forgotten Confederates: An Anthology about Black Southerners*. Atlanta, GA: Southern Heritage Press, 1995. (*Journal of Confederate History Series*, Volume XIV) 193p. Bibliography. Index. Photographs. /GC 975 B248f/

Beasley, Donna. *Family Pride: The Complete Guide to Tracing African-American Genealogy*. New York: Macmillan USA, 1997. 192p. Appendices. Illustrations. Index. Photographs. /GC 973 B38f/

Beginning Genealogy. Los Angeles, CA: California African American Genealogical Society, 1997. 78p. Bibliography. Illustrations. /GC 929 B329/

Bell, Janet Cheatham. *African Heritage Bibliography, Addendum*. Momence, IL: Baker & Taylor, 1988. 84p. /GC 929.11 Af82/

Berger, Graenum. *Black Jews in America: A Documentary with Commentary*. New York, NY: Federation of Jewish Philanthropies of New York, 1978. 218p. Index. /GC 929.102 J55b/

Bergeron, Arthur Jr. et al. *Black Southerners in Gray: Essays on Afro-Americans in Confederate Armies*. Murfreesboro, TN: Southern Heritage Press, 1994. 172p. Notes. One photograph. /GC 973.74 Aa1rol/

Berlin, Ira & Leslie S. Rowland, eds. *Families and Freedom: A Documentary History of African-American Kinship in the Civil War Era*. New York: The New Press, 1997. 259p.

Bibliography. Drawings. Index. Notes. Photographs. /GC 973 F875a/

Berlin, Ira & Ronald Hoffman. *Slavery and Freedom in the Age of the American Revolution*. Charlottesville, VA: University Press of Virginia, 1983. 314p. Index. Tables. /GC 973 Sl12/

Billington, Monroe Lee and Roger D. Hardaway. *African Americans on the Western Frontier*. Niwot, CO: University Press of Colorado, 1998. 275p. Appendix. Bibliography. Index. Map. Notes. Photographs. /GC 978 B489a/

Black Americans in Defense of Our Nation. Washington, DC: U. S. Government Printing Office, 1985. 189p. /GC 973.001 Aa1bl/

Black Americans Information Directory. Detroit, MI: Gale Research, Inc., 1990. /GC 929.11 B556/

Black Elected Officials: A National Register. Washington, DC: Joint Center for Political Studies Press, 1988. 481p. Index. /GC 929.11 B558 1988/

Black History News & Notes. Indianapolis, IN: Indiana Historical Society, 198-. /Periodical/

Black Resource Guide. Washington, DC: Johnson, 1985. 281p. /GC 929.11 B56/

Black Women in the Middle West Project: A Comprehensive Resource Guide, Illinois and Indiana. Indianapolis, IN: Indiana Historical Bureau, 1986. 238p. Bibliography. Index. Photographs. /GC 977 B56/

Blassingame, John W. *The Slave Community: Plantation Life in the Antebellum South*. New York: Oxford University Press, 1979. 414p. Appendices. Bibliography. Index. /GC 975 B61s 1979/

Blassingame, John W., ed. *Slave Testimony: Two Centuries of Letters, Speeches, Interviews, and Autobiographies*. Baton Rouge, LA: Louisiana State University Press, 1977. 777p. Illustrations. Index. Photographs. /GC 973 Sl1/

Blockson, Charles L. *African Americans in Pennsylvania: A History and Guide*. Baltimore, MD: Black Classic Press, 1994. 199p. Bibliography. Glossary. Index. Photographs. /GC 974.8 B62a/

Blockson, Charles L. *Hippocrene Guide The Underground Railroad*. New York: Hippocrene Books, 1994. 380p. Index. Maps. Narratives. Photographs. /GC 973 B62h/

Blockson, Charles L. *The Underground Railroad*. New York: Prentice Hall Press, 1987. 308p. Index. First person narratives of escapes to freedom. /GC 929.11 B595u/

Blockson, Charles L. and Ron Fry. *Black Genealogy*. Englewood Cliffs, NJ: Prentice-Hall Company, Inc., 1977. 232p. Index. Illustrations. Bibliography. /GC 929 B62b/

Boles, John B. *Black Southerners, 1619-1869*. Lexington, KY: The University Press of Kentucky, 1984. 244p. Bibliography. Index. /GC 975 B638b/

Bowers, William T., William M. Hammond and George L. MacGarrigle. *Black Soldier, White Army*. Washington, DC: Center for Military History, United States Army, 1996. 294p. Appendices.

Bibliography. Index. Maps. Photographs. /GC 951.9042 Aa1bo/

Bowley, Freeman S. *A Boy Lieutenant: Memoirs of Freeman S. Bowley, 30th United States Colored Troops Officer.* Fredericksburg, VA: Sergeant Kirkland's Museum and Historical Society, Inc., 1997. 124p. Appendices. Bibliography. Illustrations. Index. Notes. Photographs. /GC 973.74 Aa1bov/

Bragg, George F. *History of the Afro-American Group of the Episcopal Church.* Baltimore, MD: Church Advocate Press, 1922. 319p. /GC 929.102 Ep4br/

Branche, Juanita Odom. *Lost Identities, Ancestors of the Past: Bailey, Branche, Clarke, Floyd, Harley, Holmes, Odom, Reynolds, Walker.* Baltimore, MD: Gateway Press, 1996. 114p. Maps. Photographs. Charts and tables. Much data regarding tracing an African American family. /GC 929.2 Od47b/

Bristol, Africa and the Eighteenth-Century Slave Trade to America. England: Bristol Record Society, 1991. 249p. Index. (Volume 3: The Years of Decline, 1746-1769) /GC 942.4102 B861p V. 42/

Brown, Larissa V. *Africans in the New World, 1493-1834.* Providence, RI: The John Carter Brown Library, 1988. 61p. Bibliography. /GC 970 B81a/

Burton, Art T. *Black, Buckskin, and Blue: African American Scouts and Soldiers on the Western Frontier.* Austin, TX: Eakin Press, 1999. 286p. Appendices. Bibliography. Index. Photographs. /GC 978 B953b/

Byers, Paula K. *African American Genealogical Sourcebook.* Detroit, MI: Gale Research, Inc., 1995. 244p. /GC 973 Af83/

Campbell, Edward D. C., Jr. and Kym S. Rice, eds. *Before Freedom Came: African-American Life in the Antebellum South*. Richmond, VA: Museum of the Confederacy, 1991. 220p. Bibliography. Index. Notes. Photographs. /GC 975 B39/

Carroll, John M. *The Black Military Experience in the American West*. New York: Liveright, 19--. 591p. Bibliography. Index. Notes. Sketches. /GC 973.001 Aa1cara/

Cashin, Herschel V., et al. *Under Fire with the Tenth U. S. Cavalry*. Niwot, CO: University Press of Colorado, 1993. 361p. Official Roll. Photographs. /GC 973.894 Aa1cas/

Catteral, Helen H. T. *Judicial Cases Concerning American Slavery and the Negro*. Washington, DC: s.n., 1926-37. Five volumes on one roll of microfilm. /Microfilm/

Chuks-orji, Ogonna. *Names from Africa: Their Origin, Meaning, and Pronunciation*. Chicago: Johnson Publishing Company, Inc., 1972. 91p. Bibliography. /GC 929.4 C27n/

Clarke, Robert L., ed. *Afro-American History: Sources for Research*. Washington, DC: Howard University Press, 1981. 236p. Documents. Index. Notes. /GC 973 N21a/

Clem, Dee. *Tracing African-American Roots*. Las Vegas, NV: Gator Publishing, Inc., 1999. 232p. Bibliography. Index. Photographs. /GC 973 C59t/

Cofer, Loris D. *Black Genealogy*. Glennville, GA: Glennville Printing & Office Supply, 1991. 897p. /GC 929.11 C56b/

Cohen, David W. and Jack P. Greene. *Neither Slave Nor Free: The Freedmen of African Descent in the Slave Societies of the New*

World. Baltimore, MD: The Johns Hopkins University Press, 1972. 344p. Appendix. Index. Notes. /GC 973 N319/

Collum, Danny Duncan, ed. *African Americans in the Spanish Civil War: "This Ain't Ethiopia, But It'll Do."* New York: G.K. Hall & Company, 1992. 234p. Bibliography. Index. Photographs. /GC 929.11 Af81/

Cornelius, Janet Duitsman. *Slave Missions and the Black Church in the Antebellum South*. Columbia, SC: University of South Carolina Press, 1999. 305p. Bibliography. Illustrations. Index. Notes. Photographs. /GC 975 C81s/

Cornish, Dudley Taylor. *The Sable Arm: Black Troops in the Union Army, 1861-1865*. Lawrence, KS: University Press of Kansas, 1987. 342p. Bibliography. Index. Notes. /GC 973.73 Aa1con/

Cottrol, Robert J. *From African to Yankee: Narratives of Slavery and Freedom in Antebellum New England*. Armonk, NY: M. E. Sharpe, 1998. 222p. Bibliography. Index. /GC 974 F925/

Cowan, Tom and Jack Maguire. *Timelines of African-American History: 500 Years of Black Achievement*. New York: The Berkley Publishing Group, 1994. 368p. Index. /GC 973 C83t/

Crawford, Marion Golightly. *African-American Genealogy: A Handbook of Reference Sources*. Detroit, MI: M. G. Crawford, 1988. 72p. /GC 929 C85a/

Curtis, Nancy C. *Black Heritage Sites: An African American Odyssey and Finder's Guide*. Chicago, IL: American Library Association, 1996. 677p. /GC 973 C945b/

Daniels, Nathan W. *Thank God My Regiment an African One: The Civil War Diary of Colonel Nathan W. Daniels*. Baton Rouge: Louisiana State University Press, 1998. 214p. Appendices. Bibliography. Index. Photographs. /GC 973.74 Aa1dan/

Danky, James P. & Maureen E. Hady, eds. *African-American Newspapers and Periodicals: A National Bibliography*. Cambridge, MA: Harvard University Press, 1998. 740p. Indices. /GC 973 Af83da/

Davis, Burke. *Black Heroes of the American Revolution*. New York: Harcourt Brace Jovanovich, 1976. 80p. Bibliography. Illustrations. Index. /GC 973.34 Aa1dav/

Davis, Charles T. and Henry Louis Gates, Jr. *The Slave's Narrative*. New York: Oxford University Press, 1985. 342p. Bibliography. Index. /GC 973 SL16/

Davis, Cyprian O.S.B. *The History of Black Catholics in the United States*. New York: Crossroad Publishing Company, 1990. 347p. Bibliography. Index. Notes. /GC 973 D2914h/

Davis, Harry E. *A History of Freemasonry Among Negroes in America*. S.l.: s.n., 1946. 333p. Index. /GC 929.11 D291h/

Davis, John. P., ed. *The American Negro Reference Book*. Englewood Cliffs, NJ: Prentice-Hall, Inc., 1966. 969p. Charts. Index. Notes. /GC 973 Am356/

Dillon, Merton Lynn. *Slavery Attacked: Southern Slaves and Their Allies, 1619-1865*. Baton Rouge, LA: Louisiana State University Press, 1990. 300p. Bibliography. Index. /GC 975 D587s/

Dinnerstein, Leonard, Roger L. Nichols and David M. Reimers. *Natives and Strangers: Blacks, Indians, and Immigrants in America*.

New York: Oxford University Press, 1990. 362p. Bibliography. Index. Photographs. /GC 973 D61n/

Documentary History of the Negro People in the United States. New York: The Citadel Press, 1968. 2 volumes. Index. Notes. /GC 973 Ap84d V. 1-2/

Donnan, Elizabeth. *Documents Illustrative of the History of the Slave Trade to America*. New York: Octagon Books, Inc., 1965. /GC 973 D713d V. 1-4/

Dow, George Francis. *Slave Ships and Slaving*. Cambridge, MD: Cornell Maritime Press, Inc., 1927. 386p. Drawings. Index. /GC 973 D745s/

Drotning, Philip T. *A Guide to Negro History in America*. New York: Doubleday & Company, Inc., 1968. 247p. Index. /GC 929.11 D83g/

Durham, Philip and Everett L. Jones. *The Negro Cowboys*. New York: Dodd, Mead & Company, 1965. 278p. Bibliography. Index. Maps. Notes. Photographs. /GC 978 N312/

Eisenberg, Marcia J. *African-American Genealogy: Some Unique Records and Basic Sources*. Pittsfield, MA: Berkshire Family History Association, 198-. 60 minutes. /Cassette Tape/

Eldridge, Thelma Strong. *Selected Ethnic Genealogical Sources at Woodson*. Chicago, IL: T. S. Eldridge, 1996. 96p. /GC 929 St88s/

Essig, James David. *Break Every Yoke: American Evangelicals Against Slavery, 1770-1808*. S.l.: J. D. Essig, 1978. 235p. Bibliography. Notes. /GC 973.4 Es77b/

41

Fears, Mary L. Jackson. *Slave Ancestral Research: It's Something Else*. Bowie, MD: Heritage Books, Inc., 1995. 268p. Bibliography. Charts. Index. Photographs. /GC 975.8 F31s/

Ferguson, Leland G. *Uncommon Ground: Archaeology and Early African America, 1650-1800*. Washington, DC: Smithsonian Institution Press, 1992. 186p. Bibliography. Illustrations. Index. Maps. /GC 973 F381u/

Finkleman, Paul. *Slavery & The Law*. Madison, WI: Madison House Publishers, Inc., 1997. 465p. Index. Notes. /GC 973 F495s/

Fleischner, Jennifer. *Mastering Slavery: Memory, Family and Identity in Women's Slave Narratives*. New York: New York University Press, 1996. 232p. Bibliography. Index. Notes. /GC 973 F619m/

Fleming, John E. *Grand Opening of the Afro-American Museum*. Cincinnati, OH: FGS Conference, 1987. 60 minutes. /Cassette Tape/

Flower of the Forest: Black Genealogical Journal. Baltimore, MD: Agnes Kane Callum, 1982-. /Periodical/

Foner, Eric. *Freedom's Lawmakers: A Directory of Black Officeholders During Reconstruction*. Baton Rouge, LA: Louisiana State University Press, 1996. 298p. Indices. Photographs. /GC 929.11 F73fa/

Forbes, Ella. *African American Women During the Civil War*. New York: Garland Publishing, Inc., 1998. 272p. Bibliography. Index. Notes. Photographs. /GC 973.74 Aa1fao/

Forbes, Jack D. *Africans and Native Americans: The Language of Race and the Evolution of Red-Black Peoples*. Urbana, IL: University of Illinois Press, 1993. 344p. Bibliography. Index. Notes. /GC 970.1 F74af/

Foster, Frances Smith. *Witnessing Slavery: The Development of Antebellum Slave Narratives*. Madison, WI: The University of Wisconsin Press, 1979. 194p. Bibliography. Index. Notes. /GC 975 F812w/

Fowler, Arlen L. *The Black Infantry in the West, 1869-1891*. Norman, OK: University of Oklahoma Press, 1996. 167p. Bibliography. Index. Notes. /GC 973.001 Aa1fow/

Fox-Genovese, Elizabeth. *Within the Plantation Household: Black and White Women of the Old South*. Chapel Hill, NC: The University of North Carolina Press, 1988. 544p. Bibliography. Index. Notes. /GC 975 F83w/

Francis, Charles E. *The Tuskegee Airmen: The Story of the Negro in the U.S. Air Force*. Boston, MA: Bruce Humphries, Inc., 1968. 225p. Notes. Photographs. /GC 940.5410 Aa1f/

Franklin, John Hope & Alfred A. Moss, Jr. *From Slavery to Freedom: A History of African Americans*. New York: Alfred A. Knopf, Inc., 1994. 680p. Appendices. Bibliographical notes. Index. Photographs. /GC 973 F845f/

Franklin, John Hope & Loren Schweninger. *Runaway Slaves: Rebels on the Plantation*. New York: Oxford University Press, 1999. 455p. Appendices. Bibliography. Illustrations. Notes. /GC 975 F854r/

Frazier, E. Franklin. *The Negro in the United States*. New York: The Macmillan Company, 1968. 769p. Bibliography. Illustrations. Indices. Notes. /GC 973 F869n/

Frey, Sylvia R. *Water from the Rock: Black Resistance in a Revolutionary Age*. Princeton, NJ: Princeton University Press, 1992. 376p. Bibliography. Index. Notes. /GC 975 F897w/

The Frontier Freedman's Journal: An African American Genealogical & Historical Journal of the South, Indian Territory, and the Southwest. Baltimore, MD: A.Y. Walton-Taji, v.1-, 1992-. /Periodical/

Gaspar, David Berry and Darlene Clark Hine. *More than Chattel: Black Women and Slavery in the Americas*. Bloomington, IN: Indiana University Press, 1996. 341p. Bibliography. Index. Notes. /GC 973 M813/

Genovese, Eugene D. *Roll, Jordan, Roll: The World the Slaves Made*. New York: Pantheon Books, 1974. 873p. Index. Notes. /GC 973 G288r/

Gibson, Lyle Eric. *The Reed-Walker Family: Descendants of Savannah Reed-Walker*. Pine Bluff, AR: L. E. Gibson, 1995. 133p. Illustrations. /GC 929.2 R25g/

Gladstone, William A. *Men of Color*. Gettysburg, PA: Thomas Publications, 1993. 227p. Appendices. Bibliography. Drawings. Index. Photographs. /GC 973.74 Aa1gw/

Glasrud, Bruce A. *African Americans in the West: A Bibliography of Secondary Sources*. Alpine, TX: Sul Ross State University, Center for Big Bend Studies, 1998. Center for Big Bend Studies Occasional Papers, No. 2. 189p. Index. Photographs. /GC 978 G463af/

Glover, Denise M. *Voices of the Spirit: Sources for Interpreting the African American Experience*. Chicago, IL: American Library Association, 1995. 211p. Indices. /GC 929 G49v/

Gould, Lois Virginia Meacham. *In Full Enjoyment of Their Liberty: The Free Women of Color of the Gulf Ports of New Orleans, Mobile, and Pensacola, 1769-1860*. Ann Arbor, MI: University Microfilms International, 1992. 375p. Bibliography. /GC 975 G73i/

Gourdin, J. Raymond. *Voices from the Past: 104th Infantry Regiment, USCT, Colored Civil War Soldiers from South Carolina*. Bowie, MD: Heritage Books, Inc., 1997. 242p. Appendices. Index. Notes. /GC 973.74 So8g/

Gray, C. Jarrett. *The Racial and Ethnic Presence in American Methodism: A Bibliography*. Madison, NJ: General Commission on Archives and History, The United Methodist Church, 1991. 89p. /GC 929.102 M56gr/

Greenberg, Kenneth S. *The Confessions of Nat Turner and Related Documents*. Boston, MA: Bedford Books of St. Martin's Press, 1996. 148p. Bibliography. Index. /GC 973 C76/

Green, Lorenzo Johnston. *The Negro in Colonial New England, 1620-1776*. New York, Columbia University Press, 1942. 1998 facsimile reprint. 404p. Appendices. Bibliography. Index. Notes. /GC 974 G833n/

Greene, Robert Ewell. *Black Courage, 1775-1783: Documentation of Black Participation in the American Revolution*. Washington, DC: National Society of the Daughters of the American Revolution, 1984. 141p. /GC 973.34 Aa1gr/

Greene, Robert Ewell. *Black Defenders of America, 1775-1973*. Chicago, IL: Johnson Publishing Company, Inc., 1974. 416p. Index. Photographs. Bibliography. /GC 973.001 Aa1gr/

Grimshaw, William H. *Official History of Freemasonry Among the Colored People in North America.* New York: Negro University Press, 1969. 392p. Photographs. /GC 929.11 G871o/

A Guide to Records of Ante-bellum Southern Plantations, From the Revolution Through the Civil War. Frederick, MD: University Publications of America, Inc., 1985-. Guides to primary source microfilmed records. /GC 975 R24 Series A-M/

A Guide to the Microfilm Edition of Slavery in Ante-bellum Southern Industries. Frederick, MD: University Publications of America, 199-. Guides to primary source microfilmed records. /GC 975 Sl1 Series A-C/

Guide to the Microfilm Edition of the Ivy Leaf, 1921-1998: A Chronicle of Alpha Kappa Alpha Sorority. Bethesda, MD: University Publications of America, 2000. 209p. Guide to microfilmed newspapers. /GC 929.11 AL755i/

Gutman, Herbert G. *The Black Family in Slavery and Freedom, 1750-1925.* New York: Vintage Books, 1977. 664p. Appendices. Charts. Index. Notes. /GC 973 G98b/

Haizlip, Shirlee Taylor. *The Sweeter The Juice: A Family Memoir in Black and White.* New York: Simon & Schuster, 1994. 271p. Bibliography. Photographs. /GC 929.2 T21hs/

Haley, James. *Afro-American Encyclopedia or, The Thoughts, Doings, and Sayings of the Race.* Nashville, TN: Winston-Derek Publishers, Inc., 1992. 2 volumes. Drawings. /GC 929.11 H127a Book 1-2/

Hall, Gwendolyn Midlo. *Love, War, and the 96th Engineers (Colored): The World War II New Guinea Diaries of Captain Hyman*

Samuelson. Urbana, IL: University of Illinois Press, 1995. 319p. Index. Notes. /GC 940.5410 Aalhg/

Halliburton, R., Jr. *Red Over Black: Black Slavery Among the Cherokee Indians*. Westport, CT: Greenwood Press, 1977. 218p. Appendices. Index. Bibliography. /GC 975 H15r/

Halter, Marilyn. *Between Race and Ethnicity: Cape Verdean American Immigrants, 1860-1965*. Urbana, IL: University of Illinois Press, 1993. 213p. Appendix. Bibliography. Index. Photographs. /GC 929.19 H16b/

Ham, Debra Newman. *The African-American Mosaic: A Library of Congress Resource Guide for the Study of Black History and Culture*. Washington, DC: Library of Congress. 1993. 300p. Index. Photographs. /GC 973 H17a/

Hardaway, Roger D. *A Narrative Bibliography of the African-American Frontier: Blacks in the Rocky Mountain West, 1535-1912*. Lampeter, Dyfed, Wales: The Edwin Mellen Press, Ltd., 1995. 242p. Indices. /GC 978 H216n/

Hargrove, Hondon B. *Buffalo Soldiers in Italy: Black Americans in World War II*. Jefferson, NC: McFarland & Company, Inc., 1985. 199p. Bibliography. Index. Notes. Photographs. Tables. /GC 940.5410 Aa1ha/

Harris, Milton Stephen. *Black Family Tree: "Slavery to 1984."* Owensboro, KY: M. S. Harris, 1984. 60p. Photographs. /GC 929.2 Si47ha/

Harris, Robert L., Jr. *Teaching Afro-American History*. Washington, DC: American Historical Association, 1985. 67p. Notes. Reference Guide. /GC 973.07 H24t/

Harvard Encyclopedia of American Ethnic Groups. Cambridge, MA: The Belknap Press of Harvard University Press, 1981. 1076p. Appendices. Bibliographies. Maps. Tables. /GC 973.004 H26/

Hawkins, Walter L. *African American Generals and Flag Officers: Biographies of Over 120 Blacks in the United States Military*. Jefferson, NC: McFarland & Company, Inc., 1993. 264p. Index. Photographs. /GC 973.001 Aa1haw/

Heard, J. Norman. *The Black Frontiersmen: Adventures of Negroes Among American Indians, 1528-1918*. New York: The John Day Company, 1969. 128p. Bibliography. Index. /GC 929.11 H35b/

Heinegg, Paul. *Free African Americans of North Carolina and Virginia*. Baltimore, MD: Clearfield Company, Inc., 1992. 462p. Bibliography. Index. /GC 975 H36f/

Henderson, Edwin B. *The Black Athlete: Emergence and Arrival*. New York: Publishers Company, Inc., 1968. 306p. Bibliography. Index. Photographs. /GC 929.11 H38b/

Henritze, Barbara K. *Bibliographic Checklist of African American Newspapers*. Baltimore, MD: Genealogical Publishing Company, 1995. 206p. Bibliography. Title Index. /GC 973.004 H39b/

Higginson, Thomas Wentworth. *Army Life in a Black Regiment*. New York: W. W. Norton & Company, 1984. 287p. Appendices. Index. /GC 973.74 Aa1higa/

Higginson, Thomas Wentworth. *Black Rebellion: Five Slave Revolts*. New York: Da Capo Press, 1998. 221p. /GC 973 H5354b/

Hine, Darlene Clark. *Black Women in America: An Historical Encyclopedia.* Brooklyn, NY: Carlson Publishing, Inc., 1993. 2 volumes. Bibliography. Chronology. Index. Photographs. /GC 973 B561/

Hodges, Graham Russell. *The Black Loyalist Directory: African Americans in Exile after the American Revolution*. New York: Garland Publishing in association with the New England Historic Genealogical Society, 1996. 318p. Appendices. Bibliography. Index. /GC 973 H665b/

Holway, John B. *Red Tails, Black Wings: The Men of America's Black Air Force*. Las Cruces, NM: Yucca Tree Press, 1997. 345p. Bibliography. Index. Notes. Photographs. /GC 940.5410 Aa1hj/

Hoobler, Dorothy and Thomas. *The African American Family Album.* New York: Oxford University Press, 1995. 127p. Bibliography. Index. Photographs. /GC 973 H76a/

Hood, J. W. *One Hundred Years of the African Methodist Episcopal Zion Church; the Centennial of African Methodism*. New York: A. M. E. Zion Book Concerns, 1895. 625p. Photographs. /Microfiche/

Horton, James Oliver and Lois E. *In Hope of Liberty: Culture, Community, and Protest Among Northern Free Blacks, 1700-1860*. New York: Oxford University Press, 1997. 340p. Index. Notes. /GC 973 H78i/

Index to Compiled Service Records of Volunteer Union Soldiers Who Served with United States Colored Troops. Washington, DC: National Archives and Records Service, 1964. 98 rolls. /Microfilm/

Intercom: Afro-Americans Communicating—Preserving Legacies.
Atlanta, GA: Rainbow Associates, Afro-American Genealogists.
V. 1-, January 1986-. /Periodical/

International Society of Sons and Daughters of Slave Ancestry Newsletter. Chicago, IL: ISDSA, V. 1-, Summer 1998-. /Periodical/

Ivy Leaf. Bethesda, MD: University Publications of America, 1999. 14 rolls. Alpha Kappa Alpha Sorority chronicle covering 1921-1998. /Microfilm/

Jacobs, Donald M. *Antebellum Black Newspapers.* Westport, CT: Greenwood Press, 1976. 587p. Index to: "Freedom's Journal," "The Rights of All," "The Weekly Advocate," and "The Colored American." /GC 016.9747 J15a/

Jacobs, Donald M. *Index to the American Slave.* Westport, CT: Greenwood Press, 1981. 274p. /GC 929.11 In2/

Johnson, Anne E. & Adam Merton Cooper. *A Student's Guide to African American Genealogy.* Phoenix, AZ: The Oryx Press, 1996. 170p. Index. Photographs. Selected bibliographies. /GC 929 J629a/

Johnson, Charles, Jr. *African American Soldiers in the National Guard: Recruitment and Deployment During Peacetime and War.* Westport, CT: Greenwood Press, 1992. 218p. Bibliography. Index. /GC 973.001 Aa1j/

Johnson, Jeff G. *Black Christians: The Untold Lutheran Story.* St. Louis, MO: Concordia Publishing House, 1991. 262p. Appendices. Notes. Tables. /GC 973 J631b/

Jordan, Lewis G. *Negro Baptist History, U.S.A., 1750-1930*. Nashville, TN: The Sunday School Publishing Board, 1995. 464p. Appendices. Bibliography. Photographs. Tables. /GC 929.102 B22jo/

Kaplan, Sidney and Emma Nogrady Kaplan. *The Black Presence in the Era of the American Revolution*. Amherst, MA: The University of Massachusetts Press, 1989. 305p. Bibliography. Index. Photographs. /GC 973.34 Aa1ka/

Katz, William Loren. *Black Indians: A Hidden Heritage*. New York: Aladdin Paperbacks, 1997. 198p. Bibliography. Index. Photographs. /GC 973 K159b/

Katz, William Loren. *Black People Who Made the Old West*. Trenton, NJ: Africa World Press, Inc., 1992. 181p. Bibliography. Index. Photographs. /GC 978 K15bl/

Katz, William Loren. *The Black West*. Garden City, NY: Doubleday & Company, Inc., 1971. 336p. Appendices. Bibliography. Drawings. Index. Photographs. /GC 978 K15b/

Katz, William Loren. *The Black West: A Documentary and Pictorial History of the African American Role in the Westward Expansion of the United States*. New York: Simon & Schuster, 1996. 348p. Appendices. Bibliography. Drawings. Index. Photographs. /GC 978 K15ba/

Kemble, Jean. *American Slavery: Pre-1866 Imprints*. London: Eccles Centre for American Studies, The British Library, 1995. 84p. Index. /GC 973 K31a/

Kenner, Charles L. *Buffalo Soldiers and Officers of the Ninth Cavalry, 1867-1898*. Norman, OK: University of Oklahoma Press, 1999.

384p. Bibliography. Index. Notes. Photographs. /GC 973.001 Aa1ke/

King, Wilma. *Stolen Childhood: Slave Youth in Nineteenth-Century America*. Bloomington, IN: Indiana University Press, 1995. 253p. Appendices. Bibliography. Index. Notes. Photographs. /GC 973 K58s/

Kulikoff, Allan. *Tobacco and Slaves: The Development of Southern Cultures in the Chesapeake, 1680-1800*. Chapel Hill, NC: University of North Carolina Press, 1986. 449p. Index. /GC 975 K95t/

Lakey, Othal Hawthorne. *The History of the CME Church (Revised)*. Memphis, TN: The CME Publishing House, 1996. 756p. Appendices. Index. Notes. Photographs. /GC 929.102 M56lake/

Lakey, Othal Hawthorne. *The Rise of "Colored Methodism:" A Study of the Background and the Beginnings of the Christian Methodist Episcopal Church*. Dallas, TX: Crescendo Book Publications, 1972. 128p. Appendices. Bibliography. Notes. /GC 929.102 M65lak/

Larrie, Reginald R. *Makin' Free: African-Americans in the Northwest Territory*. Detroit, MI: B. Ethridge Books, 1981. 133p. Bibliography. Index. Photographs. /GC 977 L32m/

Law, Nova. *African-American Genealogy Workbook*. Birmingham, AL: Legacy Publishing Company, 1994. 3rd ed. 113p. Lists. Maps. /GC 929 L411a/

Lawson, Jacqueline A. *An Index of African Americans Identified in Selected Records of the Bureau of Refugees, Freedmen, and*

Abandoned Lands. Bowie, MD: Heritage Books, Inc., 1995. Various pagination. /GC 973 L44i/

Leckie, William H. *The Buffalo Soldiers: A Narrative of the Negro Cavalry in the West*. Norman, OK: University of Oklahoma Press, 1981. 290p. Bibliography. Index. Photographs. /GC 973.001 Aa11/

Lerner, Gerda, ed. *Black Women in White America: A Documentary History*. New York: Random House, 1972. 630p. Bibliography. /GC 929.11 L556b/

Lincoln, Charles Eric. *The Black Muslims in America*. Boston, MA: Beacon Press, 1961. 276p. Index. Notes. /GC 973 L637b/

Littlefield, Daniel F., Jr. *Africans and Creeks: From the Colonial Period to the Civil War*. Westport, CT: Greenwood Press, 1979. 286p. Bibliography. Index. Maps. /GC 970.1 L73a/

Littlefield, Daniel F., Jr. *Africans and Seminoles: From Removal to Emancipation*. Westport, CT: Greenwood Press, 1977. 278p. Bibliography. Index. Lists. /GC 970.1 L73af/

Littlefield, Daniel F., Jr. *The Cherokee Freedmen: From Emancipation to American Citizenship*. Westport, CT: Greenwood Press, 1978. Bibliography. Index. /GC 970.1 L73c/

Littlefield, Daniel F., Jr. *The Chickasaw Freedmen: A People Without a Country*. Westport, CT: Greenwood Press, 1980. 248p. Bibliography. Index. Photographs. /GC 976.6 L727c/

Litwack, Leon F. *Trouble in Mind: Black Southerners in the Age of Jim Crow*. New York: Alfred A. Knopf, 1998. 599p. Bibliography. Index. Notes. /GC 973 L737t/

Lowery, I. E. *Life on the Old Plantation in Ante-Bellum Days, Or A Story Based on Facts*. Columbia, SC: The State Company Printers, 1911. 185p. Appendix. /GC   975   L95l/

Lucas, Ernestine. *Black Genealogical Research*. Dayton, OH: MVCGH Conference, 1983. 40 minutes. /Cassette Tape/

Lucas, Ernestine. *Forces and Destinations of Black Migration*. Columbus, OH: NGS Conference, 1986. /Cassette Tape/

Lyda, Chester H. *The Negro Soldier in the American Revolution*. Chicago, IL: University of Chicago, 1922. 67p. Dissertation. Notes. /GC   973.3   L983n /

McKivigan, John R., ed. *The Roving Editor, or Talks with Slaves in the Southern States, by James Redpath*. University Park, PA: The Pennsylvania State University Press, 1996. 356p. Appendices. Index. Notes. /GC   975   R249r/

Madubuike, Ihechukwu. *A Handbook of African Names*. Washington, DC: Three Continents Press, 1976. 233p. /GC   929.4   M25h/

Majors, M. A. *Noted Negro Women*. Chicago: Donohue & Henneberry, 1893. 365p. Photographs. Pictures. /GC   929.19   M28n/

Mather, Frank Lincoln, ed. *Who's Who of the Colored Race: A General Biographical Dictionary of Men and Women of African Descent*. Chicago, IL: s. n., 1915. 296p. /GC   929.11   W62co/

Meier, August. *The Making of Black America: Essays in Negro Life & History*. New York: Atheneum, 1976. 507p. Bibliography. /GC   973   M2895   V. 2/

Meillassoux, Claude. *The Anthropology of Slavery: The Womb of Iron and Gold*. Chicago, IL: The University of Chicago Press, 1991.

421p. Bibliography. Glossary. Indices. Notes. /GC 973 M469a/

Melish, Joanne Pope. ***Disowning Slavery: Gradual Emancipation and "Race" in New England, 1780-1860.*** Ithaca, NY: Cornell University Press, 1998. 296p. Illustrations. Index. Notes. /GC 974 M486d/

Miller, Randall M. & John David Smith. ***Dictionary of Afro-American Slavery.*** New York: Greenwood Press, 1988. 866p. Bibliographies. Charts. Chronology. Index. Maps. /GC 973 D562/

Moebs, Thomas Truxtun. ***Black Soldiers–Black Sailors–Black Ink: Research Guide on African Americans in U. S. Military History, 1526-1900.*** Williamsburg, VA: Moebs Publishing Company, 1994. 1654p. Bibliography. Master Index. /GC 973 M722b/

Mullin, Michael. ***Africa in America: Slave Acculturation and Resistance in the American South and the British Caribbean, 1736-1831.*** Urbana, IL: University of Illinois Press, 1994. 412p. Appendices. Bibliography. Index. Notes. /GC 973 M91a/

Murdza, Peter J., Jr. ***Immigration to Liberia, 1865 to 1904.*** Newark, DE: University of Delaware, 1975. 76p. /GC 929.19 M94i/

Nankivell, John H. ***History of the Twenty-fifth Regiment United States Infantry, 1869-1926.*** New York: Negro Universities Press, 1969. 212p. Appendices. Photographs. /GC 973.001 Aa1n/

The Negro in American History: Slaves and Master, 1567-1854. S.l.: William Benton, 1969. 466p. Index. Photographs. /GC 973 N31295 V. 3/

The Negro in American History: A Taste of Freedom, 1854-1927. S.l.: William Benton, 1969. 452p. Photographs. /GC 973 N31295 V.2/

The Negro Year Book, 1952: A Review of Events Affecting Negro Life. New York: Wm. H. Wise & Company, Inc., 1952. 424p. Index. /GC 973 N313 1952/

Nell, William C. *The Colored Patriots of the American Revolution.* New York: Arno Press & The New York Times, 1968. 396p. /973.34 Aa1nel/

Newman, Debra L. *Black History: A Guide to Civilian Records in the National Archives.* Washington, DC: National Archives Trust Fund Board, 1984. 379p. Index. Photographs. /GC 016.973 N458b/

Newman, Debra L. *List of Black Servicemen Compiled From the War Department Collection of Revolutionary War Records.* Washington, DC: National Archives and Records Service, 1974. 29p. Bibliography. /GC 973.34 Aa1new/

Newman, Debra L. *List of Free Black Heads of Families in the First Census of the United States.* Washington, DC: The National Archives, 1973. 44p. Bibliography. /GC 929.11 N46l/

Nichols, Elaine, ed. *The Last Miles of the Way: African American Homegoing Traditions, 1890-Present.* Columbia, SC: Commissioners of the South Carolina State Museum, 1989. 73p. Bibliography. Index. /GC 973 L339/

Paradis, James M. *Strike the Blow for Freedom: The 6th United States Colored Infantry in the Civil War.* Shippensburg, PA: White Mane Books, 1998. 203p. Appendices. Bibliography. Illustrations. Index. Maps. Notes. /GC 973.74 Aa1pj/

Patterson, Lindsay. *Anthology of the American Negro in the Theatre.*
New York: Publishers Company, Inc., 1967. 306p. Bibliography.
Index. Photographs. /GC 973 An81/

Pease, Jane H. and William H. Pease. *They Who Would Be Free:
Black's Search for Freedom, 1830-1861.* New York: Atheneum,
1974. 331p. Bibliography. Index. Notes. /GC 973 P324t/

Phillips, Ulrich B. *Plantation and Frontier Documents: 1641-1863.*
Cleveland, OH: The Arthur H. Clark Company, 1909. 756p.
Charts. Maps. Tables. /GC 975 P54p/

Piersen, William D. *Black Yankees: The Development of an
Afro-American Subculture in Eighteenth-Century New
England.* Amherst, MA: University of Massachusetts Press,
1988. 237p. Index. Notes. /GC 974 P61b/

Porter, Kenneth Wiggins. *The Black Seminoles: History of a Freedom-
Seeking People.* Gainesville, FL: University Press of Florida,
1996. 284p. Bibliography. Index. /GC 970.3 Se52p/

Postell, William Dosite. *The Health of Slaves on Southern Plantations.*
Baton Rouge, LA: Louisiana State University Press, 19--. 231p.
Bibliography. Index. Photographs. /GC 975 P84h/

Potter, Joan. *African-American Firsts: Famous, Little-Known and
Unsung Triumphs of Blacks in America.* Elizabethtown, NY:
Pinto Press, 1994. 336p. Bibliography. Index. Photographs.
/GC 973 P853a/

Potts, Howard E. *A Comprehensive Name Index for "The American
Slave."* Westport, CT: Greenwood Press, 1997. 390p. /GC 975
P858c/

Proceedings of the Black State Conventions, 1840-1865. Philadelphia, PA: Temple University Press, 1979-. 2 volumes. /GC   929.11   P938   V. 1-2/

Profile of Black Museums. Washington, DC: African American Museums Association, 1988. 54p. /GC   929   P94/

Quarles, Benjamin. *The Negro in the Civil War*. New York: Da Capo Press, Inc., 1989. 379p. Bibliography. Index. /GC   973   Aalq/

Ravage, John W. *Black Pioneers: Images of the Black Experience on the North American Frontier*. Salt Lake City, UT: The University of Utah Press, 1997. 224p. Bibliography. Index. Notes. Photographs. /GC   978   R197bl/

Rawick, George P., ed. *The American Slave: A Composite Autobiography–From Sundown to Sunup: The Making of the Black Community*. Westport, CT: Greenwood Publishing Company, 1972. 208p. Bibliography. Index. /GC   973   R19f/

Rawick, George P., ed. *The American Slave: A Composite Autobiography–God Struck Me Dead*. Westport, CT: Greenwood Publishing Company, 1971. 218p. /GC   929.11   G54/

Rawick, George P., ed. *The American Slave: A Composite Autobiography–Unwritten History of Slavery*. Westport CT: Greenwood Publishing Company, 1972. 322p. /GC   929.11   Un9/

Redfern, Bernice. *Women of Color in the United States: A Guide to the Literature*. New York: Garland Publishing, Inc., 1989. 156p. Indices. /GC   016.3054   R24w/

Reiss, Oscar. *Blacks in Colonial America*. Jefferson, NC: McFarland & Company, 1997. 293p. Index. Notes. /GC 973.2 R278b/

Reynolds, Edward. *Stand the Storm: A History of the Atlantic Slave Trade*. Chicago, IL: I. R. Dee, 1993. 182p. Bibliography. Index. Map. Notes. /GC 973 R334s/

Richardson, Ben. *Great American Negroes*. New York: Thomas Y. Crowell Company, 1956. 339p. Index. /GC 973 R393g/

Richardson, David, ed. *Bristol, Africa and the Eighteenth-Century Slave Trade to America*. Bristol, England: Bristol Record Society, 1987, 1996. 157p. Index. Volume 2: The Years of Ascendancy, 1730-1745; Volume 4: The Final years, 1770-1807. Contains many lists of ships. /GC 942.4102 B861p V. 39 & V. 47/

Robinson, Wilhelmena S. *Historical Negro Biographies*. New York: Publishers Company, Inc., 1967. (International Library of Negro Life and History) 291p. Bibliography. Drawings. Index. Photographs. /GC 929.11 R568h/

Rose, James and Alice Eichholz. *Black Genesis*. Detroit, MI: Gale Research Company, 1978. 326p. Illustrations. Bibliographies. Indices. /GC 929 R72b/

Ross, Joseph B. *Tabular Analysis of the Records of the U. S. Colored Troops and Their Predecessor Units in the National Archives of the United States*. Washington, DC: National Archives and Records Service, 1973. 27p. /GC 973.74 Aa1una/

Saunders, Doris. *Black Newspapers as a Source for Afro-Americans*. Salt Lake City, UT: NGS Conference, 1985. 90 minutes. /Cassette Tape/

Saunders, Doris. *Value of Family History for Afro-Americans*. Salt Lake City, UT: NGS Conference, 1985. 60 minutes. /Cassette Tape/

Savage, W. Sherman. *Blacks in the West*. Westport, CT: Greenwood Press, 1976. 230p. Contributions in Afro-American and African Studies Number 23. Bibliography. Index. Notes. /GC 978 Sa9bl/

Schmal, John P. *An African-American Family: The Williams-Lear Family History*. S.l.: s.n., 1993. 50p. Notes. /GC 929.2 W671sc/

Schweninger, Loren. *Black Property Owners in the South, 1790-1915*. Urbana, IL: University of Illinois Press, 1990. 426p. Appendices. Bibliography. Index. Notes. Photographs. /GC 975 Sch98b/

Scott, Edward Van Zile. *The Unwept: Black American Soldiers and the Spanish-American War*. Montgomery, AL: The Black Belt Press, 1996. 240p. Bibliography. Index. Notes. /GC 973.894 Aa1sc/

Scott, Emmett J. *Scott's Official History of the American Negro in the World War*. S.l.: E. J. Scott, 1919. 512p. /GC 940.410 Aa1sc/

Scott, Jean S. *Afro-American Genealogical Research*. Albany, NY: New York Conference, 1983. 55 minutes. /Cassette Tape/

Scott, Jean S. *Beginning an Afro-American Genealogical Pursuit*. New York: Eppress Printers, 1985. 27p. Bibliography. /GC 929 Sco8b/

Schubert, Frank N. *Black Valor: Buffalo Soldiers and the Medal of Honor, 1870-1898*. Wilmington, DE: Scholarly Resources, Inc.,

1997. 231p. Bibliography. Index. Notes. Photographs. /GC 973 Sch78b/

Secret, Jeanette Braxton. *Guide to Tracing Your African American Civil War Ancestor*. Bowie, MD: Heritage Books, Inc., 1997. 3rd ed. Bibliography. /GC 973 Se25y/

Sigler, Phil Samuel. *The Attitudes of Free Blacks Towards Emigration to Liberia*. Ann Arbor, MI: University Microfilms, Inc., 1973. 209p. Bibliography. /GC 973 Si255a/

Six Women's Slave Narratives. New York: Oxford University Press, 1988. A compilation of previously published works. /GC 973 Si97/

Slattery, Kenneth M. *Negro Theatre in America Prior to the Civil War*. Fort Wayne, IN: Fort Wayne Public Library, 1972. 23p. Bibliography. Notes. /GC 973 N3138/

Slavery and Abolition of the Slave Trade, 1700-1890. New York: Schomburg Collection, New Public Library, 1971. Manuscript collection from the Schomburg Collection of Negro Literature and History. 1 roll. /Microfilm/

Sloan, Irving J. *The Blacks in America, 1492-1977: A Chronology & Fact Book*. Dobbs Ferry, NY: Oceana Publications, Inc., 1977. 169p. Index. /GC 973 Sl5b/

Smith, Gloria L. *Beginning Black–Indian Genealogy–The Seminoles*. Tucson, AZ: G. L. Smith, 1994. 135p. Bibliography. Lists. /GC 929.11 Sm57b/

Smith, Gloria L. *Black American Genealogy for Beginners*. Tucson, AZ: G. L. Smith, 1979. 31p. /GC 929 Sm51b/

Smith, Jessie Carney, ed. *Ethnic Genealogy*. Westport, CT: Greenwood Press, 1983. /GC 929 Et3/

Smith, Jonathan Kennon. *Death Notices in the CME Christian Index, 1885-1905*. S. l.: J. K. Smith, 1999. 68p. Index. /GC 973 Sm58d/

Southern Genealogist's Exchange Quarterly, The. Hampton, GA: Armchair Publications, 1957-. /Periodical/

Southern States Armchair Researcher, The. Hampton, GA: Armchair Publications, 1983-. /Periodical/

State Slavery Statutes. Frederick, MD: University Publications of America, 1989. 354 microfiche. /Microfiche/

State Slavery Statutes: Guide to the Microfiche Collection. Frederick, MD: University Publications of America, 1989. 565p. Index. /GC 973 St2/

Stephenson, Wendell Holmes. *Isaac Franklin: Slave Trader and Planter of the Old South*. Baton Rouge, LA: Louisianna University Press, 1938. 368p. Index. Plantation records. /GC 975 St4i/

Sterling, Dorothy. *The Trouble They Seen: The Story of Reconstruction in the Words of African Americans*. New York: Da Capo Press, 1994. 491p. Drawings. Index. Photographs. /GC 929.11 T75/

Stewart, Jeffrey C. *1001 Things Everyone Should Know About African American History*. New York: Doubleday, 1996. 406p. Bibliography. Index. Photographs. /GC 973 St49o/

Stewart, Paul W. and Wallace Y. Ponce. *Black Cowboys*. Broomfield, CO: Phillips Publishing, Inc., 1986. Bibliography. Photographs. /GC 929.11 St49b/

Streets, David H. *Slave Genealogy: A Research Guide With Case Studies*. Bowie, MD: Heritage Books, Inc., 1986. 87p. Appendices. Bibliography. /GC 929 St78s/

Tadman, Michael. *Speculators and Slaves: Masters, Traders, and Slaves in the Old South*. Madison, WI: The University of Wisconsin Press, 1996. 317p. Appendices. Bibliography. Index. /GC 975 T12s/

Tanner, Benjamin Tucker. *An Apology for African Methodism*. Baltimore, MD: s.n., 1867. 468p. /GC 929.102 M56t/

Taylor, Yuval, ed. *I Was Born a Slave: An Anthology of Classic Slave Narratives, Volume One, 1770-1849*. Chicago, IL: Lawrence Hill Books, 1999. 764p. Bibliography. Notes. /GC 975 I1 V. 1/

Thackery, David T. *Afro-American Family History at The Newberry Library: A Research Guide and Bibliography*. Chicago, IL: The Newberry Library, 1988. 28p. /GC 016.929 T32a/

Thackery, David T. and Dee Woodtor. *Case Studies in Afro-American Genealogy*. Chicago, IL: The Newberry Library, 1989. 43p. /GC 929 T32c/

The Trans-Atlantic Slave Trade: A Database on CD-ROM. Cambridge, England: Press Syndicate of the University of Cambridge. 89 page booklet with 1 CD-ROM. /CD-ROM/

Trudeau, Noah Andre. *Like Men of War: Black Troops in the Civil War, 1862-1865*. New York: Little, Brown and Company, 1998.

548p. Bibliography. Index. Maps. Notes. Photographs. /GC 973.74 Aa1tr/

Valuska, David L. *The African American in the Union Navy: 1861-1865*. New York: Garland Publishing, Inc., 1993. 353p. Appendices. Bibliography. Index. Lists. /GC 973.74 Aalvd/

Vaughn, Emily E. *Black Snow(den), Warsaw–Benjamin Snowden and the Related Lines: A Wee Bit 'o' History of the Snowdens from Maryland to Ohio and to Warsaw, New York, by the Underground Railroad*. Buffalo, NY: E. E. Vaughn, 1997. 198p. Family Group Sheets. Photographs. /GC 929.2 Sn635v/

Vlach, John Michael. *Back of the Big House: The Architecture of Plantation Slavery*. Chapel Hill, NC: The University of North Carolina Press, 1993. 258p. Drawings. Index. Notes. Photographs. /GC 975 V84b/

Walker, James D. *Afro-American Genealogy*. Kansas City, MO: FGS Conference, 1985. 60 minutes. /Cassette Tape/

Walker, James D. *Afro-Americans in the American Revolution*. Salt Lake City, UT: NGS Conference, 1985. 60 minutes. /Cassette Tape/

Walker, James D. *Black Genealogy: How to Begin*. Athens, GA: University of Georgia Center for Continuing Education, 1977. 52p. Bibliography. /GC 929 W15b/

Walker, James D. *Researching Blacks in the Region–Mid-Atlantic*. Baltimore, MD: s.n., 198-. 65 minutes. /Cassette Tape/

Walker, James D. *Searching for Black Ancestors*. Cincinnati, OH: FGS Conference, 1987. 60 minutes. /Cassette Tape/

Walls, William J. *The African Methodist Episcopal Zion Church: Reality of the Black Church*. Charlotte, NC: A.M.E. Zion Publishing House, 1974. 669p. Bibliography. Illustrations. Index. Photographs. /GC 929.102 Af8w/

Walton-Raji, Angela Y. *Black Indian Genealogy Research*. Bowie, MD: Heritage Books, Inc., 1993. 167p. Bibliography. Index. /GC 929 W17b/

Warner, Lee H. *Free Men in an Age of Servitude: Three Generations of a Black Family*. Lexington, KY: The University Press of Kentucky, 1992. 168p. Bibliography. Index. Notes. /GC 929.2 P942w/

Watson, Alan. *Slave Laws in the Americas*. Athens, GA: The University of Georgia Press, 1989. 179p. Index. Notes. /GC 929.11 W328s/

Wesley, Charles H. *In Freedom's Footsteps: From the African Background to the Civil War*. New York: Publishers Company, Inc., 1968. 307p. Bibliography. Index. Photographs. /GC 973 W51i/

Wesley, Charles H. *The Quest for Equality: From Civil War to Civil Rights*. New York: Publishers Company, Inc., 1968. 307p. Bibliography. Index. Photographs. /GC 973 W51q/

Wesley, Charles H. & Patricia W. Romero. *Negro Americans in the Civil War: From Slavery to Citizenship*. New York: Publishers Company, Inc., 1967. 307p. Bibliography. Index. Photographs. /GC 973.7 W51n/

Westward Soul! Denver, CO: Black American West Foundation, Inc., 1976. 59p. /GC 978.8 P97/

White, Barnetta McGhee. *In Search of Kith and Kin: The History of a Southern Black Family*. Baltimore, MD: Gateway Press, Inc., 1986. 208p. Appendices. Index. /GC 929.2 M1729w/

Who's Who in Colored America: A Biographical Directory of Notable Living Persons of African Descent in America. Brooklyn, NY: Thomas Yenser, 1940. 608p. /GC 929.11 W619 1938-1940/

Wiencek, Henry. *The Hairstons: An American Family in Black and White*. New York: St. Martin's Press, 1999. Bibliography. Index. Maps. Notes. Photographs. /GC 929.2 H1264w/

Wiley, Bell Irvin. *Southern Negroes, 1861-1865*. NY: Rinehart & Company, Inc., 19--. 366p. Illustrations. Index. Photographs. /GC 975 W64s/

Williams, Ethel L. and Clifton F. Brown. *The Howard University Bibliography of African and Afro-American Religious Studies*. Wilmington, DE: Scholarly Resources, Inc., 1977. 525p. Index. /GC 973 W67h/

Williams, Gilbert Anthony. *The Christian Recorder, Newspaper of the African Methodist Episcopal Church: History of a Forum for Ideas, 1854-1902*. Jefferson, NC: McFarland & Company, 1996. 165p. Bibliography. Index. /GC 929.102 Af78wi/

Williamson, Joel. *New People: Miscegenation and Mulattoes in the United States*. New York: The Free Press, 1980. 221p. Bibliography. Index. /GC 973 W683n/

Wilson, Joseph T. *The Black Phalanx: A History of the Negro Soldiers of the United States in the Wars of 1775-1812, 1861-1865*. Hartford, CT: American Publishing Company, 1890. 528p. Illus. /GC 973.001 Aa1wi/

Woodson, Carter G. *Free Negro Heads of Families in the United States in 1830*. Washington, DC: Association for the Study of Negro Life and History, Inc., 1925. 296p. /GC 929.11 W86f/

Woodson, Carter G. *Free Negro Owners of Slaves in the United States in 1830: Together with Absentee Ownership of Slaves in the United States in 1830*. New York: Negro University Press, 1968. 78p. /GC 973 W868f/

Woodtor, Dee. *Finding a Place Called Home: A Guide to African-American Genealogy and Historical Identity*. New York: Random House, 1999. 452p. Bibliography. Index. Maps. Photographs. /GC 973 W8682f/

World Conference on Records: Preserving Our Heritage, August 12 - 15, 1980. Salt Lake City, UT: Corporation of the President of the Church of Jesus Christ of Latter-day Saints, 1980. /GC 929 W88 V. 11 Nos. 901-903/

Wright, Roberta Hughes. *Lay Down Body: Living History in African American Cemeteries*. Detroit, MI: Visible Ink Press, 1996. Bibliography. Index. /GC 973 H869L/

Yetman, Norman R., ed. *Voices from Slavery*. NY: Holt, Rinehart, and Winston, 19--. 368p. Index. Photographs. /GC 973 Y48v/

Young, Tommie Morton. *African-American Genealogy: Exploring and Documenting the Black Family*. Clarksville, TN: Jostens Publishers, 19--. 70p. Charts. Photographs. /GC 929 Y87a/

Young, Tommie Morton. *Afro-American Genealogy Sourcebook*. New York: Garland Publishing Company, 1987. 199p. /GC 929 Y87af/

ALABAMA

Andrews, Johnnie Jr. *Non-Whites in Colonial Alabama: A Compendium of Indian, Black, Mulatto and Quadroon Records, 1704-1813*. Prichard, AL: Bienville Historical Society, 1989. 43p. /GC 976.102 M71ab/

Boothe, Charles Octavius. *The Cyclopedia of the Colored Baptists of Alabama*. Birmingham, AL: Alabama Publishing Company, 1895. /GC 976.1 B64c/

Brown, Alan & David Taylor, eds. *Gabr'l Blow Sof': Sumter County, Alabama Slave Narratives*. Livingston, AL: Livingston Press, The University of West Alabama, 1997. 123p. Index. Photographs. /GC 976.101 Su6g/

East Alabama Colored Musical Convention. *Minutes of the Fourth Annual Session of the East Alabama Colored Musical Convention, Held with New Bethel Church, White Oak Springs, Barbour County, Ala., August 8, 9, and 10, 1890*. S.l.: The Convention, 1890. 7p. /GC 976.1 Ea77m/

Feldman, Lynne B. *A Sense of Place: Birmingham's Black Middle-Class Community, 1890-1930*. Tuscaloosa, AL: University of Alabama Press, 1999. 326p. Bibliography. Illustrations. Index. /GC 976.102 B53f/

Fuller, Willie J. *Blacks in Alabama, 1528-1865*. OH: W. J. Fuller, 1976. 30p. Bibliography. /GC 976.1 F95b/

Hester, Gwendolyn Lynette. *Freedmen and Colored Marriage Records, 1865-1890, Sumter County, Alabama*. Bowie, MD: Heritage Books, Inc., 1996. 315p. Appendices. /GC 976.101 Su6h/

Hollins, Frances D., ed. *The Stone Street Baptist Church—Alabama's First, 1806-1982*. S.l.: s.n., 1982. 149p. /GC 976.102 M71s/

Johnson, Charles S. *Shadow of the Plantation*. New Brunswick, NJ: Transaction Publishers, 1996. 215p. Index. /GC 976.101 M23j/

Leaders of the Colored Race in Alabama. Mobile, AL: The News Publishing Company, Inc., 1928. 99p. Index. Photographs. /GC 976.1 L46/

Miller, Randall M., ed. *"Dear Master:" Letters of a Slave Family*. Athens, GA: The University of Georgia Press, 1990. 297p. Bibliography. Drawings. Index. Photographs. /GC 976.101 82d/

Rawick, George P., ed. *The American Slave: A Composite Autobiography—Alabama & Indiana Narratives*. Westport, CT: Greenwood Pub. Co., 1972. /GC 976.1 AL17 Sec. 1/

Rawick, George P., ed. *The American Slave: A Composite Autobiography—Alabama Narratives*. Westport, CT: Greenwood Publishing Co., 1977. /GC 976.1 AL16/

Rawick, George P., ed. *The American Slave: A Composite Autobiography—Alabama... Narratives*. Westport, CT: Greenwood Publishing Co., 1979. /GC 929.11 AL113 Sec. 1/

Records of Ante-Bellum Southern Plantations from the Revolution through the Civil War. Frederick, MD: University Publications of America, Inc., 198-.
Alabama--Archibald H. Arrington papers, 1754-1865. /Series J, Part 12, Rolls 15-16/
Alabama--Hamilton Brown papers, 1752-1907. /Series J, Part 14, Rolls 5-8/
Alabama--Bruce family papers, 1746-1871. /Series E, Part 3, Rolls 7-30/

Alabama--Bullock & Hamilton papers, 1757-1971. /Series J, Part 13, Rolls 5-8/
Alabama--Davidson family papers, 1827-1935. /Series J, Part 13, Rolls 28-34/
Alabama--Gilliam family papers, 1794-1865. /Series E, Part 2, Rolls 19-21/
Alabama--Chillab Smith Howe papers, 1814-1899. /Series J, Part 6, Rolls 20-23/
Alabama--Jackson family papers, 1784-1880. /Series J, Part 4, Rolls 25-36/
Alabama--Isaac Jarratt papers, 1832-1979. /Series J, Part 13, Roll 40/
Alabama--William Johnson papers, 1760-1888. /Series J, Part 13, Rolls 2-3/
Alabama--Lewis family papers, 1730-1956. /Series F, Part 12, Rolls 13-14/
Alabama--George Washington Polk papers, 1793-1857. /Series J, Part 8, Rolls 13-14/
Alabama--Prince family papers, 1784-1880. /Series J, Part 4, Rolls 25-36/
Alabama--Ruffin & Meade papers, 1796-1906. /Series J, Part 9, Rolls 28-30/
Alabama--Francis Gildart Ruffin papers, 1802-1860. /Series J, Part 9, Rolls 30-32/
Alabama--Tayloe family papers, 1708-1861. /Series M, Part 1, Rolls 1-57/
Autauga co., AL--Benjamin Fitzpatrick papers, 1819-1892. /Series J, Part 7, Roll 5/
Baldwin co., AL--Henry Alderson papers, 1848-1882. /Series J, Part 7, Roll 1/
Barbour co., AL--John Fletcher Comer journal, 1844-1847. /Series J, Part 7, Roll 1/
Benton co., AL--Lipscomb family papers, 1791-1867. /Series J, Part 7, Roll 8/
Butler co., AL--Marcus Joseph Wright papers, 1831-1860. /Series J, Part 7, Roll 7/
Chambers co., AL--Geo. Washington Allen papers, 1832-1865. /Series J, Part 7, Rolls 4-5/
Clarke co., AL--William Stump Forwood papers, 1836-1861. /Series J, Part 7, Rolls 1-2/
Covington co., AL--Julien S. Devereux papers, 1787-1865. /Series G. Part 1, Rolls 36-42/
Dallas co., AL--William M. Byrd papers, 1832-1914. /Series J, Part 7, Roll 5/
Franklin co., AL--Thompson family papers, 1809-1924. /Series J, Part 7, Roll 8/
Greene co., AL--John Gideon Harris diary, 1859. /Series J, Part 7, Roll 6/
Greene co., AL--Ernest Haywood papers, 1830-1860. /Series J, Part 7, Rolls 12-20/
Greene co., AL--Johnston & McFaddin family papers, 1839-1890. /Series J, Part 7, Roll 6/
Greene co., AL--Walton family papers, 1804-1868. /Series J, Part 7, Rolls 3-4/
Greene co., AL--Marcus J. Wright papers, 1831-1860. /Series J, Part 7, Roll 7/

Hale co., AL--Benjamin Fitzpatrick papers, 1819-1892. /Series J, Part 7, Roll 5/
Hale co., AL--John Gideon Harris diary, 1859. /Series J, Part 7, Roll 6/
Hale co., AL--Johnston & McFaddin family papers, 1839-1890. /Series J, Part 7, Roll 6/
Hale co., AL--Henry Watson, Jr., papers, 1744-1870. /Series F, Part 1, Rolls 9-18/
Limestone co., AL--Buchanan & McClellan papers, 1816-1872. /Series J, Part 7, Roll 8/
Lowndes co., AL--Leonard M. Burford papers, 1837-1868. /Series J, Part 7, Roll 3/
Macon co., AL--Julien S. Devereux papers, 1787-1865. /Series G. Part 1, Rolls 36-42/
Madison co., AL--Clement Claiborne Clay family papers, 1811-1866. /Series F, Part 1, Rolls 18-22/
Madison co., AL--Wyche & Otey family papers, 1824-1900 & 1935-1936. /Series J, Part 7, Rolls 9-12/
Marengo co., AL--William M Byrd papers, 1832-1914. /Series J, Part 7, Roll 5/
Marengo co., AL--Ernest Haywood papers, 1830-1860. /Series J, Part 7, Rolls 12-20/
Marengo co., AL--Johnston & McFaddin family papers, 1839-1890. /Series J, Part 7, Roll 6/
Marengo co., AL--Ruffin, Roulhac & Hamilton family papers [James H. Ruffin plantation records], 1841-1848. /Series J, Part 7, Roll 7/
Marengo co., AL--Samuel O. Wood papers, 1847-1862. /Series F, Part 1, Roll 9/
Mobile co., AL--Dorman family papers, 1838-1897. /Series J, Part 7, Roll 1/
Mobile co., AL--James McKibbin Gage papers, 1835-1876. /Series J, Part 7, Roll 8/
Mobile co., AL--Herbert C. Peabody papers, 1845-1849. /Series J, Part 7, Roll 3/
Mobile co., AL--Henry Lee Reynolds papers, 1851-1864. /Series J, Part 7, Roll 3/
Montgomery co., AL--W. J. Ridgill papers, 1851-1853. /Series J, Part 7, Roll 3/
Perry co., AL--Philip Henry Pitts papers, 1814-1889. /Series J, Part 7, Rolls 6-7/
Russell co., AL--George Washington Allen papers, 1832-1865. /Series J, Part 7, Rolls 4-5/
Russell co., AL--Tillman & Norwood ledgers, 1859-1868. /Series J, Part 7, Roll 7/
Sumter co., AL--Turner Reavis account book, 1842-1890. /Series C, Part 2, Roll 1/
Tuscaloosa co., AL--John Gideon Harris diary, 1859. /Series J, Part 7, Roll 6/
Wilcox co., AL--Wm. H. Gilliland papers, 1829-1868. /Series F, Part 1, Roll 8/

Records of the Assistant Commissioner for the State of Alabama, Bureau of Refugees, Freedmen, and Abandoned Lands, 1865-1870. Washington, DC: National Archives and Records Service, 1969. Microcopy M809. Endorsements Sent. Annual Reports. Miscellaneous Reports. Personal Reports. Consolidated Tri-monthly Reports. Monthly Reports. Register of Letters. /Microfilm Rolls 3-16, 19-20/

Registers of Signatures of Depositors in Branches of the Freedman's Savings and Trust Company, 1865-1874. Washington, DC: National Archives and Records Service, 1969. Microcopy M816. Huntsville. Mobile. /Microfilm Rolls 21-22/

Sellers, James Benson. *Slavery in Alabama.* Tuscaloosa, AL: The University of Alabama Press, 1950. 426p. Bibliography. Index. Notes. Photographs. /GC 976.1 Se4s/

Slave Schedules for 1850–Alabama. Washington, DC: The National Archives, 1964. Microcopy 432. /Microfilm Rolls 17-24/

Slave Schedules for 1860–Alabama. Washington, DC: The National Archives, 1967. Microcopy 653. /Microfilm Rolls 27-36/

Slavery in Ante-Bellum Southern Industries. Frederick, MD: University Publications of America, 199-.
Alabama--Bryan & Leventhorpe Family Papers, 1797-1860. /Series B, Rolls 2-3/

Todd, Jerrie. *Slave Abstracts from Will Book III.* Athens, AL: Limestone County Commission, Department of History and Archives, 1993. 62p. Index. /GC 976.101 L62ta/

Tuskegee Institute News Clippings File. Tuskegee Institute, AL: Tuskegee Institute, 1978. 66p. /GC 976.102 T87g/

ARIZONA

Luckingham, Bradford. *Minorities in Phoenix: A Profile of Mexican American, Chinese American, and African American Communities, 1860-1992*. Tucson, AZ: The University of Arizona Press, 1994. 258p. Index. Notes. Tables. /GC 979.102 P56lu/

Rawick, George P., ed. *The American Slave: A Composite Autobiography–Arizona... Narratives*. Westport, CT: Greenwood Publishing Company, 1979. /GC 929.11 AL113 Sec. 2/

Smith, Gloria L. *African Americans & Arizona's Three C's: Cotton, Copper, Cattle*. Tucson, AZ: G. L. Smith, 1994. 18p. Bibliography. /GC 979.101 P64s Suppl. 1994/

Smith, Gloria L. *Arizona's Black Americana: A Survey of Black American History in Arizona*. Tucson, AZ: G. L. Smith, 197-. 118p. /GC 979.1 Sm52a/

Smith, Gloria L. *Black Americana in Arizona*. Tucson, AZ: G. L. Smith, 1977. 120p. Bibliographies. /GC 979.1 Sm52b/

Smith, Gloria L. *Black Heritage Trails and Tales of Tucson and Fort Huachuca*. 52p. Appendices. Bibliography. /GC 979.101 P64s/

ARKANSAS

Patterson, Ruth Polk. *The Seed of Sally Good'n: A Black Family of Arkansas, 1833-1953*. Lexington, KY: The University Press of Kentucky, 1985. 183p. Bibliography. Index. Notes. Photographs. /GC 929.2 P759pa/

Rawick, George P., ed. *The American Slave: A Composite Autobiography–Arkansas Narratives.* Westport, CT: Greenwood Publishing Company, 1972. /GC 976.7 Ar486 Pts. 1-6/

Rawick, George P., ed. *The American Slave: A Composite Autobiography–Arkansas Narratives and Missouri Narratives.* Westport, CT: Greenwood Publishing Company, 1972. /GC 976.7 Ar486 Pt. 7 Sec. 1/

Rawick, George P., ed. *The American Slave: A Composite Autobiography–Arkansas...Narratives.* Westport, CT: Greenwood Publishing Company, 1977. /GC 929.11 Ar486 Sec. 1/

Rawick, George P., ed. *The American Slave: A Composite Autobiography–Arkansas...Narratives.* Westport, CT: Greenwood Publishing Company, 1979. /GC 929.11 AL113 Sec. 3/

Records of Ante-Bellum Southern Plantations from the Revolution through the Civil War. Frederick, MD: University Publications of America, Inc., 198-.
Arkansas--Burwell Benson papers, 1804-1914. /Series J, Part 13, Rolls 11-12/
Arkansas--Berkeley family papers, 1536-1868. /Series E, Part 2, Rolls 1-18/
Arkansas--Mary Jeffreys Bethell diary, 1853-1873. /Series J, Part 13, Roll 12/
Arkansas--Thomas W. Butler papers, 1842-1913. /Series I, Part 5, Rolls 4-9/
Arkansas--Leonidas Chalmers Glenn papers, 1752-1907. /Series J, Part 13, Roll 35/
Arkansas--Hannah family papers, 1760-1967. /Series M, Part 5, Rolls 21-28/
Arkansas--Gustavus A. Henry papers, 1804-1895. /Series J, Part 6, Rolls 18-20/
Arkansas--Robert Hall Morrison papers, 1820-1888. /Series J, Part 8, Rolls 18-19/
Arkansas--Shanks family papers, 1801-1923. /Series J, Part 13, Rolls 4-5/
Arkansas--Wyche & Otey papers, 1824-1900 & 1935-1936. /Series J, Part 7, Rolls 9-12/

Jefferson co., AR--James Trooper Armstrong papers, 1832-1891. /Series J, Part 6, Roll 29/

Miller co., AR--Geo. Travis Wright papers, 1824-1865. /Series G, Part 1, Roll 42-44/

Records of the Assistant Commissioner for the State of Arkansas, Bureau of Refugees, Freedmen, and Abandoned Lands, 1865-1869. Washington, DC: National Archives and Records Service, 1974. Records Relating to Freedmen's Labor. Register of Letters. /Microfilm Rolls 4-20, 31-44, 49-50/

Registers of Signatures of Depositors in Branches of the Freedman's Savings and Trust Company, 1865-1874. Washington, DC: National Archives and Records Service, 1969. Microcopy M816. Little Rock. /Microfilm Roll 51/

Slave Schedules for 1850–Arkansas. Washington, DC: The National Archives, 1964. Microcopy 432. /Microfilm Roll 32/

Slave Schedules for 1850–Arkansas. Washington, DC: The National Archives, 1967. Microcopy 653. /Microfilm Rolls 53-54/

Thomas, Charles E. *Jelly Roll: A Black Neighborhood in a Southern Mill Town.* Little Rock, AR: Rose Publishing Company, 1986. 157p. Appendix. Bibliography. /GC 976.702 C12t/

CALIFORNIA

African Americans in Los Angeles and Los Angeles Township: Extracts from U.S. Censuses, Volume 1: 1850-1880. Los Angeles, CA: California African American Genealogical Society, 1995. 24p. /GC 979.402 L882af V.1/

African Americans in Los Angeles and Los Angeles Township: Extracts from U.S. Censuses, Volume 2: 1900. Los Angeles, CA: California African American Genealogical Society, 1997. 170p. /GC 979.402 L882af V.2/

Beasley, Delilah L. *Negro Trail Blazers of California*. New York: Negro University Press, 1969. 317p. Photographs. /GC 979.4 B375n/

Calhoon, F. D. *Coolies, Kanakas, and Cousin Jacks, and Eleven Other Ethnic Groups Who Populated the West During the Gold Rush Years*. Sacramento, CA: CAL-CON Publishers, 1986. 322p. Appendix. /GC 979.4 C113c/

Cole, Olen, Jr. *The African-American Experience in the Civilian Conservation Corps*. Gainesville, FL: University Press of Florida, 1999. 114p. Appendices. Bibliography. Index. Notes. Photographs. /GC 979.4 C675a/

From the Baobab Tree. Oakland, CA: African American Genealogical and Historical Society of Northern California, v.1-, 1997-. /Periodical/

History of Black Americans in Santa Clara Valley. San Jose, CA: Garden City Women's Club, 1978. 220p. Appendices. Index. Photographs. /GC 979.401 Sa68g/

Johnson, Geralyn. *California African American Genealogical Society Surname Directory*. Los Angeles, CA: CAAGS, 1995. 127p. /GC 979.402 L882caa/

Lapp, Rudolph M. *Blacks in Gold Rush California*. New Haven, CT: Yale University Press, 1977. 321p. Bibliography. Index. Notes. Photographs. /GC 979.4 L31b/

Parker, Elizabeth L. and James Abajian. *A Walking Tour of the Black Presence in San Francisco During the Nineteenth Century*. San Francisco, CA: San Francisco African American Historical and Cultural Society, 1974. 23p. Index. /GC 979.402 Sa519pa/

Shover, Michele. *Blacks in Chico, 1860-1935: Climbing the Slippery Slope*. Chico, CA: Association for Northern California Records and Research, 1991. 56p. Notes. /GC 979.402 C43s/

Thurman, Sue Bailey. *Pioneers of Negro Origin in California*. San Francisco, CA: Acme Publishing Company, 1971. 70p. Illustrations. /GC 979.4 T42p/

COLORADO

Ball, Wilbur P. *Black Pioneers of the Prairie*. Greeley, CO: Greeley Printing Company, 1992. 48p. Appendix. Photographs. /GC 978.801 W45ba/

Black Settlers of the Pikes Peak Region, 1850-1899. Colorado Springs, CO: NHACS, Inc., 1986. 34p. Photographs. /GC 978.801 El6bl/

Black Tracks. Denver, CO: Black Genealogy Search Group, v.1-, 1992-. /Periodical/

Childers, Joy and Gertrude Sauter. *African-American Genealogy at the Denver Public Library*. Denver, CO: Denver Public Library, 1994. 18p. /GC 978.802 D43gab/

Rawick, George P., ed. *The American Slave: A Composite Autobiography—Colorado...Narratives*. Westport, CT: Greenwood Publishing Company, 1977. /GC 929.11 Ar486 Sec. 2/

CONNECTICUT

Brown, Barbara W. and James M. Rose. *Black Roots in Southeastern Connecticut, 1650-1900*. Detroit, MI: Gale Research Company, 1980. 722p. Indices. /GC 974.6 B81b/

Minority Military Service, Connecticut, 1775-1783. Washington, DC: National Society Daughters of the American Revolution, 1988. 17p. /GC 973.34 C76m/

Nason, Mary. *African-Americans in Simsbury, 1725-1925*. Simsbury, CT: M. L. Nason, 1996. 20p. Bibliography. /GC 974.602 Si5n/

Rose, James M. *Tapestry: A Living History of the Black Family in Southwestern Connecticut*. New London, CT: New London County Historical Society, 1979. 163p. Bibliography. Index. Notes. /GC 974.6 R715t/

Stewart, Daniel Y. *Black New Haven*. New Haven, CT: D. Y. Stewart, 1977. 72p. Photographs. /GC 974.602 N41st/

White, David O. *Connecticut's Black Soldiers, 1775-1783*. Chester, CT: Pequot Press, 1973. 71p. Illustrations. Lists. Notes. /GC 973.74 C76wh/

DELAWARE

Essah, Patience. *A House Divided: Slavery and Emancipation in Delaware, 1638-1865*. Charlottesville, VA: University Press of Virginia, 1996. 216p. Carter G. Woodson Institute Series in Black Studies. Index. Notes. /GC 975.1 Es73h/

Williams, William H. *Slavery and Freedom in Delaware, 1639-1865.* Wilmington, DE: Scholarly Resources, Inc., 1996. 270p. Appendix. Bibliography. Index. Maps. Notes. Photographs. /GC 975.1 W67s/

DISTRICT OF COLUMBIA

Brown, Letitia Woods. *Free Negroes in the District of Columbia, 1790-1846.* New York: Oxford University Press, 1972. 226p. Appendices. Index. Notes. /GC 975.3 B81f/

Clark-Lewis, Elizabeth. *Living In, Living Out: African American Domestics in Washington, DC, 1910-1940.* Washington, DC: Smithsonian Institution Press, 1994. 242p. Index. Notes. Photographs. /GC 975.302 W27cl/

Emancipation in the District of Columbia—Letter from the Secretary of the Treasury, in Answer to a Resolution of the House of Representatives, of the 11th of January, Transmitting the Report and Tabular Statements of the Commissioners Appointed in Relation to Emancipated Slaves in the District of Columbia. Washington, DC: Government Printing Office, 1864. 79p. Lists of names. /GC 975.3 Em11/

Habeas Corpus Case Records of the United States Circuit Court for the District of Columbia, 1820-1863. Washington, DC: National Archives and Records Service, 1963. Microcopy M434. /Microfilm Rolls 28-29/

Hilyer, Andrew F. *The Twentieth Century Union League Directory...A Historical, Biographical and Statistical Study of Colored Washington.* Washington, DC: The Union League, 1901. 174p. Index. /GC 975.3 H56t/

Rawick, George P., ed. *The American Slave: A Composite Autobiography–District of Columbia...Narratives.* Westport, CT: Greenwood Publishing Company, 1979. /GC 929.11 AL113 Sec. 4/

Records of Ante-Bellum Southern Plantations from the Revolution through the Civil War. Frederick, MD: University Publications of America, Inc., 198-.
District of Columbia--Carter papers, 1667-1862. /Series L, Part 1, Rolls 1-18/
District of Columbia--Clingman & Puryear papers, 1810-1940. /Series J, Part 13, Roll 40/
District of Columbia--John Steele papers, 1716-1846. /Series J, Part 13, Rolls 13-19/
District of Columbia--Tayloe family papers, 1708-1861. /Series L, Part 1, Roll 18 & Series M, Part 1, Rolls 1-57/

Records of the Assistant Commissioner for the District of Columbia Bureau of Refugees, Freedmen, and Abandoned Lands, 1865-1869. Washington, DC: National Archives and Records Service, 1978. Microcopy M1055. Letters Sent. Endorsements Sent and Received. Register of Letters Received. Records Relating to the Issuing of Rations. Monthly Reports of Rations, Clothing, and Medicine Issued. Records Relating to the Relief of Destitute Freedmen, Reports of Operations of the Special Relief Commission. Records Relating to Abandoned or Confiscated Lands. Records Relating to Transportation of Freedmen and Bureau Personnel. /Microfilm Rolls 2-12, 15-18/

Records of the Board of Commissioners for the Emancipation of Slaves in the District of Columbia, 1862-1863. Washington, DC: National Archives and Records Service, 1963. Microcopy M520. Minutes. Lists of Petitions and Awards. Final Report. /Microfilm Rolls 19-24/

Records of the United States District Court for the District of Columbia Relating to Slaves, 1851-1863. Washington, DC: National

Archives and Records Service, 1963. Microcopy M433. Emancipation & Manumission Papers. Fugitive Slave Case Papers. /Microfilm Rolls 25-27/

Registers of Signatures of Depositors in Branches of the Freedman's Savings and Trust Company, 1865-1874. Washington, DC: National Archives and Records Service, 1969. Microcopy M816. /Microfilm Rolls 30-31/

Slavery in Ante-Bellum Southern Industries. Frederick, MD: University Publications of America, 199-.
District of Columbia--Bryan & Leventhorpe Family Papers, 1797-1860. /Series B, Rolls 2 - 3/

Sluby, Paul E. Sr. *Columbian Harmony Cemetery Records, District of Columbia, 1831-1899*. Washington, DC: Columbian Harmony Society, 197-. 357p. /Microfilm/

FLORIDA

The Black Experience: A Guide to Afro-American Resources in the Florida State Archives. Tallahassee, FL: Florida Department of State, 1991. 52p. Index. Photographs. /GC 975.9 B561/

Brown, Canter Jr. *Florida's Black Public Officials, 1867-1924*. Tuscaloosa, AL: The University of Alabama Press, 1998. 252p. Appendix. Bibliography. Biographical Dictionary. Drawings. Index. Notes. Photographs. /GC 975.9 B7999f/

Colburn, David R. and Jane L. Landers. *The African American Heritage of Florida*. Gainesville, FL: University Press of Florida, 1995. 392p. Index. Notes. Photographs. /GC 975.9 C67a/

Dunn, Marvin. *Black Miami in the Twentieth Century*. Gainesville, FL: University Press of Florida, 1997. 414p. Bibliography. Illustrations. Index. Notes. Photographs. Tables /GC 975.902 M58du/

Evans, Arthur S., Jr. and David Lee. *Pearl City, Florida: A Black Community Remembers*. Boca Raton, FL: Florida Atlantic University Press, 1990. 162p. Bibliography. Index. Photographs. /GC 975.902 B63e/

Jones, Maxine D. and Kevin M. McCarthy. *African Americans in Florida*. Sarasota, FL: Pineapple Press, Inc., 1993. 189p. Index. Photographs. /GC 975.9 J721a/

Landers, Jane. *Black Society in Spanish Florida*. Urbana, IL: University of Illinois Press, 1999. 390p. Blacks in the New World Series. Appendices. Illustrations. Index. Maps. Notes. Photographs. Tables. /GC 975.9 L233b/

Landers, Jane. *Fort Mose, Gracia Real de Santa Teresa de Mose: A Free Black Town in Spanish Colonial Florida*. St. Augustine, FL: St. Augustine Historical Society, 1992. 34p. Notes. /GC 975.902 Sa11la/

McDonogh, Gary W., ed. *The Florida Negro: A Federal Writers' Project Legacy*. Jackson, MS: University Press of Mississippi, 1993. 177p. Appendices. Bibliography. Index. Notes. Photographs. /GC 975.9 F6625/

Negroes, &c, Captured from Indians in Florida, &c. Washington, DC: War Department, 1839. (25th Congress, 3rd Session, House of Reps., War Dept.) 126p. Lists. /GC 975.9 Un31n/

Registry of negro prisoners captured by the troops commanded by Major General Thomas S. Jesup, in 1836 and 1837, and owned by Indians, or who claim to be free.

No.	Names.	Sex.	Tribe, town, or owner.	Estimated age. Years.	Estimated age. M'ths.	Remarks.
1	Jacob	Male	Toon-a-hi-ta	25	.	Wounded in right knee.
2	Rina	Female	Mic-a-po-to-ka	18	.	} Wife and children to Jacob; Clauds died May 27, 1837.
3	Venice	Female	Do	2	2	
4	Clauds	Female	Do	.	.	
5	Jane	Female	Do	40	.	} Mother to Rina and Molly.
6	Molly	Female	Do	23	.	
7	Billy	Male	Do	12	.	} Mother and son.
8	Chloe	Female	Do	19	.	
9	Sarah	Female	Do	2	.	Sister to Jacob; mother and children.
10	Dennis	Male	Do	1	.	
11	Pompey	Male	Do	70	.	} Husband and wife.
12	Dolly	Female	Do	50	.	
13	Lilla	Female	Do	20	.	} Mother and children.
14	Tom	Male	Do	11	.	
15	Bella	Female	Do	9	.	
16	Hagar	Female	Do	30	.	
17	Ned	Male	Do	3	.	
18	Fanny	Female	Do	27	.	} Mother and children.
19	Charles	Male	Do	6	.	
20	Margaret	Female	Do	4	.	
21	Sylvia	Female	Do	1	.	
22	Buno	Male	Do	19	.	Daughter to Pompey and Dolly; mother to Hagar.
23	Peggy	Female	Do	45	.	
24	Bob	Male	Do	30	.	
25	Margaret	Female	Do	21	.	
26	Cyrus	Male	Do	13	.	
27	Rose	Female	Harriet Bowlegs	70	.	} Grandmother to Jacob and Chloe; sold by Mr. Forrester, of Six-mile creek, to Bowlegs, several years since; Juba cousin to Jacob.
28	Juba	Female	Do	30	.	

Negroes, &c, Captured from Indians in Florida, &c. Washington, DC: War Department, 1839, document no. 225, p. 66.

Phelts, Marsha Dean. *An American Beach for African Americans*. Gainesville, FL: University Press of Florida, 1997. 188p. Bibliography. Notes. Photographs. /GC 975.901 N17p/

Phillips, Ulrich Bonnell and James David Glunt, eds. *Florida Plantation Records from the Papers of George Noble Jones*. St. Louis, MO: Missouri Historical Society, 1927. 596p. Index. /GC 975.9 J71f/

Rawick, George P., ed. *The American Slave: A Composite Autobiography–Florida Narratives*. Westport, CT: Greenwood Publishing Company, 1972. /GC 975.9 F662/

Rawick, George P., ed. *The American Slave: A Composite Autobiography–Florida...Narratives*. Westport, CT: Greenwood Publishing Company, 1979. /GC 929.11 AL113 Sec. 5/

Records of Ante-Bellum Southern Plantations from the Revolution through the Civil War. Frederick, MD: University Publications of America, Inc., 198-.
Florida--Farish Carter papers, 1794,1806-1868. /Series J, Part 4, Rolls 38-43/
Florida--Davidson family papers, 1827-1935. /Series J, Part 13, Rolls 28-34/
Florida--Isaac Jarratt papers, 1832-1979. /Series J, Part 13, Roll 40/
Florida--James Jones Philips papers, 1814-1892. /Series J, Part 12, Roll 17/
Florida--William Henry Wills papers, 1712-1892. /Series J, Part 12, Rolls 41-43/
Alachua co., FL--James B. Bailey papers, 1847-1885. /Series J, Part 4, Rolls 44-45/
Leon co., FL--Branch family papers, 1788-1866. /Series J, Part 4, Rolls 45-47/
Leon co., FL--Absalom Benton Whitaker papers, 1814-1845. /Series J, Part 4, Roll 47/
Madison co., FL--Geo. Noble Jones papers, 1786-1872. /Series F, Part 2, Roll 1/

Registers of Signatures of Depositors in Branches of the Freedman's Savings and Trust Company, 1865-1874. Washington, DC:

National Archives and Records Service, 1969. Microcopy M186. Tallahassee. /Microfilm Roll 31/

Slave Schedules for 1850–Florida. Washington, DC: National Archives and Records Service, 1964. Microcopy 432. /Microfilm Roll 60/

Slave Schedules for 1860–Florida. Washington, DC: National Archives and Records Service, 1967. Microcopy 653. /Microfilm Roll 110/

Smith, Julia Floyd. *Slavery and Plantation Growth in Antebellum Florida, 1821-1860.* Gainesville, FL: University of Florida Press, 1973. 249p. Appendix. Bibliography. Index. Photographs. /GC 975.9 Sm6s/

Struggle for Survival: A Partial History of the Negroes of Marion County, 1865 to 1976. Marion County, FL: Black Historical Organization of Marion County, 1977. 111p. Photographs. /GC 975.901 M33s/

Wells, Sharon. *Forgotten Legacy: Blacks in Nineteenth Century Key West.* Key West, FL: Historic Key West Preservation Board, 1982. 60p. Bibliography. Notes. Photographs. /GC 975.902 K52we/

GEORGIA

Bullard, Mary R. *Black Liberation on Cumberland Island in 1815.* DeLeon Springs, FL: E. O. Painter Printing Company, 1983. 141p. Appendices. Bibliography. Index. Photographs. /GC 975.801 C14b/

Bullard, Mary R. *Robert Stafford of Cumberland Island: Growth of a Planter*. DeLeon Springs, FL: E. O. Painter Printing Company, 1986. 349p. Appendix. Bibliography. Index. Photographs. /GC 975.8 B79b/

Caldwell, A. B., ed. *History of the American Negro and His Institutions: Georgia Edition*. Atlanta, GA: A. B. Caldwell Publishing Company, 1917. 688p. Photographs. /GC 975.8 C12h Parts 1-2/

Carter, E. R. *Biographical Sketches of Our Pulpit*. Chicago: Afro-Am Press, 1969. 216p. Portraits. /GC 975.8 C244b/

Carter, E. R. *Black Side: A Partial History of the Business, Religious and Educational Side of the Negro in Atlanta, GA*. Atlanta, GA: s.n., 1894. 323p. Drawings. Index. Photos. /GC 975.802 At6ca/

Clifton, James M., ed. *Life and Labor on Argyle Island: Letters and Documents of a Savannah River Rice Plantation, 1833-1867*. Savannah, GA: The Beehive Press, 1978. 365p. /GC 975.801 C61L/

Davidson, William H. *Books of Honey and Butter: Plantations and People of Meriwether County, Georgia*. Alexander City, AL: Outlook Publishing Company, 1971. Bibliography. Index. Maps. Photographs. /GC 975.801 M54 Vol. 1-2/

Drums and Shadows: Survival Studies Among the Georgia Coastal Negroes. Athens, GA: University of Georgia Press, 1940. 274p. Appendix. Bibliography. Index. Photographs. /GC 975.8 W93d/

Durett, Dan and Dana F. White. *An-Other Atlanta Tour: The Black Heritage*. Atlanta, GA: The History Group, Inc., 1900. 48p. Photographs. /GC 975.802 At6du/

Gunn, Victoria Reeves. *Hofwyl Plantation*. Atlanta, GA: Department of Natural Resources, 1974. 216p. Bibliography. Charts. Lists. /GC 975.8 G95h/

Gunn, Victoria Reeves. *Jarrell Plantation: A History*. Atlanta, GA: Department of Natural Resources, 1974. 166p. Bibliography. Lists. /GC 975.801 J71g/

Journal and Account Book, 1834-1861, of Hugh Fraser Grant of Elizafield Plantation, Glynn County, Georgia. S.n.: s.l., 19--. Slave Lists. /GC 975.8 G76j/

Kemble, Frances Ann. *Journal of a Residence on a Georgian Plantation in 1838-1839*. New York: Alfred A. Knopf, 1961. 415p. Index. Map. /GC 975.8 K31j/

Mason, Herman "Skip," Jr. *Atlanta in the Roaring Twenties*. Dover, NH: Arcadia Publishing, 1997. 128p. Bibliography. Photographs. /GC 975.802 At6ma/

Merritt, Carole. *Homecoming: African-American Family History in Georgia*. Atlanta, GA: African-American Family History Association, 1982. 122p. Notes. Photographs. /GC 975.8 M55h/

Metro-Atlanta Black Pages, 1993. College Park, GA: Ken Reid, 1993. 221p. /GC 975.802 At6me 1993/

Morgan, Dorothy Henderson. *When Servants Ride Horses: One Version of the David Dickson Story*. Dublin, GA: D. H. Morgan, 1992. 185p. Bibliography. Illustrations. /GC 975.801 H19m/

Rathbun, Fred C. *Names From Georgia, 1865-1866, Freedmens Bureau Letters, Roll 13*. Littleton, CO: F. C. Rathbun, 1986. 58p. /GC 975.8 R184n/

Rawick, George P., ed. *The American Slave: A Composite Autobiography—Georgia Narratives*. Westport, CT: Greenwood Publishing Company, 1972. /GC 975.8 G2975 Parts 1-4/

Rawick, George P., ed. *The American Slave: A Composite Autobiography—Georgia Narratives*. Westport, CT: Greenwood Publishing Company, 1977. /GC 975.8 G2976 Parts 1-2/

Rawick, George P., ed. *The American Slave: A Composite Autobiography—Georgia...Narratives*. Westport, CT: Greenwood Publishing Company, 1979. /GC 929.11 AL113 Sec. 6/

Records of Ante-Bellum Southern Plantations from the Revolution through the Civil War. Frederick, MD: University Publications of America, Inc., 198-.

Georgia--George Washington Allen papers, 1832-1865. /Series J, Part 7, Rolls 4-5/

Georgia--Branch family papers, 1788-1866. /Series J, Part 4, Rolls 45-47/

Georgia--Hamilton Brown papers, 1752-1907. /Series J, Part 14, Rolls 5 - 8/

Georgia--James Evans papers, 1826-1927. /Series J, Part 12, Rolls 2-6/

Georgia--James McKibbin Gage papers, 1835-1876. /Series J, Part 7, Roll 8/

Georgia--Leonidas Chalmers Glenn papers, 1752-1907. /Series J, Part 13, Roll 35/

Georgia--Wm. Polk papers, 1840-1867. /Series J, Part 5, Roll 15/

Georgia--William Henry Wills papers, 1712-1892. /Series J, Part 12, Rolls 41-43/

Baker co., GA--Jackson family papers, 1784-1880. /Series J, Part 4, Rolls 25-36/

Baker co., GA--Prince family papers, 1784-1880. /Series J, Part 4, Rolls 25-36/

Baldwin co., GA--Farish Carter papers, 1794, 1806-1868. /Series J, Part 4, Rolls 38-43/

Bibb co., GA--Jackson family papers, 1784-1880. /Series J, Part 4, Rolls 25-36/

Bibb co., GA--Prince family papers, 1784-1880. /Series J, Part 4, Rolls 25-36/
Bryan co., GA--Arnold family papers, 1758-1915. /Series J, Part 4, Rolls 7-11/
Bryan co., GA--Screven family papers, 1758-1915. /Series J, Part 4, Rolls 7-11/
Camden co., GA--Duncan Clinch letterbook, 1834-1859. /Series C, Part 2, Roll 1/
Cass co., GA--Geo. Scarborough Barnsley papers, 1837-1918. /Series J, Part 4, Rolls 43-44/
Cass co., GA--Mackay family papers, 1790-1861. /Series J, Part 4, Rolls 3-7/
Cass co., GA--Stiles family papers, 1790-1861. /Series J, Part 4, Rolls 3-7/
Chatham co., GA--Arnold family papers, 1758-1915. /Series J, Part 4, Rolls 7-11/
Chatham co., GA--William Gibbons, Jr. papers, 1728-1803. /Series F, Part 2, Roll 1/
Chatham co., GA--George N. Jones papers, 1786-1872. /Series F, Part 2, Roll 1/
Chatham co., GA--Geo. J. Kollock plantation books, 1837-1861. /Series J, Part 4, Rolls 2-3/
Chatham co., GA--Mackay family papers, 1790-1861. /Series J, Part 4, Rolls 3-7/
Chatham co., GA--Manigault family papers, 1825-1897. /Series J, Part 4, Rolls 1-2/
Chatham co., GA--John Orme letterbook, 1821-1845. /Series H, Roll 28/
Chatham co., GA--Screven family papers, 1758-1915. /Series J, Part 4, Rolls 7-11/
Chatham co., GA--Stiles family papers, 1790-1861. /Series J, Part 4, Rolls 3-7/
Clarke co., GA--Jackson family papers, 1784-1880. /Series J, Part 4, Rolls 25-36/
Clarke co., GA--Prince family papers, 1784-1880. /Series J, Part 4, Rolls 25-36/
Creek Nation, GA--Rebecca M. H. Hagerty papers, 1823-1880. /Series G, Part 1, Roll 42/
Glynn co., GA--James Hamilton Couper plantation records, 1818-1854. /Series J, Part 4, Rolls 16-17/
Glynn co., GA--William Audley Couper plantation records, 1795-1865. /Series J, Part 4, Rolls 17-20/
Glynn co., GA--Elizafield plantation records, 1834-1861. /Series J, Part 4, Roll 20/
Glynn co., GA--Roswell King, Jr. diary, 1838-1845. /Series I, Part 2, Roll 20/
Glynn co., GA--William Page papers, 1786-1825. /Series J, Part 4, Rolls 21-25/
Glynn co., GA--Woolley family papers, 1788-1869, 1917. /Series J, Part 4, Roll 25/

Habersham co., GA--Geo. J. Kollock plantation books, 1837-1861. /Series J, Part 4, Rolls 2-3/

Jasper co., GA--Iveson Lewis Brookes papers, 1785-1868. /Series J, Part 4, Rolls 37-38/

Jones co., GA--Iveson Lewis Brookes papers, 1785-1868. /Series J, Part 4, Rolls 37-38/

Liberty co., GA--Alexander family papers, 1758-1915. /Series J, Part 4, Rolls 11-16/

Liberty co., GA--Bonaventure Plantation book, 1850-1851. /Series H, Roll 1/

Liberty co., GA--Hillhouse family papers, 1758-1915. /Series J, Part 4, Rolls 11-16/

Liberty co., GA--Charles Colcock Jones plantation books, 1834-1849. /Series H, Roll 28/

Liberty co., GA--Joseph Jones slave records, 1834-1861. /Series H, Roll 28/

Liberty co., GA--Roswell King, Jr. diary, 1838-1845. /Series I, Part 2, Roll 20/

McIntosh co., GA--Butler's Island Plantation Hospital book, 1838-1843. /Series H, Roll 1/

McIntosh co., GA--Joseph Jones slave records, 1834-1861. /Series H, Roll 28/

McIntosh co., GA--Roswell King, Jr. diary, 1838-1845. /Series I, Part 2, Roll 20/

Morgan co., GA--Douglas Watson Porter papers, 1819-1862. /Series J, Part 4, Roll 38/

Murray co., GA--Farish Carter papers, 1794,1806-1868. /Series J, Part 4, Rolls 38-43/

Richmond co., GA--Slave Import Register, 1820-1821. /Series F, Part 2, Roll 1/

Savannah, GA--Geo. Noble Jones papers, 1786-1872. /Series F, Part 2, Roll 1/

Records of the Assistant Commissioner for the State of Georgia, Bureau of Refugees, Freedmen, and Abandoned Lands, 1865-1869. Washington, DC: National Archives and Records Service, 1968. Microcopy M798. Letters Received. Unregistered Letters. Telegrams Received. Appointments. Test Oaths. Murders and Outrages. Freedmen Murdered or Assaulted. /Microfilm Rolls 11-32/

Registers of Signatures of Depositors in Branches of the Freedman's Savings and Trust Company, 1865-1874. Washington, DC:

National Archives and Records Service, 1969. Microcopy M816. Atlanta. Augusta. Savannah. /Microfilm Rolls 33-37/

Reidy, Joseph P. *From Slavery to Agrarian Capitalism in the Cotton Plantation South: Central Georgia, 1800-1880*. Chapel Hill, NC: The University of North Carolina Press, 1992. 360p. Appendix. Bibliography. Index. Notes. Photographs. /GC 975.8 R27f/

Scipio, L. Albert. *The 24th Infantry at Fort Benning*. Silver Spring, MD: Roman Publications, 1986. 373p. /GC 975.801 M97s/

Slave Bills of Sale Project. Altanta, GA: African-American Family History Association, Inc., 1986. 246p. /GC 975.8 SL1 V. 1-2/

Slave Schedules for 1850–Georgia. Washington, DC: The National Archives, 1964. Microcopy 432. /Microfilm Rolls 88-96/

Slave Schedules for 1860–Georgia. Washington, DC: The National Archives, 1967. Microcopy 653. /Microfilm Rolls 142-153/

Slavery in Ante-Bellum Southern Industries. Frederick, MD: University Publications of America, 199-.
Georgia--Peck, Welford & Company papers, 1834-1844. /Series C, Part 2, Roll 39/
Cherokee co., GA--Mary G. Franklin account books, 1842-1855. /Series A, Roll 4/
Columbia co., GA--Joseph Belknap Smith papers, 1802-1916. /Series A, Roll 1-3/
McDuffie co., GA--Joseph Belknap Smith papers, 1802-1916. /Series A, Roll 1-3/
Wilkes co., GA--Joseph Belknap Smith papers, 1802-1916. /Series A, Roll 1-3/

Terrell, Lloyd P. and Marguerite S. C. *Blacks in Augusta: A Chronology, 1741-1977.* Augusta, GA: Preston Publications, 1977. 50p. Index. /GC   975.802   Au4t/

Troup, Cornelius V. *Distinguished Negro Georgians.* Dallas, TX: Royal Publishing Company, 19--. 203p. Index. /GC   975.8   T75d/

Wagner, Clarence M. *Profiles of Black Georgia Baptists.* Gainesville, GA: Bennett Brothers Printing Company, 1980. 268p. Photographs. /GC   975.8   W12p/

Wood, Betty. *Women's Work, Men's Work: The Informal Slave Economies of Lowcountry Georgia.* Athens, GA: University of Georgia Press, 1995. 247p. Index. Notes. /GC   975.8   W8494w/

ILLINOIS

Afro-American Genealogical and Historical Society. *Constitution.* Chicago, IL: Afro-American Genealogical and Historical Society, 1984. 7p. /GC   977.302   C43af/

Afro-American Genealogical and Historical Society of Chicago Newsletter. Chicago, IL: Afro-American Genealogical and Historical Society of Chicago, v.1-, 1980-. /Periodical/

Afro-American Historical and Genealogical Society Cleveland Chapter Newsletter. Cleveland, OH: Afro-American Historical and Genealogical Society Cleveland Chapter, v.1-5, 1990-95. /Periodical/

Black, Ford S. *Black's Blue Book: Business and Professional Directory (Chicago).* Chicago: s. n., 1918, 1919, 1921, 1923/4. /GC   977.302   C43blu/

Colored People's Blue-Book and Business Directory of Chicago, IL, 1905. Chicago: Celerity Printing Company, 1905. 140p. /GC 977.302 C43co/

Dorsey, James. *Up South: Blacks in Chicago's Suburbs, 1719-1983*. Bristol, IN: Wyndham Hall Press, Inc., 1986. 113p. Notes. /GC 977.302 C43do/

1927 Intercollegian Wonder Book or 1779 - The Negro in Chicago - 1927. Chicago, IL: The Washington Intercollegiate Club, 1927. 232p. /GC 977.302 C43neg V.1/

Miller, Edward A., Jr. *The Black Civil War Soldiers of Illinois: The Story of the Twenty-ninth U.S. Colored Infantry*. Columbia, SC: The University of South Carolina Press, 1998. 267p. Appendix. Bibliography. Index. Notes. Photographs. /GC 973.34 IL5mil/

Ogden, Mary Elaine. *The Chicago Negro Community: A Statistical Description*. Chicago: W. P. A., 1939(?). 246p. Index. Bibliography. /GC 977.302 C43un/

The Patricia Liddell Researchers News Journal. Chicago, IL: Patricia Liddell Researchers, 1991-. /Periodical/

Records of Ante-Bellum Southern Plantations from the Revolution through the Civil War. Frederick, MD: University Publications of America, Inc., 198-.
Illinois--John Augustine Washington papers, 1824-1860. /Series M, Part 6, Roll 14/

Sutton, Raleigh. *The African American Heritage of Elgin, Illinois and the Greater Kane County Area: A Genealogy of Most of the First Families from the Days as Contrabands to the Present*

Time–1856-1996. Elgin, IL: R. Sutton, 1996. 185p. "A Collection of Family Relationships." /GC 977.301 K13s/

Weems, Robert E., Jr. ***Black Business in the Black Metropolis: The Chicago Metropolitan Assurance Company, 1925-1985***. Bloomington, IN: Indiana University Press, 1996. 158p. Bibliography. Index. Notes. Photographs. Tables. /GC 977.302 C43we/

INDIANA

Afro-Americans in Fort Wayne and the Surrounding Area. S. l.: s. n., 19--. 105p. (Manuscript) /GC 977.202 F77af/

Bigham, Darrel E. ***We Ask Only a Fair Trial: A History of the Black Community of Evansville, Indiana***. Bloomington, IN: Indiana University Press, 1987. 286p. Index. Notes. Photographs. /GC 977.202 Ev17bi/

Black History News and Notes. Indianapolis, IN: Indiana Historical Society, n.1-, 1979-. /Periodical/

Boone County, Indiana: Enumeration of White and Colored Males Over the Age of 21 for the Years 1907, 1913, 1919, 1925. [Boone County, IN]: s. n., 1907, 1913, 1919, 1925. 4 vols. /GC 977.201 B64boa/

Clifford, Eth and John McDowell. ***Freedom's Road: A History of Black People in Indiana***. Indianapolis, IN: David-Stewart Publishing Company, 1970. 50p. /GC 977.2 C612f/

Crenshaw, Gwendolyn J. ***"Bury Me in a Free Land:" The Abolitionist Movement in Indiana, 1816-1865***. Indianapolis, IN: Indiana

Historical Bureau, 1993. 68p. Illustrations. Notes. Photographs. /GC 977.2 C863bu/

Ebony Lines. Bloomington, IN: Indiana African American Historical and Genealogical Society, v.2-4, 1990-92. Previously published as *Indiana African American Historical and Genealogical Society Newsletter*. /Periodical/

Eliza Harris Marker: The Story of the Underground Slave Railroad in Jay County, Indiana. S. l.: s. n., 1997. 23 pages. /GC 977.201 J33han/

Enumeration of White and Colored Males Over the Age of Twenty-one in Licking Township, Blackford County, Indiana, 1919. [Blackford County, IN]: s. n., 1919. /GC 977.201 B56e/

Fort Wayne Black Pages and Professional Directory, Fall 1994-Spring 1995. Fort Wayne, IN: Fort Wayne Black Pages and Professional Directory, Inc., 1995. /GC 977.202 F77fora/

Gibbs, Wilma L., ed. *Guide to African American Printed Sources at the Indiana Historical Society*. Indianapolis, IN: Indiana Historical Society, 1997. 68p. /GC 977.2 In2ahg/

Gibbs, Wilma L., ed. *Indiana's African-American Heritage: Essays from "Black History News & Notes."* Indianapolis, IN: Indiana Historical Society, 1993. 243p. Index. Photographs. /GC 977.2 In923/

Goodall, Hurley and J. Paul Mitchell. *A History of Negroes in Muncie*. Muncie, IN: Ball State University, 1976. 58p. /GC 977.202 M92g/

Hine, Darlene Clark. *When the Truth is Told: A History of Black Women's Culture and Community in Indiana, 1875-1950*.

Indianapolis, IN: National Council of Negro Women, 1981. 90p. Appendices. /GC 977.2 H58w/

Holmes, Maurice. *Miscellaneous Records of Jennings County, Indiana.* [Jennings Co., IN]: s. n., 1976. Negro Registry on p.42-64. /GC 977.201 J44ho/

Indiana African American Historical and Genealogical Society Newsletter. Bloomington, IN: Indiana African American Historical and Genealogical Society, v.1-2, 1989-90. Continued as *Ebony Lines.* /Periodical/

McDougald, Lois. *Negro Migration into Indiana, 1800-1860.* Bloomington, IN: L. McDougald, 1945. 92p. Bibliography. Maps. /GC 977.2 M14n/

Miller, Marion Clinton. *The Antislavery Movement in Indiana.* Ann Arbor, MI: M. M. Clinton, 19--. 290p. Bibliography. Notes. /GC 977.2 M614a/

People in Fort Wayne. Fort Wayne, IN: Fort Wayne Urban League, Inc., 1964. Photographs. /GC 977.202 F77plo/

Peterson, Roger A. *African Americans found in Owen County, Indiana Records, 1819-1880.* Owen County, IN: R. A. Peterson, 1996. 94p. Index. /GC 977.201 Ow2petc/

Rawick, George P., ed. *The American Slave: A Composite Autobiography—Alabama and Indiana Narratives.* Westport, CT: Greenwood Publishing Company, 1972. /GC 976.1 AL17 Sec. 2/

Rawick, George P., ed. *The American Slave: A Composite Autobiography—Indiana and Ohio Narratives.* Westport, CT:

Greenwood Publishing Company, 1977. /GC 977.2 In2455 Sec. 1/

Rawick, George P., ed. *The American Slave: A Composite Autobiography–Indiana...Narratives*. Westport, CT: Greenwood Publishing Company, 1979. /GC 929.11 AL113 Sec. 7/

Register of Negro Slaves and Masters for 1805-1807, Knox County, Indiana Territory. Chicago, IL: Barrackman Family Association, 1970. 5p. /GC 977.2 B233r/

Researching African-American History in the Indiana State Library and Historical Building. Indianapolis, IN: Indiana Historical Bureau, 1997. 24p. Illustrations. Photographs. /GC 977.2 In2683r/

Robbins, Coy D. *African-American Soldiers From Indiana with the Union Army in the Civil War, 1863-1865*. Bloomington, IN: C. D. Robbins, 1989. 46p. /GC 973.74 In2rob/

Robbins, Coy D. *Black Heritage in Westfield, Indiana*. Bloomington, IN: C. D. Robbins, 1984. 41p. Appendix. Bibliography. Index. /GC 977.201 H18ro/

Robbins, Coy D. *Black Pioneers in Indiana*. Bloomington, IN: Indiana African American Historical and Genealogical Society, 1990. 8p. /GC 977.2 B56/

Robbins, Coy D. *Indiana Negro Registers, 1852-1865*. Bowie, MD: Heritage Books, Inc., 1994. 185p. Index. /GC 977.2 In24572 1852-1865/

Robbins, Coy D. *Reclaiming African Heritage at Salem, Indiana*. Bowie, MD: Heritage Books, Inc., 1995. 234p. Appendices. Bibliography. Index. /GC 977.202 Sa32ro/

Robbins, Coy D. *Source Book: African American Genealogy in Indiana*. Bloomington, IN: C. D. Robbins, 1989. 37p. /GC 977.2 R53s/

Spears, Jean E. and Dorothy Paul. *Admission Record, Indianapolis Asylum for Friendless Colored Children, 1871-1900*. Indianapolis, IN: Indiana Historical Society, 1978. 159p. Index. /GC 977.202 In3sp/

Tanner, David. *Focus: Fort Wayne's Roots*. S. l.: D. Tanner, 1978. 35p. Bibliography. Maps. /GC 977.202 F77tan/

Taylor, Robert M. & Connie A. McBirney, ed. *Peopling Indiana: The Ethnic Experience*. Indianapolis, IN: Indiana Historical Society, 1996. Pages 12 - 36. Notes. /GC 977.2 P39/

Thornbrough, Emma Lou. *This Far by Faith: Black Hoosier Heritage*. Indianapolis, IN: Indiana Committee for the Humanities, 1982. 24p. Bibliography. Photographs. /GC 977.2 T349/

W. P. A. *Index to Enumeration of Male Voters of Miami County, Indiana, 1850-1920*. S. l.: Indiana Works Progress Administration, 1938. /GC 977.201 M58unro/

Wallis, Don. *All We Had Was Each Other: The Black Community of Madison, Indiana*. Bloomington, IN: Indiana University Press, 1998. 136p. "An Oral History of the Black Community of Madison, Indiana." /GC 977.202 M26wa/

Zeigler, Sarah Parham. *The History of the Negro Church in Indianapolis*. Indianapolis, IN: Butler University, 1943. 203p. Bibliography. Map. Notes. /GC 977.202 In3z/

IOWA

Bergmann, Leola Marjorie Nelson. *The Negro in Iowa.* Iowa City, IA: State Historical Society of Iowa, 1969. 96p. Editorial addendum by Wm. J. Petersen. Bibliography. Notes. Tables. /GC 977.7 B454n/

KANSAS

Black Historic Sites: A Beginning Point. Topeka, KS: Kansas State Historical Society, 1977. 45p. Illus. Index. /GC 978.1 K13bl/

Cornish, Dudley Taylor. *Kansas Negro Regiments in the Civil War.* Kansas: Commission on Civil Rights, 1969. 15p. Photographs. /GC 973.74 K13co/

Cox, Thomas C. *Blacks in Topeka, Kansas, 1865-1915: A Social History.* Baton Rouge, LA: Louisiana State University Press, 1982. 236p. Bibliography. Index. Tables. /GC 978.102 T62co/

Gordon, Jacob U. *Narrative of African Americans in Kansas, 1870-1992.* Lewiston, NY: The Edwin Mellen Press, 1993. 302p. Bibliography. /GC 978.1 G65n/

Rawick, George P., ed. *The American Slave: A Composite Autobiography–Kansas...Narratives.* Westport, CT: Greenwood Pub. Company, 1972. /GC 929.11 K136 Sec. 1/

Rawick, George P., ed. *The American Slave: A Composite Autobiography–Kansas...Narratives.* Westport, CT: Greenwood Publishing Company, 1979. /GC 929.11 AL113 Sec. 8/

Robertson, Clara Hamlet. *Kansas Territorial Settlers of 1860 Who Were Born in Tennessee, North Carolina, and South Carolina.* Baltimore, MD: Genealogical Publishing Company, Inc., 1976. 187p. Maps. /GC 978.1 R54k/

KENTUCKY

Dunnigan, Alice A. *The Fascinating Story of Black Kentuckians: Their Heritage and Traditions.* Washington, DC: Association For the Study of Afro-American Life and History, Inc., 1982. 528p. Bibliography. Index. Notes. Photographs. /GC 976.9 D92f/

Garrison, Gwendolyn. *Black Marriages of Fayette County, Kentucky, 1866-1876.* Lexington, KY: Kentucky Tree-Search, 1985. Index. /GC 976.901 F29g/

Gorin, Michelle. *Afro-American Marriage Bonds, January 1870 through December 1873, From the Files of the Barren County, Kentucky County Clerk's Office.* Glasgow, KY: Gorin Genealogical Publishing, 1992. 229p. Index. /GC 976.901 B27goq/

Gorin, Michelle. *Barren's Black Roots.* Glasgow, KY: Gorin Genealogical Publishing, 1992. 167p. Index. /GC 976.901 B27gop/

A History of Blacks in Kentucky. Frankfort, KY: Kentucky Historical Society, 1992. 2 volumes. Bibliography. Index. Notes. Photographs. /GC 976.9 L96h v. 1 - 2/

Johnson, W. D. *Biographical Sketches of Prominent Negro Men and Women of Kentucky.* Lexington, KY: Standard Print, 1897. 132p. Index. Portraits. /GC 976.9 J632b/

Montell, William Lynwood. *The Saga of Coe Ridge, Cumberland County, Kentucky*. S. l.: Harper Torchbooks, 19--. 289p. Bibliography. Illustrations. Index. /GC 976.901 C91m/

1988 Kentucky Directory of Black Elected Officials. Frankfort, KY: Kentucky Commission on Human Rights, 1988. 7th Report. /GC 976.9 N62/

Parrish, C. H., ed. *Golden Jubilee of the General Association of Colored Baptists in Kentucky*. Louisville, KY: Mayes Printing Company, 1915. 304p. Photographs. /GC 976.9 G56/

Rawick, George P., ed. *The American Slave: A Composite Autobiography–Kentucky...Narratives*. Westport, CT: Greenwood Publishing Company, 1972. /GC 929.11 K136 Sec. 2/

Records of Ante-Bellum Southern Plantations from the Revolution through the Civil War. Frederick, MD: University Publications of America, Inc., 198-.
Kentucky--Walter Alves papers, 1771-1858. /Series J, Part 13, Rolls 10-11/
Kentucky--Langdon, Young, & Meares family papers, 1771-1877. /Series J, Part 12, Roll 1/
Kentucky--Llangollen School records, 1806-1849. /Series M, Part 4, Rolls 38-39/
Kentucky--McDowell family papers, 1777-1963, /Series M, Part 6, Rolls 4-5/
Kentucky--James McDowell papers, 1770-1915. /Series J, Part 9, Rolls 19-27/
Kentucky--Meriwether family papers, 1791-1880s. /Series J, Part 9, Roll 27/
Jefferson co., KY--Louis Marshall papers, 1816-1878. /Series J, Part 8, Roll 20/
Woodford co., KY--Louis Marshall papers, 1816-1878. /Series J, Part 8, Roll 20/

Registers of Signatures of Depositors in Branches of the Freedman's Savings and Trust Company, 1865-1874. Washington, DC: National Archives and Records Service, 1969. Microcopy M816. Lexington. Louisville. /Microfilm Roll 1/

Robinson, Lottie Offett. *The Bond-Washington Story: The Education of Black People, Elizabethtown, Kentucky*. S.l.: Bond-Washington School(?), 1983. 152p. Photographs. /GC 976.902 El4r/

Sanders, Carol L. *Russell County, Kentucky Black Marriages, Bk. 1 & 2, 1866-1876 & 1875-1914*. Blue Ash, OH: C. L. Sanders, 1987-. 43p. & 35p. /GC 976.901 R91sd/

Slave Schedules for 1850–Kentucky. Washington, DC: The National Archives, 1964. Microcopy 432. /Microfilm Rolls 223-228/

Slave Schedules for 1860–Kentucky. Washington, DC: The National Archives, 1967. Microcopy 653. /Microfilm Rolls 401-406/

Slavery in Ante-Bellum Southern Industries. Frederick, MD: University Publications of America, 199-.
Kentucky--Henry Banks papers, 1781-1817. /Series C, Part 2, Rolls 1-4/
Kentucky--Preston family papers, 1727-1896. /Series C, Part 1, Rolls 5-16/

Smith, Leslie Shively. *Around Muhlenberg County, Kentucky: A Black History*. Evansville, IN: Unigraphic, Inc., 1979. 283p. Index. Photographs. /GC 976.901 M89s/

Tippie, Gwendolyn. *Afro-American Births of Adair Thru Ballard County, Kentucky, 1852-1862*. S.l.: G. Tippie, 198-. 47p. /GC 976.9 T49ab/

Tippie, Gwendolyn. *Afro-American Births of Barren Thru Bath County, Kentucky, 1852-1862*. S.l.: G. Tippie, 198-. 52p. /GC 976.9 T49aba/

Tippie, Gwendolyn. *Afro-American Births of Boone Thru Bourbon County, Kentucky, 1852- 1862*. S.l.: G. Tippie, 198-. 64p. /GC 976.9 T49abb/

Tippie, Gwendolyn. *Afro-American Deaths of Adair Thru Bath County, Kentucky, 1852-1862*. S.l.: G. Tippie, 198-. 52p. /GC 976.9 T49a/

Tippie, Gwendolyn. *Afro-American Deaths of Boone Thru Boyle County, Kentucky, 1852-1862*. S.l.: G. Tippie, 198-. 38p. /GC 976.9 T49aa/

Vanderpool, Montgomery. *Colored Marriage Bonds, Logan County, KY to 1900*. Russellville, KY: M. Vanderpool, 1985. 80p. Index. /GC 976.901 L82co/

Walker, Juliet E. K. *Free Frank: A Black Pioneer on the Antebellum Frontier*. Lexington, KY: The University Press of Kentucky, 1983. 223p. Index. Photographs. Illustrations. Charts. /GC 976.9 W145f/

LOUISIANA

Afro-Louisiana Historical and Genealogical Society Journal. Baton Rouge, LA: Afro-Louisiana Historical and Genealogical Society, v.1-, 1989-. /Periodical/

Black Bicentennial Committee of Ouachita Parish. *Contributors of Ouachita Parish: A History of Blacks*. Ouachita Parish, LA: Black Bicentennial Committee of Ouachita Parish, 1976. 42p. /GC 976.301 Ou1b/

Brasseaux, Carl A., Keith P. Fontenot, and Claude F. Oubre. *Creoles of Color in the Bayou Country*. Jackson, MS: University Press of Mississippi, 1994. 174p. Appendices. Bibliography. Index. /GC 976.3 B73c/

Childs, Marleta. *The 1850 Slave Schedule of Natchitoches Parish, Louisiana*. Ville Platte, LA: Provincial Press, 1998. North Louisiana Census Reports, Volume V. 91p. Index. /GC 976.301 N19c/

Clark, Peter Wellington. *Delta Shadows: A Pageant of Negro Progress in New Orleans*. New Orleans, LA: Graphic Arts Studios, 1942. 200p. Photographs. /GC 976.302 N43c/

Clement, William Edwards and Stuart Omer Landry. *Plantation Life on the Mississippi*. New Orleans, LA: Pelican Publishing Company, 1961. 235p. Index. Maps. Photographs. /GC 976.301 Ib34c/

Davis, Edwin Adams. *Plantation Life in the Florida Parishes of Louisiana, 1836-1846 (West Feliciana Parish) as Reflected in the Diary of Bennet Hilliard Barrow*. New York: AMS Press, Inc., 1967. Accounts. Bibliography. Slave lists. /GC 976.301 W54b/

DeHart, Jess. *Plantations of Louisiana*. Gretna, LA: Pelican Publishing Company, 1982. 176p. Index. Sketches. /GC 976.3 D355p/

DeVille, Winston. *Slaves and Masters of Pointe Coupee, Louisiana: A Calendar of Civil Records, 1762-1823*. Ville Platte, LA: W. DeVille, 1988. 74p. Index. /GC 976.301 P75da/

Dill, Harry F. *African American Inhabitants of Rapides Parish, Louisiana, 1 June - 4 September 1870*. Bowie, MD: Heritage Books, Inc., 1998. 373p. Index. /GC 976.301 R18di/

Dill, Harry F. and William Simpson. *Some Slaveholders and Their Slaves, Union Parish, Louisiana 1839-1865*. Bowie, MD: Heritage Books, Inc., 1997. 195p. Indices. /GC 976.301 Un3d/

Guide to the Heartman Manuscripts on Slavery. Boston, MA: G. K. Hall & Company, 1982. 221p. Index. /GC 976.302 N43x/

Hall, Gwendolyn Midlo. *Africans in Colonial Louisiana: The Development of Afro-Creole Culture in the Eighteenth Century*. Baton Rouge, LA: Louisiana State University Press, 1992. 434p. Appendices. Index. Notes. /GC 976.3 H14a/

Hardy, Linell L. *Abstract of Account Information of Freedman's Savings and Trust, New Orleans, LA, 1866-1869*. Bowie, MD: Heritage Books, Inc., 1999. 183p. Index. /GC 976.302 N43gy/

Hebert, Donald J. *Southwest Louisiana Records: Church and Civil Records*. Baton Rouge, LA: Claitor's Publishing Division, 1984. Volume 33–Supplement. Slave and Black Records (1765 - 1886). /GC 976.3 H35s V.33 p. 106 - 307/

Hicks, William. *History of Louisiana Negro Baptists from 1804 to 1914*. Nashville, TN: National Baptist Publishing Company, 19--. 251p. Photographs. /GC 976.3 H529h/

Hollandsworth, James. G., Jr. *The Louisiana Native Guard: The Black Military Experience During the Civil War*. Baton Rouge, LA: Louisiana State University Press, 1995. 140p. Appendix. Bibliography. Index. Photographs. /GC 973.74 L93ho/

Kilbourne, Richard Holcombe Jr. *Debt, Investment, Slaves: Credit Relations in East Feliciana Parish, Louisiana, 1825-1885*. Tuscaloosa, AL: The University of Alabama Press, 1995. 201p. Bibliography. Index. Notes. /GC 976.301 Ea74k/

Lathrop, Barnes Fletcher. *The Pugh Plantations, 1860-1865, A Study of Life in Lower Louisiana*. Austin, TX: B. F. Lathrop, 1945. 477p. Bibliography. /GC 976.3 L34p/

MacDonald, Robert R. et al. *Louisiana's Black Heritage*. New Orleans, LA: Louisiana State Museum, 1979. 239p. Bibliography. /GC 976.3 L934/

Malone, Ann Patton. *Sweet Chariot: Slave Family and Household Structure in Nineteenth-Century Louisiana*. Chapel Hill, NC: The University of North Carolina Press, 1992. 369p. Bibliography. Index. Notes. Tables. /GC 976.3 M29s/

Menn, Joseph Karl. *The Large Slaveholders of Louisiana–1860*. New Orleans, LA: Pelican Publishing Company, 1964. 432p. Bibliography. /GC 976.3 M52m/

Mills, Gary B. *The Forgotten People: Cane River's Creoles of Color*. Baton Rouge, LA: Louisiana State University Press, 1977. 277p. Index. Photographs. Maps. Charts. /GC 976.301 N19mj/

Ochs, Stephen J. *A Black Patriot and a White Priest: Andre Cailloux and Claude Paschal Maistre in Civil War New Orleans*. Baton Rouge, LA: Louisiana State University Press, 2000. 304p. Appendix. Bibliography. Illustrations. Index. Maps. Notes. Photographs. /GC 973.73 L93ny/

Perkins, A. E. *Who's Who in Colored Louisiana*. Baton Rouge, LA: Douglas Loan Company, Inc., 1930. 155p. Portraits. /GC 976.3 W62/

Records of Ante-Bellum Southern Plantations from the Revolution through the Civil War. Frederick, MD: University Publications of America, Inc., 198-.
Louisiana--Slavery Manuscript Series, 1784-1865. /Series H, Roll 20/
Louisiana--Mary Jeffreys Bethell diary, 1853-1873. /Series J, Part 13, Roll 12/
Louisiana--Hamilton Brown papers, 1752-1907. /Series J, Part 14, Rolls 5-8/
Louisiana--Canebroke Plantation, 1856-1858. /Series G, Part 1, Roll 11/
Louisiana--Capehart family papers, 1782-1983. /Series J, Part 12, Rolls 20-21/
Louisiana--Farish Carter papers, 1794,1806-1868. /Series J, Part 4, Rolls 38-43/

Louisiana--William Dunbar account book, 1776-1847. /Series J, Part 6, Roll 1/
Louisiana--Guion family papers, 1789-1927. /Series J, Part 6, Roll 1/
Louisiana--Hughes family papers, 1790-1860. /Series J, Part 6, Rolls 23-24/
Louisiana--Jackson, Riddle, and Company papers, 1835-1839. /Series J, Part 5, Roll 19/
Louisiana--Francois Mignon papers, 1825-1854. /Series J, Part 6, Roll 15/
Louisiana--Minor family papers, 1763-1900. /Series J, Part 6, Rolls 1-2/
Louisiana--Norton, Chilton, & Dameron papers, 1760-1926. /Series J, Part 6, Rolls 3-5/
Louisiana--Pegram-Johnson-McIntosh family papers, 1825-1941. /Series M, Part 5, Rolls 47-48/
Louisiana--Quitman family papers, 1760-1926. /Series J, Part 6, Rolls 5-12/
Louisiana--Randolph & Yates family papers, 1815-1865,1952. /Series J, Part 6, Roll 27/
Louisiana--Frederick Seip papers, 1808-1908. /Series J, Part 6, Roll 15/
Louisiana--Thompson family papers, 1809-1924. /Series J, Part 7, Roll 8/
Louisiana--Lewis Thompson papers, 1723-1894. /Series J, Part 12, Rolls 32-38/
Louisiana--Wickham family papers. 1766-1945. /Series M, Part 4, Rolls 51-55/
Ascension parish, LA--Ashland plantation record, 1852. /Series I, Part 1, Roll 13/
Ascension parish, LA--Louis Bringier family papers, 1826-1847. /Series I, Part 1, Roll 13/
Ascension parish, LA--H. M. Seale diary, 1853-1857. /Series I, Part 1, Roll 13/
Ascension parish, LA--Trist Wood papers, 1800-1898. /Series J, Part 5, Roll 6/
Assumption parish, LA--Landry family papers, 1831-1865. /Series I, Part 1, Roll 8/
Assumption parish, LA--Pugh family papers, 1807-1882. /Series G, Part 1, Rolls 1-11 & Series I, Part 1, Rolls 6-7/
Caddo parish, LA--Hubbard S. Bosley papers, 1825-1865. /Series I, Part 2, Roll 19/
Carroll parish, LA--Ashton Plantation auction broadside, 1859. /Series I, Part 1, Roll 10/
Concordia parish, LA--Geo. W. Sargent books, 1840-1900. /Series J, Part 6, Rolls 12-15/
De Soto parish, LA--Sidney Harding diary, 1863-1865. /Series I, Part 1, Roll 4/
East Carroll parish, LA--Airlie Plantation, 1862. /Series G, Part 1, Roll 11/
East Carroll parish, LA--Bruce, Seddon & Wilkins, 1741-1865. /Series I, Part 1, Rolls 9-10/
East Feliciana parish, LA--Abel John Norwood record books, 1844-1880. /Series I, Part 2, Rolls 12-13/

East Feliciana parish, LA--Benjamin Kendrick papers, 1806-1894. /Series I, Part 2, Rolls 11-12/

Iberia parish, LA--Avery family papers, 1796-1924. /Series J, Part 5, Rolls 10-11/

Iberia parish, LA--Bayside plantation records, 1846-1866. /Series J, Part 5, Roll 6/

Iberia parish, LA--Caffery family papers, 1838-1859. /Series J, Part 5, Roll 7/

Iberia parish, LA--Frank Liddell Richardson papers, 1851-1869. /Series J, Part 5, Roll 7/

Iberia parish, LA--Eliza Anne (Marsh) Robertson family papers, 1849-1872. /Series J, Part 5, Roll 12/

Iberia parish, LA--David Weeks family papers, 1782-1957. /Series I, Part 6, Rolls 1-19/

Iberville parish, LA--Franklin A. Hudson diaries, 1852-1859. /Series J, Part 5, Rolls 12-13/

Iberville parish, LA--Joseph Kleinpeter papers, 1813-1894. /Series I, Part 1, Roll 9/

Iberville parish, LA--LeBlanc family papers, 1812-1866. /Series I, Part 2, Roll 17/

Iberville parish, LA--John H. Randolph papers, 1822-1865. /Series I, Part 1, Rolls 14-15/

Iberville parish, LA--Slack family papers, 1805-1944. /Series J, Part 5, Rolls 13-14/

Jefferson parish, LA--John McDonogh papers, 1789-1860, 1929. /Series H, Rolls 2-11/

Lafourche parish, LA--Robert O. Butler papers, 1848-1888. /Series I, Part 5, Rolls 3-4/

Lafourche parish., LA--Mathews papers, 1797-1865. /Series I, Part 2, Rolls 14-17/

Lafourche parish., LA--Pugh family papers, 1807-1882. /Series G, Part 1, Rolls 1-11 & Series I, Part 1, Rolls 6-7/

Natchitoches parish, LA--Pre Aux Cleres plantation records, 1852-1854. /Series I, Part 2, Roll 19/

Natchitoches parish, LA--Lestan Prudhomme papers, 1826-1854. /Series H, Rolls 20-21/

Natchitoches parish, LA--Phanor Prudhomme family papers, 1804-1940. /Series J, Part 5, Rolls 15-17/

Orleans parish, LA--Gustave Aivilien Breaux diaries, 1859, 1863-1865. /Series H, Roll 30/

Orleans parish, LA--Citizens Bank of Louisiana minute books & records, 1833-1868. /Series H, Rolls 13-17/
Orleans parish, LA--Thomas Durnford estate, 1827-1901. /Series H, Roll 13/
Orleans parish, LA--Eugene Forstall letterbooks, 1851-1864. /Series H, Roll 20/
Orleans parish, LA--Rosemonde E. & Emile Kuntz papers, 1837-1838 & 1850-1857. /Series H, Rolls 12-13/
Orleans parish, LA--Hugues Lavergne letterbooks, 1829-1842. /Series H, Roll 30/
Orleans parish, LA--John McDonogh papers, 1789-1860, 1929. /Series H, Rolls 2-12/
Orleans parish, LA--Wm. Page Saunders papers, 1854-1856. /Series J, Part 5, Roll 14/
Orleans parish, LA--Samuel Walker diary, 1856-1878. /Series H, Roll 24/
Orleans parish, LA--Maunsell White papers, 1802-1912. /Series J, Part 5, Roll 1/
Orleans parish, LA--Trist Wood papers, 1800-1898. /Series J, Part 5, Roll 6/
Plaquemines parish, LA--Andrew Durnford Plantation journal, 1840-1868. /Series H, Roll 13/
Plaquemines parish, LA--Geo. Lanaux papers, 1830-1865. /Series I, Part 1, Rolls 11-13/
Plaquemines parish, LA--Samuel McCutchon family papers, 1832-1874. /Series I, Part 1, Rolls 5-6/
Plaquemines parish, LA--Ross/Stackhouse records, 1804-1881. /Series H, Roll 1/
Plaquemines parish, LA--Ste. Sophie/Live Oak Plantation records, 1823-1829. /Series H, Roll 1/
Plaquemines parish, LA--Maunsell White papers, 1802-1912. /Series J, Part 5, Roll 1/
Pointe Coupee parish, LA--John Boyd diary, 1850-1871. /Series J, Part 5, Roll 14/
Pointe Coupee parish, LA--John G. Devereux papers, 1791-1890. /Series J, Part 5, Roll 14/
Pointe Coupee parish, LA--Ledoux & Co. plantation journal, 1856-1857. /Series I, Part 1, Roll 9/
Pointe Coupee parish, LA--Julien Poydras papers, 1794-1800. /Series H, Roll 1/
Pointe Coupee parish, LA--William Page Saunders family papers, 1854-1856. /Series J, Part 5, Roll 14/
Rapides parish, LA--Mathews papers, 1797-1865. /Series I, Part 2, Rolls 14-17/
Rapides parish, LA--Thomas O. Moore papers, 1832-1865. /Series I, Part 2, Rolls 18-19/

Rapides parish, LA--Wm. Polk papers, 1840-1867. /Series J, Part 5, Roll 15/
Red River parish, LA--Joseph Toole Robinson papers, 1830s, 1853-1861. /Series I, Part 2, Roll 20/
Red River parish, LA--Hubbard S. Bosley papers, 1825-1865. /Series I, Part 2, Roll 19/
St. Bernard parish, LA--Geo. Lanaux papers, 1830-1865. /Series I, Part 1, Rolls 11-13/
St. Bernard parish, LA--John McDonogh papers, 1789-1860, 1929. /Series H, Rolls 2-11/
St. Charles parish, LA--Kenner family papers, 1844-1892. /Series I, Part 1, Roll 5/
St. Charles parish, LA--Saml. McCutchon papers, 1832-1874. /Series I, Part 1, Rolls 5-6/
St. James parish, LA--Valcour Aime slave records, 1821-1850. /Series H, Roll 1/
St. James parish, LA--Boucry family record books, 1814-1884, 1910. /Series I, Part 1, Roll 8/
St. James parish, LA--Bruce, Seddon & Wilkins, 1741-1865. /Series I, Part 1, Rolls 9-10/
St. James parish, LA--Octave Colomb Plantation journal, 1849-1866. /Series H, Roll 20/
St. James parish, LA--Jean Baptiste Ferchand journal, 1858. /Series H, Roll 30/
St. James parish, LA--Eugene Forstall letterbooks, 1851-1864. /Series H, Roll 20/
St. James parish, LA--George Mather account books, 1782-1845. /Series I, Part 1, Roll 8/
St. James parish, LA--William Webb Wilkins papers, 1848-1852. /Series I, Part 1, Roll 10/
St. Landry parish, LA--Bayside plantation records, 1846-1866. /Series J, Part 5, Roll 6/
St. Landry parish, LA--John Close papers, 1802-1872. /Series I, Part 2, Rolls 17-18/
St. Landry parish, LA--Jean Baptiste Meullion papers, 1798-1889. /Series H, Roll 13/
St. Martin parish, LA--Gustave A. Breaux diaries, 1859, 1863-1865. /Series H, Roll 30/
St. Martin parish, LA--Willis P. Griffith papers, 1840-1865. /Series H, Roll 29/
St. Martin parish, LA--Palfrey family papers, 1776-1918. /Series I, Part 1, Rolls 1-4/
St. Martin parish, LA--David Rees papers, 1803-1835. /Series H, Rolls 29-30/

St. Mary parish, LA--Brashear & Lawrence family papers, 1804-1982. /Series J, Part 5, Rolls 7-10/

St. Mary parish, LA--Caffery family papers, 1838-1859. /Series J, Part 5, Roll 7/

St. Mary parish, LA--Sidney Harding diary, 1863-1865. /Series I, Part 1, Roll 4/

St. Mary parish, LA--Palfrey family papers, 1776-1918. /Series I, Part 1, Rolls 1-4/

St. Mary parish, LA--Simpson & Brumby papers, 1847-1865. /Series J, Part 5, Roll 7/

St. Mary parish, LA--Stirling, 1784-1865. /Series I, Part 2, Rolls 21-25/

Tangipahoa parish, LA--John W. Gurley papers, 1858-1866. /Series I, Part 2, Roll 13/

Tensas parish, LA--Alexander Blanche plantation journal, 1851-1856. /Series I, Part 3, Roll 14/

Tensas parish, LA--Richardson & Farrar papers, 1860-1876. /Series J, Part 6, Roll 12/

Tensas parish, LA--John Perkins papers, 1822-1864. /Series J, Part 5, Roll 18/

Terrebonne parish, LA--Robert Ruffin Barrow papers, 1749-1858. /Series H, Rolls 17-19 & Series J, Part 5, Roll 2/

Terrebonne parish, LA--Robert O. Butler papers, 1848-1888. /Series I, Part 5, Rolls 3-4/

Terrebonne parish, LA--Andrew McCollam family papers, 1792-1873. /Series J, Part 5, Rolls 3-5/

Terrebonne parish, LA--Wm. A. Shaffer papers, 1818-1921. /Series J, Part 5, Rolls 2-3/

West Baton Rouge parish, LA--Stirling papers, 1784-1865. /Series I, Part 2, Rolls 21-25/

West Feliciana parish, LA-- Coert R. Barrow papers, 1749-1858. /Series H, Rolls 17-19/

West Feliciana parish, LA--Butler family papers, 1663-1950. /Series I, Part 5, Rolls 13-27/

West Feliciana parish, LA--Anna and Sarah Butler papers, 1838-1861. /Series I, Part 5, Roll 1/

West Feliciana parish, LA--Margaret Butler papers, 1847-1880. /Series I, Part 5, Roll 2/

West Feliciana parish, LA--Richard Butler papers, 1795-1889. /Series I, Part 5, Rolls 2-3/

West Feliciana parish, LA--Robert O. Butler papers, 1848-1888. /Series I, Part 5, Rolls 3-4/

West Feliciana parish, LA--Thomas Butler papers, 1804-1945. /Series I, Part 5, Rolls 9-13/

West Feliciana parish, LA--Thomas W. Butler papers, 1842-1913. /Series I, Part 5, Rolls 4-9/

West Feliciana parish, LA--Benjamin Kendrick papers, 1806-1894. /Series I, Part 2, Rolls 11-12/

West Feliciana parish, LA--Mathews papers, 1797-1865. /Series I, Part 2, Rolls 14-17/

West Feliciana parish, LA--John M. Pintard papers, 1796-1825. /Series I, Part 2, Roll 14/

West Feliciana parish, LA--Stirling papers, 1784-1865. /Series I, Part 2, Rolls 21-25/

Records of the Assistant Commissioner for the State of Louisiana, Bureau of Refugees, Freedmen, and Abandoned Lands, 1865-1869. Washington, DC: National Archives and Records Service, 1976. Microcopy M1027. Endorsements Sent. Records Relating to the Condition of Freedmen and Refugees. Records of Indigent Refugees and Freedmen from Subordinate Officers. Letters and Telegrams Received. Records Relating to Confiscated Lands. Murders and Outrages. Personnel Records. Monthly Reports. /Microfilm Rolls 3-25, 32-35/

Records of the Superintendent of Education of the State of Louisiana, Bureau of Refugees, Freedmen, and Abandoned Lands, 1864-1869. Washington, DC: National Archives and Records Service, 1977. Microcopy M1026. Ledger and Journal Accounts of the Board of Education. School Supplies. Tax Base. Tax Assessment in New Orleans. Reports from School Directors. Financial Reports. Miscellaneous Reports. /Microfilm Rolls 36-38/

Register of Free Colored Persons, 1840-1864, New Orleans, LA. New Orleans, LA: New Orleans Public Library, 198-. /Microfilm/

Registers of Signatures of Depositors in Branches of the Freedman's Savings and Trust Company, 1865-1874. Washington, DC: National Archives and Records Service, 1969. Microcopy M816. New Orleans. Shreveport. /Microfilm Roll 39/

Record for Andrew Hunter

Date ~~and No.~~ of Application, Mch 19, 1867
~~Name of Master,~~ formerly lived at Memphis,
~~Name of Mistress,~~ Tenn. Has been here since
~~Plantation,~~ the War.
Age
~~Height~~ and Complexion, About 47 – Black
wears Wig Lily
Father or Mother? Married? Wife Margaret Shield
Name of Children, Ellen about 14. Alfred 21 yo.
Regiment and Company; 7th USCT. Co. E.
Place of Birth, Sumner Co. above Nashville Tenn.
Residence, No 203 (forgot name of street)
Occupation, Steward private house

REMARKS, Son Robert died 10 yrs ago.
(Andrew has other children by Louisa Sanders.
John 24 + William 22 + Patsy 23 – + Nell (dead). They
all were sold away from Memphis to Ala. – William
was here about 6 mos ago.
his Father was in Houston Texas – 20 yrs ago – when he was
there – his mother died there 21 yo ago. Last August.
Bro. John in N.O. + William (dont know when he is) + Frederick
dont know where he is – Sister Mary + Martha wife of Robin
Signature,
Burrill – Has a Bro. Philip. Dont know where he is)

Andrew ×his Hunter
mark

N° 304

Slave Schedules for 1850–Louisiana. Washington, DC: The National Archives, 1964. Microcopy 432. /Microfilm Rolls 242-247/

Slave Schedules for 1860–Louisiana. Washington, DC: The National Archives, 1967. Microcopy 653. /Microfilm Rolls 427-431/

Slavery in Ante-Bellum Southern Industries. Frederick, MD: University Publications of America, 199-.
Louisiana--Allmand family papers, 1796-1891. /Series C, Part 2, Rolls 19-20/
Louisiana--Hawkins family papers, 1738-1865. /Series B, Rolls 8-21/
Louisiana--Talcott family papers, 1814-1915. /Series C, Part 2, Rolls 12-19/

Vincent, Charles. ***Black Legislators in Louisiana During Reconstruction.*** Baton Rouge, LA: Louisiana State University Press, 1976. 262p. Bibliography. Index. Pictures. /GC 976.3 V742b/

Watts, Gwendolyn P. ***Against All Odds: McDonogh 35 High School, 1917-1937.*** New Orleans, LA: University of New Orleans, 1998. 60p. Appendices. Bibliography. Notes. Tables. /GC 976.302 N43wa/

MAINE

Minority Military Service, Maine, 1775-1783. Washington, DC: National Society Daughters of the American Revolution, 1990. 24p. /GC 973.34 M28mi/

MARYLAND

Adams, Carolyn Greenfield. *Hunter Sutherland's Slave Manumissions and Sales in Harford County, Maryland, 1775-1865.* Bowie, MD: Heritage Books, Inc., 1999. 121 p. Index. /GC 975.201 H22su/

Annual Baltimore County African American Cultural Festival. Baltimore, MD: Baltimore County African American Cultural Festival, Inc., 1997-. Photographs. /GC 975.201 B21af 1997-./

Blackford, John. *The Ferry Hill Plantation Journal: January 4, 1838 - January 15, 1839, Washington County, Maryland.* Chapel Hill, NC: University of North Carolina Press, 1961. (The James Sprunt Studies in History and Political Science. Vol. 43) 139p. Index. /GC 975.2 B564f/

Carothers, Bettie Stirling. *Maryland Slave Owners and Superintendents, 1978.* Lutherville, MD: B. S. Carothers, 1974/5. 2v. Index. /GC 975.2 C22ma/

Clayton, Ralph. *Black Baltimore, 1820-1870.* Bowie, MD: Heritage Books, Inc., 1987. 199p. Indices. /GC 975.201 B21cl/

Clayton, Ralph. *Free Blacks of Anne Arundel County, Maryland, 1850.* Bowie, MD: Heritage Books, Inc., 1987. 51p. Index. /GC 975.201 An7cla/

Clayton, Ralph. *Slavery, Slaveholding, and the Free Black Population of Antebellum Baltimore.* Bowie, MD: Heritage Books, Inc., 1993. 353p. Index. Notes. /GC 975.202 B21cl/

Cohen, Anthony. *The Underground Railroad in Montgomery County, Maryland: A History and Driving Guide.* Rockville, MD:

Montgomery County Historical Society, 1997. 40p.
Bibliography. Maps. Photographs. /GC 975.201 M76coh/

Davidson, Thomas E. *Free Blacks on the Lower Eastern Shore of Maryland, The Colonial Period–1662-1775*. Crownsville, MD: Maryland Historical & Cultural Publications, 1991. 110p. Appendices. Maps. Notes. /GC 975.2 D28f/

Diggs, Louis S. *Holding On to Their Heritage*. Baltimore, MD: L. S. Diggs, 1996. 180p. Appendices. Photographs. /GC 975.202 R27d/

Fuller, Marsha Lynne. *African American Manumissions of Washington County, MD*. Hagerstown, MD: Desert Sheik Press, 1997. 295p. Appendices. Index. /GC 975.201 W276f/

Hynson, Jerry M. *The African American Collection: Kent County, Maryland*. Westminster, MD: Family Line Publications, 1998. 105p. Index. /GC 975.201 K41hy/

Hynson, Jerry M. *Free African Americans of Maryland, 1832 (Including: Allegany, Anne Arundel, Calvert, Caroline, Cecil, Charles, Dorchester, Frederick, Kent, Montgomery, Queen Ann's, and St. Mary's Counties)*. Westminster, MD: Family Line Publications, 1998. 161p. Index. /GC 975.2 H998f/

Hynson, Jerry M. *Maryland Freedom Papers*. Westminster, MD: Family Line Publications, 1997. 107p. Volume 1–Anne Arundel County. Volume 2–Kent County. Index. /GC 975.2 H99m V. 1-2/

Jacobsen, Phebe R. *Researching Black Families at the Maryland Hall of Records*. Annapolis, MD: The Maryland Hall of Records Commission, 1984. 12p. Photographs. /GC 929 J146r/

McDaniel, George W. *Black Historical Resources in Upper Western Montgomery County Community Histories*. Sugarloaf Regional Trails, MD: s.n., 1979. 163p. Charts. Photographs. /GC 975.201 M76mc/

Morgan, Philip D. *Slave Counterpoint: Black Culture in the Eighteenth-Century Chesapeake and Lowcountry*. Chapel Hill, NC: University of North Carolina Press, 1998. 703p. Illustrations. Index. Notes. /GC 975 M823s/

Papers of the Maryland State Colonization Society. (A Collection of the Maryland Historical Society) Philadelphia, PA: Rhistoric Publications, Inc., 1970. Correspondence, day books, deeds, financial records, manumission books, newspapers, and pamphlets. /Microfilm Rolls 1 - 31/

Papers of the Maryland State Colonization Society: A Guide to the Microfilm Edition. Philadelphia, PA: Rhistoric Publications, Inc., 1970. 34p. /GC 929 M362g/

Pearl, Susan G. *Prince George's County African-American Heritage Survey, 1996*. Upper Marlboro, MD: The Maryland-National Capital Park & Planning Commission, 1996. 162p. Appendices. Bibliography. Maps. Photographs. /GC 975.201 P93pea/

Phillips, Christopher. *Freedom's Port: The African American Community of Baltimore, 1790-1860*. Urbana, IL: University of Illinois Press, 1997. 350p. Bibliography. Index. Maps. /GC 975.202 B21ph/

Rawick, George P., ed. *The American Slave: A Composite Autobiography–Maryland...Narratives*. Westport, CT: Greenwood Publishing Company, 1972. /GC 929.11 K136 Sec. 3/

Rawick, George P., ed. *The American Slave: A Composite Autobiography–Maryland...Narratives.* Westport, CT: Greenwood Publishing Company, 1979. /GC 929.11 Al113 Sec. 9/

Records of Ante-Bellum Southern Plantations from the Revolution through the Civil War. Frederick, MD: University Publications of America, Inc., 198-.
Maryland--Robert Carter papers, 1760-1815. Series M, Part 2, Roll 6/
Maryland--William Stump Forwood papers, 1836-1861. /Series J, Part 7, Rolls 1-2/
Maryland--Jackson, Riddle, and Company papers, 1835-1839. /Series J, Part 5, Roll 19/
Maryland--Jennings family papers, 1737-1837. /Series M, Part 2, Roll 9/
Maryland--John McDonogh papers, 1789-1860, 1929. /Series H, Rolls 3-11/
Maryland--Shirley plantation journal, 1650-1888. /Series K, Rolls 1-26/
Maryland--Stephen Moore papers, 1767-1869. /Series J, Part 13, Rolls 9-10/
Maryland--Tayloe family papers, 1708-1861. /Series M, Part 1, Rolls 1-57/
Maryland--William Henry Wills papers, 1712-1892. /Series J, Part 12, Rolls 41-43/
Anne Arundel co., MD--Jacob Franklin papers, 1702-1818. /Series D, Roll 1/
Anne Arundel co., MD--William Henry Hall papers, 1745-1902. /Series F, Part 3, Rolls 39-40/
Anne Arundel co., MD--Jones record books, 1779-1812. /Series D, Roll 9/
Anne Arundel co., MD--Mercer family papers, 1656-1869. /Series M, Part 2, Rolls 13-15/
Baltimore co., MD--Richard Dorsey papers, 1809-1845. /Series D, Roll 11/
Baltimore co., MD--John Eager Howard papers, 1827-1828. /Series D, Roll 11/
Baltimore co., MD--Jones record books, 1779-1812. /Series D, Roll 9/
Baltimore co., MD--William Patterson account books, 1787-1837. /Series D, Roll 1/
Carroll co., MD--Susanna Warfield diaries, 1845-1885. /Series D, Roll 12/
Cecil co., MD--Martha Forman diaries, 1814-1859. /Series D, Rolls 12-14/
Frederick co., MD--L. A. Barr daybook, 1855-1858. /Series F, Part 3, Roll 43/
Frederick co., MD--Roger Johnson account books, 1806-1842. /Series D, Rolls 8-9/
Frederick co., MD--Lee family papers, 1780-1851. /Series F, Part 3, Rolls 43-44/

Frederick co., MD--Levin Winder papers, 1813-1815. /Series F, Part 3, Roll 43/
Harford co., MD--Michael family papers, 1811-1873. /Series D, Roll 10/
Harford co., MD--Neilson record books, 1798-1900. /Series D, Rolls 10-11/
Montgomery co., MD--Solomon Davis account book, 1812-1826. /Series F, Part 3, Roll 43/
Prince George's co., MD--Richard D. Burroughs papers, 1807-1859. /Series F, Part 3, Rolls 41-43/
Prince George's co., MD--Oden family papers, 1755-1835. /Series D, Rolls 7-8/
Prince George's co., MD--Thomas Wood papers, 1804-1888. /Series D, Rolls 5-7/
Queen Anne's co., MD--Edward Downes papers, 1775-1784. /Series F, Part 3, Roll 41/
Queen Anne's co., MD--Hollyday family papers, 1677-1951. /Series D, Rolls 1-4/
Talbot co., MD--Hollyday family papers, 1677-1951. /Series D, Rolls 1-4/
Washington co., MD--Blackford family papers, 1836-1858. /Series M, Part 6, Roll 1/
Washington co., MD--Thomas E. Buchanan papers, 1798-1950. /Series F, Part 3, Rolls 44-45/

Registers of Signatures of Depositors in Branches of the Freedman's Savings and Trust Company, 1865-1874. Washington, DC: National Archives and Records Service, 1969. Microcopy M816. Baltimore. /Microfilm Roll 11/

Slave Schedules for 1850–Maryland. Washington, DC: The National Archives, 1964. Microcopy 432. /Microfilm Rolls 300-302/

Slave Schedules for 1860–Maryland. Washington, DC: The National Archives, 1967. Microcopy 653. /Microfilm Rolls 484-485/

Whitman, T. Stephen. *The Price of Freedom: Slavery and Manumission in Baltimore and Early National Maryland.* Lexington, KY: University Press of Kentucky, 1997. 238p. Bibliography. Index. Maps. /GC 975.2 W59p/

Wilson, W. Emerson, ed. *Plantation Life at Rose Hill: The Diaries of Martha Ogle Forman, 1814-1845*. Wilmington, DE: The Historical Society of Delaware, 1976. 462p. Appendix. Index. /GC 975.201 C32fo/

Wright, James H. *The Free Negro in Maryland, 1634-1860*. New York: Columbia University, 1921. 362p. Bibliography. Notes. Volume 97, Number 3, Whole Number 222 of *Studies in History, Economics and Public Law*. /GC 975.2 W92f/

Yentsch, Anne Elizabeth. *A Chesapeake Family and Their Slaves: A Study in Historical Archaeology*. New York: Press Syndicate of the University of Cambridge, 1994. 433p. Appendices. Bibliography. Index. Notes. Photographs. /GC 975.202 An7v/

MASSACHUSETTS

Carvalho, Joseph, III. *Black Families in Hampden County, Massachusetts, 1650-1855*. Boston, MA: New England Historic Genealogical Society, 1984. 211p. Index. /GC 974.401 H17ca/

Cromwell, Adelaide M. *The Other Brahmins: Boston's Black Upper Class, 1750-1950*. Fayetteville, AR: The University of Arkansas Press, 1994. 284p. Bibliography. Charts. Illustrations. Index. Notes. Photographs. /GC 974.402 B65cr/

Dorman, Franklin A. *Twenty Families of Color in Massachusetts, 1742-1998*. Boston, MA: New England Historic Genealogical Society, 1998. 524p. Appendices. Bibliography. Illustrations. Index. Notes. /GC 974.4 D735t/

Emilio, Luis F. *History of the Fifty-fourth Regiment of the Massachusetts Volunteer Infantry, 1863-1865: A Brave Black Regiment*. Boston, MA: The Boston Book Company, 1894. 452p. Appendix. Index. Map. /GC 973.74 M38eml/

Levesque, George A. *Black Boston: African American Life and Culture in Urban America, 1850-1860*. New York: Garland Publishing, Inc., 1994. 537p. Appendix. Bibliography. Index. /GC 974.402 B65lev/

Minority Military Service, Massachusetts, 1775-1783. Washington, DC: National Society Daughters of the American Revolution, 1989. 34p. /GC 973.34 M38m/

The Museum-Smith Court News. Boston, MA: Museum of Afro-American History, Abiel Smith School, v.1-, 1988-. /Periodical/

On the Altar of Freedom: A Black Soldier's Civil War Letters from the Front. Amherst, MA: University of Massachusetts Press, 1991. 139p. Photographs. /GC 973.74 M38goo/

Parsons, William S. & Margaret A. Drew. *The African Meeting House in Boston: A Sourcebook*. Boston, MA: Museum of Afro-American History, 19--. 225p. Index. Notes. /GC 974.402 B65par/

Smith, James Avery. *The History of the Black Population of Amherst, Massachusetts, 1728-1870*. Boston, MA: New England Historic Genealogical Society, 1999. 145p. Bibliography. Index. Photographs. /GC 974.402 Am47sm/

Trudeau, Noah Andre. *Voices of the 55th: Letters from the 55th Massachusetts Volunteers, 1861-1865*. Dayton, OH: Morningside House, Inc., 1996. 258p. Appendices. Index. Maps. Notes. Photographs. /GC 973.74 M38vo/

MICHIGAN

Brown, Frank R. *A Brief History of 33 Black Churches in Battle Creek, 1849-1997: One Hundred and Forty Eight Years of Progress*. Battle Creek, MI: F. R. Brown, 1997. Photographs. /GC 977.402 B32br/

Brown, Frank R. *Freedom, Justice and Equality: A Pictorial History of the NAACP*. Battle Creek, MI: F. R. Brown, 1996. Photographs. /GC 977.402 B32bro/

Fox, Jean M. *Tracking the Underground Railroad*. Farmington Hills, MI: The Farmington Hills Historical Commission, 1993. 38p. Notes. Photographs. /GC 977.402 F22fox/

Fred Hart Williams Genealogical Society Newsletter. Detroit, MI: Burton Collection of the Detroit Public Library, Fred Hart Williams Genealogical Society, v.1-, 1980-. /Periodical/

Lindquist, Charles N. *The Antislavery-Underground Railroad Movement in Lenawee County, Michigan, 1830-1860*. Adrian, MI: Lenawee County Historical Society, 1999. Bibliography. Illustrations. Index. Maps. Notes. /GC 977.401 L54li/

McRae, Norman. *Negroes in Michigan During the Civil War*. S. l.: Michigan Civil War Centennial Observance Committee, 196-. 124p. Lists. /GC 973.74 M58ma/

Martich, Dorothy. *Martich Black History Collection*. Battle Creek, MI: D. Martich, 1988. 87 scrapbooks on 15 reels of microfilm. Last reel includes an index to the collection. Covers Battle Creek, Calhoun County, and central Michigan. /Microfilm/

Record of Service of Michigan Volunteers in the Civil War, Volume 46: First Colored Infantry. S.l.: s. n., 19--. /GC 973.74 M58mic v. 46/

Warren, Francis H. *Michigan Manual of Freedmen's Progress*. Detroit, MI: John M. Green, 1915. 371p. Illustrations. Index. /GC 977.4 M58mih & GC 977.4 W25m/

Wilson, Benjamin C. *The Rural Black Heritage Between Chicago and Detroit: 1850-1929–A Photograph Album and Random Thoughts*. Kalamazoo, MI: New Issues Press, Western Michigan University, 1985. 245p. Appendices. Notes. Photographs. /GC 977.4 W68r/

MINNESOTA

Rawick, George P., ed. *The American Slave: A Composite Autobiography–Minnesota...Narratives*. Westport, CT: Greenwood Publishing Company, 1977. /GC 929.11 Ar486 Sec. 3/

MISSISSIPPI

Alford, Terry L. "Some Manumissions Recorded in the Adams County Deed Books in Chancery Clerk's Office, Natchez, Mississippi, 1795-1835" in *The Journal of Mississippi History*, volume 33, no. 1, February, 1971, p. 39-50. /Periodical/

Carlton, Marie Haven. *Enumeration of Black Educable Children in Tate County, Mississippi, 1925*. Senatobia, MS: Tate County, Mississippi Genealogical and Historical Society, 1994. 154p. Index. /GC 976.201 T18cb/

Crushshon, Mabel Green. *An Index to Hinds County, Mississippi Freedmen's Bureau Labor Contracts*. Carrollton, MS: Pioneer Publishing Company, 1999. 90p. /GC 976.201 H58cr/

Diamond, E. Grey and Herman Hattaway. *Letters from Forest Place: A Plantation Family's Correspondence, 1846-1881*. Jackson, MS: University Press of Mississippi, 1993. 512p. Appendix. Index. /GC 976.201 C23d/

Embrey, Syble Moore. *Educable Children, Tate County, Mississippi (Black) 1933*. Senatobia, MS: Tate County, Mississippi Genealogical and Historical Society, 1994. 190p. Index. /GC 976.201 T18emb 1933/

Embrey, Syble Moore. *Educable Children, Tate County, Mississippi (Black) 1935*. Senatobia, MS: Tate County, Mississippi Genealogical and Historical Society, 1994. 183p. Index. /GC 976.201 T18emb 1935/

Fox, Louise Cox. *Black Marriages of Tate County, Mississippi 1873-1900*. S.l.: s.n., 1997. /GC 976.201 T18fj/

Frankel, Noralee. *Freedom's Women: Black Women and Families in Civil War Era Mississippi*. Bloomington, IN: Indiana University Press, 1999. 270p. Bibliography. Index. Notes. /GC 976.2 F851f/

Griffith, Lucille. **"The Plantation Record Book of Brookdale Farm, Amite Co., MS, 1856-57"** in *The Journal of Mississippi History*, volume 7, 1945, p. 23-31. /Periodical/

Hamilton, William B. and William D. McCain. **Wealth in the Natchez Region: Inventories of the Estate of Charles Percy, 1794 and 1804"** in *The Journal of Mississippi History*, volume 10, no. 4, October, 1948, p. 290. /Periodical/

Herman, Janet Sharp. *The Pursuit of a Dream*. New York: Oxford University Press, 1981. 290p. Bibliography. Index. Notes. /GC 976.202   M86h/

Johnson, William. *William Johnson: The Ante-bellum Diary of a Free Negro*. Baton Rouge, LA: Louisiana State University Press, 1993. 812p. Index. Notes. /GC   976.202   N19jo/

Mitchell, Mozella G. *New Africa in America: The Blending of African and American Religious and Social Traditions Among Black People in Meridian, Mississippi and Surrounding Counties*. New York: Peter Lang Publishing, Inc., 1994. (*Martin Luther King, Jr. Memorial Studies in Religion, Culture and Social Development*, Volume 5) 245p. Appendix. Photographs. /GC 976.201   L36m/

Nesbany, Nettie, Betty Craft, Lettie Sabbs, and Karen Massey. *Index to the Signatures of Deposits for the Freedman's Savings and Loan Bank, 1865-1869, for the State of Mississippi: Columbia, Natchez, and Vicksburg*. Bowie, MD: Heritage Books, Inc., 1997. 134p. /GC   976.2   In25/

Rawick, Geo. P., ed. *The American Slave: A Composite Autobiography –Mississippi Narratives*. Westport, CT: Greenwood Publishing Company, 1977. /GC   976.2   M695   Parts 1-5/

Rawick, George P., ed. *The American Slave: A Composite Autobiography–Oklahoma and Mississippi Narratives*. Westport, CT: Greenwood Publishing Company, 1972. /GC 976.6   Ok55   Sec. 2/

Records of Ante-Bellum Southern Plantations from the Revolution through the Civil War. Frederick, MD: University Publications of America, Inc., 198-.
Mississippi--W. A. Britton record book, 1847.   /Series I, Part 3, Roll 18/

Mississippi--Hamilton Brown papers, 1752-1907. /Series J, Part 14, Rolls 5-8/
Mississippi--Brownrigg family papers, 1736-1944. /Series J, Part 12, Rolls 17-18/
Mississippi--Bullock & Hamilton papers, 1757-1971. /Series J, Part 13, Rolls 5-8/
Mississippi--Richard Butler papers, 1795-1889. /Series I, Part 5, Rolls 2-3/
Mississippi--William M Byrd papers, 1832-1914. /Series J, Part 7, Roll 5/
Mississippi--Clingman & Puryear family papers, 1810-1940. /Series J, Part 13, Roll 40/
Mississippi--Dorman family papers, 1838-1897. /Series J, Part 7, Roll 1/
Mississippi--James Gwyn papers, 1653-1887. /Series J, Part 14, Rolls 8-9/
Mississippi--Hairston & Wilson family papers, 1800-1895. /Series J, Part 11, Rolls 1-3/
Mississippi--George Hairston papers, 1779-1950. /Series J, Part 11, Roll 4/
Mississippi--Peter Wilson Hairston papers, 1773-1877. /Series J, Part 11, Rolls 5-8/
Mississippi--Hannah family papers, 1760-1967. /Series M, Part 5, Rolls 21-28/
Mississippi--Jackson, Riddle, and Company papers, 1835-1839. /Series J, Part 5, Roll 19/
Mississippi--Johnston & McFaddin family papers, 1839-1890. /Series J, Part 7, Roll 6/
Mississippi--Lewis family papers, 1730-1956. /Series F, Part 12, Rolls 13-14/
Mississippi--Thomas David Smith McDowell papers, 1735-1905. /Series J, Part 12, Rolls 7-12/
Mississippi--Mason family papers, 1789-1965. /Series M, Part 5, Rolls 36-46/
Mississippi--Rufus Reid papers, 1772-1911. /Series J, Part 13, Rolls 37-38/
Mississippi--Francis Gildart Ruffin papers, 1802-1860. /Series J, Part 9, Rolls 30-32/
Mississippi--Shanks family papers, 1801-1923. /Series J, Part 13, Rolls 4-5/
Mississippi--Simpson & Brumby family papers, 1847-1865. /Series J, Part 5, Roll 7/
Mississippi--Thompson family papers, 1809-1924. /Series J, Part 7, Roll 8/
Mississippi--David Weeks family papers, 1782-1957. /Series I, Part 6, Rolls 1-19/
Mississippi--Wyche & Otey papers, 1824-1900 & 1935-1936. /Series J, Part 7, Rolls 9-12/
Adams co., MS--Conner papers, 1818-1865. /Series I, Part 3, Rolls 14-18/
Adams co., MS--William Dunbar account book, 1776-1847. /Series J, Part 6, Roll 1/
Adams co., MS--Ellis-Farar family papers, 1768-1871. /Series I, Part 3, Roll 10/
Adams co., MS--Farrar papers, 1804-1865. /Series I, Part 3, Rolls 6-10/
Adams co., MS--Benjamin Farar papers, 1773-1826. /Series H, Rolls 24-25/

Adams co., MS--Gillespie papers, 1776-1865. /Series I, Part 3, Rolls 13-14/
Adams co., MS--Guion family papers, 1789-1927. /Series J, Part 6, Roll 1/
Adams co., MS--William Kenner papers, 1802-1832. /Series I, Part 3, Rolls 12-13/
Adams co., MS--John Knight papers, 1784-1891. /Series F, Part 1, Rolls 2-4/
Adams co., MS--John T. McMurran papers, 1836-1875. /Series I, Part 3, Roll 18/
Adams co., MS--Andrew Macrery papers, 1795-1855. /Series I, Part 3, Rolls 10-11/
Adams co., MS--Mandeville papers, 1815-1865. /Series I, Part 3, Rolls 3-6/
Adams co., MS--William N. Mercer papers, 1789-1865. /Series H, Roll 24 & Series I, Part 3, Rolls 1-3/
Adams co., MS--Minor family papers, 1763-1900. /Series J, Part 6, Rolls 1-2/
Adams co., MS--John Nevitt diary, 1826-1854. /Series J, Part 6, Roll 3/
Adams co., MS--Norton, Chilton, and Dameron family papers, 1760-1926. /Series J, Part 6, Rolls 3-5/
Adams co., MS--Haller Nutt papers, 1843-1859. /Series F, Part 1, Rolls 1-2/
Adams co., MS--Quitman family papers, 1760-1926. /Series J, Part 6, Rolls 5-12/
Adams co., MS--Richardson & Farrar family papers, 1860-1876. /Series J, Part 6, Roll 12/
Adams co., MS--George W. Sargent books, 1840-1900. /Series J, Part 6, Rolls 12-15/
Adams co., MS--Frederick Seip papers, 1808-1908. /Series J, Part 6, Roll 15/
Adams co., MS--Vidal papers, 1797-1869, 1936. /Series I, Part 3, Rolls 11-12/
Amite co., MS--Everett family papers, 1817-1955. /Series H, Rolls 27-28/
Amite co., MS--Randolph & Yates family papers, 1815-1865,1952. /Series J, Part 6, Roll 27/
Chickasaw co., MS--Chillab Smith Howe papers, 1814-1899. /Series J, Part 6, Rolls 20-23/
Claiborne co., MS--McCall Plantation journals, 1850-1854. /Series F, Part 1, Rolls 4-5/
Claiborne co., MS--James Fontaine Maury diary, 1861. /Series J, Part 6, Roll 27/
Covington co., MS--Duncan McLaurin papers, 1779-1932. /Series F, Part 1, Rolls 5-8/
Franklin co., MS--Pinckey Cotesworth Harrington family papers, 1829-1893. /Series J, Part 6, Roll 18/
Hinds co., MS--Everard Green Baker diaries, 1833-1876. /Series J, Part 6, Rolls 15-16/
Hinds co., MS--Gustavus A. Henry papers, 1804-1895. /Series J, Part 6, Rolls 18-20/

Hinds co., MS--Norton, Chilton, and Dameron family papers, 1760-1926. /Series J, Part 6, Rolls 3-5/

Hinds co., MS--Wm. C. F. Powell papers, 1831-1847. /Series F, Part 1, Roll 8/

Hinds co., MS--Whitaker & Snipes papers, 1780,1835-1889. /Series J, Part 6, Roll 29/

Jefferson co., MS--Everard Green Baker diaries, 1833-1876. /Series J, Part 6, Rolls 15-16/

Lowndes co., MS--Elizabeth Amis Cameron (Hooper) Blanchard papers, 1836-1858. /Series J, Part 6, Roll 17/

Lowndes co., MS--William Ethelbert Ervin diaries, 1839-1856. /Series J, Part 6, Roll 17/

Lowndes co., MS--James Thomas Harrison papers, 1770-1896. /Series J, Part 6, Roll 18/

Lowndes co., MS--Daniel W. Jordan papers, 1827-1866. /Series F, Part 2, Rolls 10-16/

Lowndes co., MS--Wm. Ruffin Smith papers, 1772-1959. /Series J, Part 6, Rolls 28-29/

Madison co., MS--George A. Fleming account book, 1838-1870. /Series I, Part 3, Roll 18/

Noxubee co., MS--Maria Dyer Davies diary, 1850-1856. /Series F, Part 1, Roll 8/

Panola co., MS--Everard Green Baker diaries, 1833-1876. /Series J, Part 6, Rolls 15-16/

Rankin co., MS--Jos. M. Jaynes plantation journals, 1854-1860. /Series F, Part 1, Roll 1/

Tippah co., MS--Francis Terry Leak papers, 1839-1865. Series J, Part 6, Rolls 24-27/

Warren co., MS--Norton, Chilton, & Dameron family papers, 1760-1926. /Series J, Part 6, Rolls 3-5/

Washington co., MS--Mary Bateman diary, 1856. /Series J, Part 6, Roll 17/

Washington co., MS--Francois Mignon papers, 1825-1854. /Series J, Part 6, Roll 15/

Washington co., MS--Frank F. Steel letters, 1859-1861. /Series J, Part 6, Roll 29/

Wilkinson co., MS--Burruss family papers, 1827-1865. /Series H, Roll 25/

Wilkinson co., MS--Joseph Embree papers, 1826-1865. /Series I, Part 2, Rolls 10-11/

Wilkinson co., MS--Nathaniel Evans papers, 1791-1865. /Series I, Part 2, Rolls 1-10/

Wilkinson co., MS--Hughes family papers, 1790-1860. /Series J, Part 6, Rolls 23-24/

Wilkinson co., MS--Benajah Inman papers, 1808-1883. /Series I, Part 2, Roll 11/
Wilkinson co., MS--Albert Lieutaud collection, 1817-1865. /Series H, Roll 28/
Wilkinson co., MS--Nancy Pinson papers, 1820-1865. /Series I, Part 2, Rolls 13-14/
Wilkinson co., MS--Randolph & Yates papers, 1815-1865,1952. /Series J, Part 6, Roll 27/
Wilkinson co., MS--George W. Sargent books, 1840-1900. /Series J, Part 6, Rolls 12-15/

Records of the Assistant Commissioner for the State of Mississippi, Bureau of Refugees, Freedmen, and Abandoned Lands, 1865-1869. Washington, DC: National Archives and Records Service, 1971. Microcopy M826. Endorsements Sent. Ration Reports. Register of Indentures of Colored Orphans. Registers of Marriages of Freedmen. Labor Contracts of Freedmen. Letters Received. /Microfilm Rolls 4-27, 35, 36, 42-50/

Registers of Signatures of Depositors in Branches of the Freedman's Savings and Trust Company, 1865-1874. Washington, DC: National Archives and Records Service, 1969. Microcopy M816. Columbus. Natchez. Vicksburg. /Microfilm Rolls 37-38/

Riley, Franklin L. **"Diary of a Mississippi Planter, January 1, 1840 to April, 1863"** in *Publications of the Mississippi Historical Society.* Oxford, MS: Mississippi Historical Society, 1909. Vol. 10. p. 305-481. /GC 976.2 M694p V.10/

Scott, Ozell D. *DeSoto County, Mississippi Black Marriages, 1866-1900.* Hernando, MS: O. D. Scott, 1997. 5 sections. /GC 976.201 D46sco/

Sewell, George A. and Margaret L. Dwight. *Mississippi Black History Makers.* Jackson, MS: University Press of Mississippi, 1984. 468p. Appendix. Bibliography. Index. Photographs. /GC 976.2 Se8m/

Slave Schedules for 1850–Mississippi. Washington, DC: The National Archives, 1964. Microcopy 432. /Microfilm Rolls 383-390/

Slave Schedules for 1860–Mississippi. Washington, DC: The National Archives, 1967. Microcopy 653. /Microfilm Rolls 595-604/

Slavery in Ante-Bellum Southern Industries. Frederick, MD: University Publications of America, 199-.
Mississippi--Fisher family papers, 1758-1896. /Series B, Rolls 28-38/
Mississippi--Hawkins family papers, 1738-1865. /Series B, Rolls 8-21/
Mississippi--Talcott family papers, 1814-1915. /Series C, Part 2, Rolls 12-19/

Terry, Brenda. *Slaves I, Claiborne County, Mississippi.* Bowie, MD: Heritage Books, 1995. 195p. Bibliography. Index. /GC 976.2 T27s/

Thompson, Cleopatra D. *The History of the Mississippi Teachers Association.* Washington, DC: NEA Teacher Rights; Jackson, MS: Mississippi Teachers Association, 1973. 184p. Photographs. Appendices. Bibliography. /GC 976.2 T37h/

Wiltshire, Betty Couch. *Carroll County, Mississippi, Estate Records, 1840-1869 with Freedman Apprenticeships.* Carrollton, MS: Pioneer Publishing Company, 1997. 168p. Index. /GC 976.201 C23wi/

MISSOURI

Bartels, Carolyn M. *Cooper County Colored Marriages, 1865-1866.* Shawnee Mission, KS: C. M. Bartels, 198-. 11p. Index. /GC 977.801 C78b/

Blattner, Teresa. *People of Color: Black Genealogical Records and Abstracts from Missouri Sources*. Bowie, MD: Heritage Books, Inc., 1993. /GC 977.8 B61p V.1-2/

Colored Paths: Historic Community Research—Transcriptions of Original Records which Legalized the Marriages of Freed People of Color in St. Charles County, Colored Marriage Records, May 25, 1865 - November 19, 1871. S. l.: RONNA, 1994. 75p. /GC 977.801 Sa21c/

Curtis Annette W. *Jackson County Missouri in Black & White*. Independence, MO: A. W. Curtis, 1995-. Volume One: "Census of Slaves, Their Owners and 'Free Colored' 1850 and 1860." Volume Two: "Jabez Smith: His Slaves, Plantations, Estate, and Heirs." /GC 977.801 J13cua V. 1-2/

Gress, Lucille D. *An Informal History of Black Families of the Warrensburg, Missouri, Area*. Warrensburg, MO: The Mid-America Press, Inc., 1997. 162p. Drawings. Photographs. /GC 977.802 W25g/

Missouri 1850 Slave Schedules: Federal Census Index. West Jordan, UT: Genealogical Services, 1988. 388p. /GC 977.8 J12mka/

O'Dell, Charles A. *Black Households in Columbia, Missouri, 1901-1909: A Directory*. Columbia, MO: C. A. O'Dell, 1988. 101p. /GC 977.802 C72o/

Rawick, George P., ed. *The American Slave: A Composite Autobiography—Arkansas Narratives and Missouri Narratives*. Westport, CT: Greenwood Publishing Company, 1972. /GC 976.7 Ar486 Part 7 Sec. 2/

Rawick, George P., ed. *The American Slave: A Composite Autobiography—Missouri...Narratives*. Westport, CT:

Greenwood Publishing Company, 1977. /GC   929.11   Ar486 Sec. 4/

Registers of Signatures of Depositors in Branches of the Freedman's Savings and Trust Company, 1865-1874. Washington, DC: National Archives and Records Service, 1969. Microcopy M816. St. Louis. /Microfilm   Roll 29/

Slave Schedules for 1850 -- Missouri. Washington, DC: The National Archives, 1964. Microcopy 432. /Microfilm   Rolls 422-424/

Slave Schedules for 1860 -- Missouri. Washington, DC: The National Archives, 1967. Microcopy 653. /Microfilm   Roll 605/

Wright, John A. *Discovering African-American St. Louis: A Guide to Historic Sites.* St. Louis, MO: Missouri Historical Society Press, 1994. 210p. Bibliography. Index. Photographs. /GC   977.802   Sa227wr/

NEBRASKA

Rawick, George P., ed. *The American Slave: A Composite Autobiography–Nebraska...Narratives.* Westport, CT: Greenwood Publishing Company, 1979. /GC   929.11   Al113 Sec. 10/

Schubert, Frank N. *Buffalo Soldiers, Braves, and the Brass: The Story of Fort Robinson, Nebraska.* Shippensburg, PA: White Mane Publishing Company, Inc., 1993. 250p. Bibliography. Index. Notes. Photographs. /GC   978.202   F77sch/

NEVADA

Rusco, Elmer. *"Good Time Coming?" Black Nevadans in the Nineteenth Century*. Westport, CT: Greenwood Press, 1975. 230p. Bibliography. Drawings. Index. Photographs. /GC 979.3 R89g/

NEW HAMPSHIRE

Minority Military Service, New Hampshire/Vermont, 1775-1783. Washington, DC: National Society Daughters of the American Revolution, 1991. 17p. /GC 973.34 Aalmin/

NEW JERSEY

Afro-American Historical and Genealogical Society New Jersey Chapter Newsletter. Jersey City, NJ: The Chapter, v.5-9, 1993-96. /Periodical/

Bilby, Joseph G. *Forgotten Warrior: New Jersey's African American Soldiers in the Civil War*. Hightstown, NJ: Longstreet House, 1993. 72p. Bibliography. Drawings. Index. Notes. Photographs. /GC 973.74 N39bi/

Fishman, George. *The African American Struggle for Freedom and Equality: The Development of a People's Identity, New Jersey, 1624-1850*. New York: Garland Publishing, 1997. 286p. Bibliography. Index. /GC 974.9 F539a/

Hodges, Graham Russell. *Slavery and Freedom in the Rural North: African Americans in Monmouth County, New Jersey, 1665-1865*. Madison, WI: Madison House, 1997. 238p. Bibliography. Index. Notes. /GC 974.901 M75ho/

Hodges, Graham Russell & Alan Edward Brown. *"Pretends to Be Free" Runaway Slave Advertisements from Colonial and Revolutionary New York and New Jersey*. New York: Garland Publishing, Inc., 1994. 369p. Appendices. Bibliography. Glossary. Indices. /GC   974.7   H665p/

Jersey Heritage. Jersey City, NJ: New Jersey Afro-American Historical and Genealogical Society, v.1-, 1992-. /Periodical/

NJ-AAHGS Newsletter. Jersey City, NJ: The Chapter, v.9-, 1996-. /Periodical/

Pawley, James A. *The Negro Church in New Jersey*. Hackensack, NJ: Works Project Administration, 1938. 55p. Bibliography. Notes. /GC   974.9   P28n/

Slave Schedules for 1850–New Jersey. Washington, DC: The National Archives, 1964. Microcopy 432. /Microfilm   Roll 466/

Wright, Giles R. *Afro-Americans in New Jersey: A Short History*. Trenton, NJ: New Jersey Historical Commission, 1988. 100p. Appendices. Photographs. /GC   974.9   W93a/

NEW MEXICO

Billington, Monroe Lee. *New Mexico's Buffalo Soldiers, 1866-1900*. Niwot, CO: University Press of Colorado, 1991. 258p. Index. Notes. /GC   978.9   B49n/

Richardson, Barbara J. *Black Directory of New Mexico, Bicentennial Edition, 1776-1976: Black Pioneers of New Mexico, A Documentary and Pictorial History*. Rio Rancho, NM: Panorama Press, 1976. 152p. Lists. Photographs. /GC   978.9   R393b/

NEW YORK

Afro-Americans in New York Life and History. Buffalo, NY: Afro-American Historical Association of the Niagara Frontier, Inc., v.1-, 1977-. /Periodical/

Bethel Missionary Baptist Church. *The Histories of Dutchess County's Predominately Black Churches: Their Histories as Told in Their Words*. Wappingers Falls, New York: Bethel Missionary Church, 1998. 55p. /GC 974.701 D95hi/

Dickenson, Richard B. *Census Occupations of Afro-American Families on Staten Island, 1840-1875*. Staten Island, NY: The Staten Island Institute of Arts and Science, St. George, 1981. 117p. Lists. Map. /GC 974.702 N422dic/

Eichholz, Alice and James M. Rose. *Free Black Heads of Households in the New York Federal Census, 1790-1830*. Detroit, MI: Gale Research Company, 1981. 301p. /GC 974.7 Ei2f/

Foote, Thelma Wills. *Black Life in Colonial Manhattan, 1664-1786*. Ann Arbor, MI: University Microfilms International, 1993. 510p. Harvard University Ph.D. Thesis, 1991. Bibliography. Notes. Tables. /GC 974.702 N421fo/

Grover, Kathryn. *Make a Way Somehow: African-American Life in a Northern Community, 1790-1965*. Syracuse, NY: Syracuse University Press, 1994. 321p. Bibliography. Index. Notes. Photographs. /GC 974.702 G26g/

Hodges, Graham Russell & Alan Edward Brown. *"Pretends to Be Free" Runaway Slave Advertisements from Colonial and Revolutionary New York and New Jersey*. New York: Garland Publishing, Inc., 1994. 369p. Appendices. Bibliography. Glossary. Indices. /GC 974.7 H665p/

King, Roger A. *The Underground Railroad in Orange County, New York: The Silent Rebellion*. Monroe, NY: Library Research Associates, 1999. 75p. Bibliography. Illustrations. Index. Maps. Photographs. /GC 974.701 Or12k/

Klees, Emerson. *Underground Railroad Tales, With Routes Through the Finger Lakes Region*. Rochester, NY: Friends of the Finger Lakes Publishing, 1997. 176p. Bibliography. Illustrations. Index. Maps. /GC 974.7 K672un/

McManus, Edgar J. *A History of Negro Slavery in New York*. Syracuse, NY: Syracuse University Press, 1966. 219p. Bibliography. Index. /GC 974.7 M215h/

Naylor, Natalie A. *Exploring African-American History, Long Island and Beyond*. Hempstead, NY: Long Island Studies Institute, Hofstra University, 1995. 66p. Bibliographies. Documents. /GC 973 N23e/

Negroes of New York. Wilmington, DE: Scholarly Resources, Inc., 1968. Five rolls of microfilm. From the Collections of the Schomburg Center, New York Public Library. A program of the Works Projects Administration in New York City. /Microfilm/

Questions and Answers on the African Burial Ground & Five Points Archaeological Projects. New York: Office of Public Education and Interpretation of the African Burial Ground, 1994. 14p. Bibliography. /GC 974.702 N422q/

Rawick, George P., ed. *The American Slave: A Composite Autobiography–New York...Narratives*. Westport, CT: Greenwood Publishing Company, 1979. /GC 929.11 Al113 Sec. 11/

Records of Ante-Bellum Southern Plantations from the Revolution through the Civil War. Frederick, MD: University Publications of America, Inc., 198-.
New York--Jackson, Riddle, and Company papers, 1835-1839. /Series J, Part 5, Roll 19/

Registers of Signatures of Depositors in Branches of the Freedman's Savings and Trust Company, 1865-1874. Washington, DC: National Archives and Records Service, 1969. Microcopy M816. New York. /Microfilm Roll 1/

Seraile, William. *New York's Black Regiments During the Civil War*. New York: W. Seraile, 1977. 273p. Appendices. Bibliography. Notes. /GC 973.74 Aa1se/

Shodell, Elly. *It Looks Like Yesterday to Me: Port Washington's Afro-American Heritage*. Port Washington, NY: Port Washington Public Library, 1984. 38p. Photographs. /GC 974.702 P835i/

Slavery in Ante-Bellum Southern Industries. Frederick, MD: University Publications of America, 199-.
New York--William B. Phillips papers, 1854-1861. /Series C, Part 1, Roll 5/

Taylor, Clarence. *Black Churches of Brooklyn*. New York: Columbia University Press, 1994. 297p. Bibliography. Index. Photographs. /GC 974.702 B792ta/

Update: African Burial Ground & Five Points Archaeological Project Newsletter. New York: Office of Public Education and Interpretation of the African Burial Ground, v.1-, 1993-. /Periodical/

White, Shane. *Somewhat More Independent: The End of Slavery in New York City, 1770-1810*. Athens, GA: University of Georgia

Press, 1991. 278p. Index. Maps. Notes. Tables. /GC 974.702 N421wh/

Williams, Lillian Serece. *Strangers in the Land of Paradise: The Creation of an African American Community, Buffalo, New York, 1900-1940*. Bloomington, IN: Indiana University Press, 1999. 273p. Bibliography. Illustrations. Index. Maps. Notes. /GC 974.702 B86wi/

Williams-Myers, A. J. *Long Hammering: Essays on the Forging of an African American Presence in the Hudson River Valley to the Early Twentieth Century*. Trenton, NJ: Africa World Press, Inc., 1994. 186p. Index. Notes. /GC 974.7 W67aj/

Wilson, Sherrill D. and Emilyn L. Brown. *African American History in Early New York: Bibliographic Resources*. New York: Office of Public Education and Interpretation of the African Burial Ground, 1996. 24p. /GC 974.702 N422ws/

NORTH CAROLINA

Africo-American Presbyterian. Charlotte, NC: D. J. Sanders, 1880-1938. 4 rolls of microfilm. Microfilm publication by Scholarly Resources, Inc. /Microfilm/

Bertie County, NC Negro Cohabitations, 1866 Acknowledgments. Raleigh, NC: North Carolina State Archives, 1960. 116p. Index. /Microfilm NC Core Collection–Bertie Co. Roll 68 (c.010-61001)/

Catawba County, NC Freedmen's Marriage Record, 1866. Raleigh, NC: North Carolina State Archives, 1968. /Microfilm NC Core Collection–Catawba Co. Roll 25 (c.021-60004)/

Catawba County, NC Marriage Register–Black, 1867-1872. Raleigh, NC: North Carolina State Archives, 1968. /Microfilm   NC Core Collection–Catawba Co.   Roll 24   (c.021-60005)/

Cecelski, David S. *Along Freedom Road: Hyde County, North Carolina and the Fate of Black Schools in the South*. Chapel Hill, NC: The University of North Carolina Press, 1994. Bibliography. Index. Notes. Photographs. /GC   975.601   H99c/

Cherokee County, NC Marriage Register, Colored, 1871-1906. White and Colored, 1872-1939. Raleigh, NC: North Carolina State Archives, 1967. /Microfilm   NC Core Collection–Cherokee Co.   Roll 38   (c.023-63001)/

Columbus County, NC Marriage Register–Colored, 1868-1974. Raleigh, NC: North Carolina State Archives, 1967/74. /Microfilm   NC Core Collection–Columbus Co.   Roll 31   (c.027-63002)/

Crow, Jeffrey J. *The Black Experience in Revolutionary North Carolina*. Raleigh, NC: Division of Archives and History, Department of Cultural Resources, 1983. 121p. Appendix. Bibliography. Notes. Photographs. /GC   975.6   C88b/

Cumberland County, NC Marriage Register–Colored, 1927-41. Raleigh, NC: North Carolina State Archives, 1974. /Microfilm   NC Core Collection–Cumberland Co.   Roll 62 (c.029-63005)/

Currituck County, NC County Court Minutes–Negro Cohabitation Certificates, 1831-1832, 1866. Raleigh, NC: North Carolina State Archives, 1972. /Microfilm   NC Core Collection–Currituck Co.   Roll 39   (c.030-60006)/

Davidson County, NC Record of Marriages–Colored, 1868-1938. Raleigh, NC: North Carolina State Archives, 1974. /Microfilm   NC Core Collection–Davidson Co.   Roll 39   (c.032-63002)/

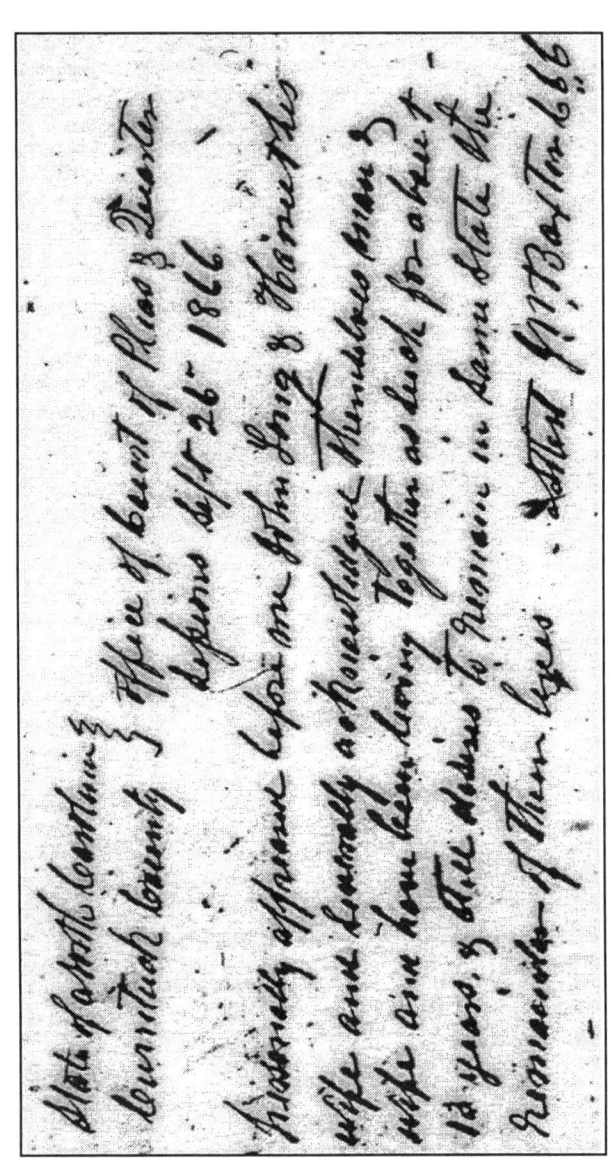

An 1866 Negro Cohabitation Certificate from Currituck County, North Carolina. (courtesy North Carolina Division of Archives and History)

Davis, Owena Hunter. *A History of Mary Potter School, Oxford, North Carolina*. Oxford, NC: s.n., 1944. /Microfilm LH 75/

Duplin County, NC Marriage of Freed People, 1866 (Cohabitation Records). Raleigh, NC: North Carolina State Archives, 1962. /Microfilm NC Core Collection–Duplin Co. Roll 43 (c.035-61001)/

Edgecombe County, NC Cohabitation Bonds, 1866. Raleigh, NC: North Carolina State Archives, 19--. /Microfilm NC Core Collection– Edgecombe Co. Roll 71 (c.037-61001)/

Forsyth County, NC Acknowledgment of Cohabitation as Man and Wife, 1820-1866. Raleigh, NC: North Carolina State Archives, 19--. /Microfilm NC Core Collection–Forsyth Co. Roll 28 (c.038-60001)/

Franklin, John Hope. *The Free Negro in North Carolina, 1790-1860*. Chapel Hill, NC: The University of North Carolina Press, 1995. 275p. Appendices. Bibliography. /GC 975.6 F85f/

Franklin County, NC Negro Cohabitation Certificates, 1866. Raleigh, NC: North Carolina State Archives, 1972. /Microfilm NC Core Collection–Franklin Co. Roll 36 (c.039-60007)/

Gates County, NC Registration of Slaves to Work in Great Dismal Swamp, 1847-1861. Raleigh, NC: North Carolina State Archives, 1974. /Microfilm NC Core Collection–Gates Co. Roll 56 (c.041-90003)/

Granville County, NC Marriage of Freed People, 1866-1867, (Cohabitation Certificates). Raleigh, NC North Carolina State Archives, 1962. /Microfilm NC Core Collection–Granville Co. Roll 63 (c.044-60011)/

Grimes, J. Bryan. *North Carolina Wills and Inventories*. Raleigh, NC: Edwards & Broughton Printing Company, 1912. 587p. Index. /GC   975.6   N816ai/

Hairston, Peter W. *The Cooleemee Plantation and Its People*. Lexington, NC: Davidson County Community College, 1986. 154p. Appendices. Bibliographies. Index. /GC   975.601   D281h/

Heinegg, Paul. *Free African Americans of North Carolina and Virginia*. Baltimore, MD: Clearfield Company, Inc., 1994. 699p. /GC   975   H36fa/

Heinegg, Paul. *Free African Americans of North Carolina and Virginia*. Baltimore, MD: Clearfield Company, Inc., 1997. 3rd edition. 825p. Index. /GC   975   H36faa/

The Heritage of Blacks in North Carolina, Volume One, 1990. Raleigh, NC: The North Carolina African-American Heritage Foundation, 1990. 492p. Index. Photographs. /GC   975.6   H42   V. 1/

Kay, Marvin L. Michael and Lorin Lee Cary. *Slavery in North Carolina, 1748-1775*. Chapel Hill, NC: The University of North Carolina Press, 1995. 402p. Appendices. Index. Notes. /GC   975.6   K18s/

Keller, Elizabeth P. *Caldwell County, NC Marriages, 1841-1872 (Including the Cohabitation Records of 1866)*. Baltimore, MD: Gateway Press, Inc., 1982. 83p. Index. /GC   975.601   C12k/

Mobley, Joe A. *James City: A Black Community in North Carolina, 1863-1900*. Raleigh, NC: North Carolina Department of Cultural Resources, Division of Archives and History, 1981. 113p. Index. Photographs. Tables. /GC   975.602   J23m/

New Hanover County, NC Marriage Register, Colored (Black), 1843-1939. Raleigh, NC: North Carolina State Archives, 1961. /Microfilm NC Core Collection–New Hanover Co. Roll 68 (c.070-63003)/

New Hanover County, NC Record of Cohabitation, 1866-1868. Raleigh, NC: North Carolina State Archives, 1974. /Microfilm NC Core Collection–New Hanover Co. Roll 65 (c.070-61001)/

North Carolina Freedman's Savings & Trust Company Records. Raleigh, NC: North Carolina Genealogical Society, 1992. 588p. Index. /GC 975.6 N8107/

Orange County, NC Marriage Register, Colored, 1867-1872; White and Colored, 1873-1962. Raleigh, NC: North Carolina State Archives, 1962. /Microfilm NC Core Collection–Orange Co. Roll 61 (c.073-60001)/

Orange County, NC Negro Cohabitation Certificates, 1866-1868. Raleigh, NC: North Carolina State Archives, 1971. /Microfilm NC Core Collection–Orange Co. Roll 63 (c.073-60014)/

Parker, Freddie L., ed. *Stealing a Little Freedom: Advertisements for Slave Runaways in North Carolina, 1791-1840*. New York: Garland Publishing, Inc., 1994. 884p. Indices. Maps. /GC 975.6 P22s/

Pasquotank County, NC Account Book/Cohabitation of Negroes. Raleigh, NC: North Carolina State Archives, 1972. /Microfilm NC Core Collection–Pasquotank Co. Roll 64 (c.075-60040)/

Perquimans County, NC Record of Marriages by Freedmen, 1866-1867. Raleigh, NC: North Carolina State Archives, 19--. /Microfilm NC Core Collection–Perquimans Co. Roll 55 (c.077-60005)/

Person County, NC Marriage Register, White and Black, 1807-1970. Raleigh, NC: North Carolina State Archives, 1966. /Microfilm NC Core Collection–Person Co. Roll 33 (c.078-63002)/

Person County, NC Record of Cohabitations, 1866. Raleigh, NC: North Carolina State Archives, 1974. /Microfilm NC Core Collection–Person Co. Roll 31 (c.078-61001)/

Pitt County, NC Cohabitation Record, 1866. Raleigh, NC: North Carolina State Archives, 1975. /Microfilm NC Core Collection–Pitt Co. Roll 41/

Rackley, Timothy Wiley. *Nash County, North Carolina, Division of Estate Slaves & Cohabitation Records, 1862-1866.* Kernersville, NC: T. W. Rackley, 1998. 86p. Index. /GC 975.601 N17re/

Rawick, George P., ed. *The American Slave: A Composite Autobiography–North Carolina and South Carolina Narratives.* Westport, CT: Greenwood Publishing Company, 1977. /GC 975.6 N8185 Sec. 1/

Rawick, George P., ed. *The American Slave: A Composite Autobiography–North Carolina Narratives.* Westport, CT: Greenwood Publishing Company, 1972. /GC 975.6 N8275 Parts 1-2/

Rawick, George P., ed. *The American Slave: A Composite Autobiography–North Carolina...Narratives.* Westport, CT: Greenwood Publishing Company, 1979. /GC 929.11 Al113 Sec. 12/

Reaves, William M. *"Strength Through Struggle:" The Chronological and Historical Record of the African-American Community in Wilmington, North Carolina, 1865-1950.* Wilmington, NC: New Hanover County Public Library, 1998. 580p. Appendices.

Bibliography. Illustrations. Index. Photographs. /GC 975.602 W67reb/

Records of Ante-Bellum Southern Plantations from the Revolution through the Civil War. Frederick, MD: University Publications of America, Inc., 198-.

North Carolina --Robert Ruffin Barrow papers, 1749-1858. /Series H, Rolls 17-19/

North Carolina--Elizabeth Amis Cameron (Hooper) Blanchard papers, 1836-1858. /Series J, Part 6, Roll 17/

North Carolina--Branch family papers, 1788-1866. /Series J, Part 4, Rolls 45-47/

North Carolina--Iveson Lewis Brookes papers, 1785-1868. /Series J, Part 4, Rolls 37-38/

North Carolina--James Thomas Harrison papers, 1770-1896. /Series J, Part 6, Roll 18/

North Carolina--Ernest Haywood papers, 1830-1860. /Series J, Part 7, Rolls 12-20/

North Carolina--Chillab Smith Howe papers, 1814-1899. /Series J, Part 6, Rolls 20-23/

North Carolina--Jackson, Riddle, & Company papers, 1835-1839. /Series J, Part 5, Roll 19/

North Carolina--Johnston & McFaddin family papers, 1839-1890. /Series J, Part 7, Roll 6/

North Carolina--Calvin Jones papers, 1785-1929. /Series J, Part 8, Rolls 1-5/

North Carolina--Hairston & Wilson papers, 1800-1895. /Series J, Part 11, Rolls 1-3/

North Carolina--Elizabeth Seawell Hairston papers, 1805-1865. /Series J, Part 11, Roll 1/

North Carolina--Robert Hall Morrison papers, 1820-1888. /Series J, Part 8, Rolls 18-19/

North Carolina--Norton, Chilton, and Dameron family papers, 1760-1926. /Series J, Part 6, Rolls 3-5/

North Carolina--Philip Henry Pitts papers, 1814-1889. /Series J, Part 7, Rolls 6-7/

North Carolina--Geo. Washington Polk papers, 1793-1857. /Series J, Part 8, Rolls 13-14/

North Carolina--Polk, Brown, & Ewell family papers, 1803-1859. /Series J, Part 8, Roll 7/

North Carolina--Polk & Yeatman family papers, 1773-1861. /Series J, Part 8, Rolls 8-13/

North Carolina--E. H. Riggan account book, 1846-1870. /Series J, Part 9, Roll 27/

North Carolina--Micahel D. Shoffner papers, 1777-1873. /Series J, Part 8, Roll 19/

North Carolina--Wm. Ruffin Smith papers, 1772-1959. /Series J, Part 6, Rolls 28-29/

North Carolina--Thompson family papers, 1809-1924. /Series J, Part 7, Roll 8/

North Carolina--Elijah Vester papers, 1813-1854. /Series J, Part 8, Roll 20/

North Carolina--Whitaker & Snipes papers, 1780,1835-1889. /Series J, Part 6, Roll 29/

North Carolina--Absalom Benton Whitaker papers, 1814-1845. /Series J, Part 4, Roll 47/

North Carolina--Wimbish family papers, 1838-1913. /Series M, Part 5, Roll 50/

Alamance co., NC--Burwell Benson papers, 1804-1914. /Series J, Part 13, Rolls 11-12/

Anson co., NC--Beall & Harper family papers, 1830-1914. /Series J, Part 13, Rolls 25-26/

Bertie co., NC--Capehart family papers, 1782-1983. /Series J, Part 12, Rolls 20-21/

Bertie co., NC--Meeta Armistead Capehart papers, 1780-1868. /Series J, Part 12, Roll 21/

Bertie co., NC--William Rhodes Capehart papers, 1791-1867. /Series J, Part 12, Roll 22/

Bertie co., NC--Margaret Mordecai Devereux papers, 1837-1856. /Series J, Part 12, Roll 22/

Bertie co., NC--Robert A. Jones account book, 1817-1829. /Series J, Part 12, Roll 27/

Bertie co., NC--Norfleet family papers, 1784-1895. /Series J, Part 12, Rolls 27-28/

Bertie co., NC--Skinner family papers, 1705-1900. /Series J, Part 12, Rolls 28-30/

Bertie co., NC--Lewis Thompson papers, 1723-1894. /Series J, Part 12, Rolls 32-38/

Bertie co., NC--Patrick Henry Winston papers, 1848-1938. /Series J, Part 12, Roll 43/

Bladen co., NC--Gillespie & Wright family papers, 1735-1877 & 1990. /Series J, Part 12, Rolls 6-7/

Bladen co., NC--Thomas David Smith McDowell papers, 1735-1905. /Series J, Part 12, Rolls 7-12/

Brunswick co., NC--John Hampden Hill papers, 1875-1880. /Series J, Part 12, Roll 1/

Brunswick co., NC--Swann family papers, 1784-1865. /Series J, Part 12, Roll 2/

Burke co., NC--Chambers family papers, 1816-1918. /Series J, Part 13, Rolls 36-37/

Burke co., NC--James Hervey Greenlee diary, 1837-1902. /Series J, Part 14, Rolls 1-4/

Burke co., NC--Thomas George Walton papers, 1779-1860. /Series J, Part 14, Rolls 9-10/

Caldwell co., NC--Beall & Harper papers, 1830-1914. /Series J, Part 13, Rolls 25-26/

Camden co., NC--Ferebee, Gregory, & McPherson family papers, 1816-1913. /Series J, Part 13, Roll 8/

Caswell co., NC--William Johnson papers, 1760-1888. /Series J, Part 13, Rolls 2-3/

Caswell co., NC--William Bethell Williamson papers, 1842-1848. /Series J, Part 13, Roll 12/

Chatham co., NC--Isaac Brooks Headen papers, 1848-1855. /Series F, Part 3, Roll 10/

Chowan co., NC--Brownrigg family papers, 1736-1944. /Series J, Part 12, Rolls 17-18/

Chowan co., NC--Skinner family papers, 1705-1900. /Series J, Part 12, Rolls 28-30/

Cleveland co., NC--Leonidas Chalmers Glenn papers, 1752-1907. /Series J, Part 13, Roll 35/

Cumberland co., NC--James Evans papers, 1826-1927. /Series J, Part 12, Rolls 2-6/

Davidson co., NC--Beall & Harper papers, 1830-1914. /Series J, Part 13, Rolls 25-26/

Davidson co., NC--Peter Wilson Hairston papers, 1773-1877. /Series J, Part 11, Rolls 5-8/

Davidson co., NC--John S. Henderson papers, 1755-1865. /Series J, Part 13, Rolls 20-25/

Davie co., NC--George Hairston papers, 1779-1950. /Series J, Part 11, Roll 4/

Davie co., NC--Peter Wilson Hairston papers, 1773-1877. /Series J, Part 11, Rolls 5-8/

Duplin co., NC--Gillespie & Wright family papers, 1735-1877 & 1990. /Series J, Part 12, Rolls 6-7/

Edgecombe co., NC--Clark family papers, 1757-1885. /Series F, Part 3, Rolls 1-2/

Edgecombe co., NC--Lewis family papers, 1730-1956. /Series F, Part 12, Rolls 13-14/

Edgecombe co., NC--James Jones Philips papers, 1814-1892. /Series J, Part 12, Roll 17/

Franklin co., NC--William Johnson papers, 1760-1888. /Series J, Part 13, Rolls 2-3/

Franklin co., NC--Nicholas Massenburg papers, 1834-1851. /Series J, Part 13, Rolls 1-2/

Franklin co., NC--Patrick Henry Winston papers, 1848-1938. /Series J, Part 12, Roll 43/

Gaston co., NC--Davidson family papers, 1827-1935. /Series J, Part 13, Rolls 28-34/

Granville co., NC--Bullock & Hamilton papers 1757-1971. /Series J, Part 13, Rolls 5-8/

Granville co., NC--Burwell family papers, 1750-1943 & 1813-1928. /Series J, Part 9, Rolls 10-15 & Series M, Part 5, Rolls 15-16/

Granville co., NC--Meeta A. Capehart papers, 1780-1868. /Series J, Part 12, Roll 21/

Granville co., NC--Samuel S. Downey papers, 1774-1912. /Series F, Part 3, Rolls 4-10/

Granville co., NC--John Rust Easton papers, 1794-1910. /Series J, Part 13, Roll 8/

Granville co., NC--Ferebee, Gregory, & McPherson family papers, 1816-1913. /Series J, Part 13, Roll 8/

Granville co., NC--Wm. Hargrove papers, 1790-1930. /Series J, Part 13, Roll 5/

Granville co., NC--Henry Jones papers, 1803-1870. /Series F, Part 3, Rolls 2-4/

Granville co., NC--Cameron family papers, 1757-1865. /Series J, Part 1, Rolls 1-69/

Granville co., NC--Person fam. papers, 1739-1907. /Series J, Part 13, Rolls 3-4/

Granville co., NC--Shanks fam. papers, 1801-1923. /Series J, Part 13, Rolls 4-5/

Guilford co., NC--Robt. Wilson account books, 1799-1822. /Series J, Part 11, Rolls 9-22/

Halifax co., NC--Archibald Davis Alston papers, 1804-1893. /Series J, Part 12, Roll 14/

Halifax co., NC--Simmons Jones Baker papers, 1800-1938. /Series J, Part 12, Roll 17/
Halifax co., NC--William Eaton papers, 1725-1893. /Series J, Part 13, Roll 1/
Halifax co., NC--Gee family papers, 1816-1850. /Series F, Part 1, Roll 22/
Halifax co., NC--Thos. Devereux Hogg papers, 1829-1910. /Series J, Part 12, Rolls 22-27/
Halifax co., NC--Robert A. Jones account book, 1817-1829. /Series J, Part 12, Roll 27/
Halifax co., NC--Peter Evans Smith papers, 1738-1869. /Series J, Part 12, Rolls 30-31/
Halifax co., NC--William Henry Wills papers, 1712-1892. /Series J, Part 12, Rolls 41-43/
Iredell co., NC--Chambers family papers, 1816-1918. /Series J, Part 13, Rolls 36-37/
Iredell co., NC--George F. Davidson papers, 1748-1887. /Series F, Part 3, Rolls 17-19/
Iredell co., NC--Benjamin Franklin Little papers, 1806-1935. /Series J, Part 13, Rolls 38-39/
Iredell co., NC--James A. Johnston papers, 1845-1867. /Series J, Part 13, Roll 36/
Iredell co., NC--Rufus Reid papers, 1772-1911. /Series J, Part 13, Rolls 37-38/
Iredell co., NC--A. J. K. Thomas papers, 1764-1920. /Series F, Part 3, Roll 19/
Lenoir co., NC--Beall & Harper family papers, 1830-1914. /Series J, Part 13, Rolls 25-26/
Lincoln co., NC--Leonidas Chalmers Glenn papers, 1752-1907. /Series J, Part 13, Roll 35/
Lincoln co., NC--Rufus Reid papers, 1772-1911. /Series J, Part 13, Rolls 37-38/
McDowell co., NC--James Hervey Greenlee diary, 1837-1902. Series J, Part 14, Rolls 1-4/
Macon co., NC--Silas McDowell papers, 1827-1961. /Series J, Part 14, Roll 10/
Martin co., NC--Thos. Devereux Hogg papers, 1829-1910. /Series J, Part 12, Rolls 22-27/
Martin co., NC--Patrick Henry Winston papers, 1848-1938. /Series J, Part 12, Roll 43/
Mecklenburg co., NC--Davidson family papers, 1827-1935. /Series J, Part 13, Rolls 28-34/
Mecklenburg co., NC--Latta fam. papers, 1799-1878. /Series J, Part 13, Roll 34/
Mecklenburg co., NC--John Osbourn diary, 1819-1821. /Series J, Part 13, Roll 34/

Mecklenburg co., NC--Rufus Reid papers, 1772-1911. /Series J, Part 13, Rolls 37-38/

Nash co., NC--Archibald Davis Alston papers, 1804-1893. /Series J, Part 12, Roll 14/

Nash co., NC--Archibald H. Arrington papers, 1754-1865. /Series J, Part 12, Rolls 15-16/

New Hanover co., NC--Burgwyn family papers, 1787-1861. /Series J, Part 12, Rolls 18-20/

New Hanover co., NC--John Hampden Hill papers, 1875-1880. /Series J, Part 12, Roll 1/

New Hanover co., NC--Levin Lane papers, 1802-1858. /Series J, Part 12, Roll 1/

New Hanover co., NC--Langdon, Young, & Meares family papers, 1771-1877. /Series J, Part 12, Roll 1/

New Hanover co., NC--Strudwick family papers, 1701-1826. /Series J, Part 12, Roll 1/

New Hanover co., NC--Swann fam. papers, 1784-1865. /Series J, Part 12, Roll 2/

Northampton co., NC--Edmonia Cabell Wilkins papers, 1782-1870. /Series J, Part 12, Rolls 39-41/

Orange co., NC--Direct Tax Assessment, 1816. /Series J, Part 13, Roll 10/

Orange co., NC--Walter Alves papers, 1771-1858. /Series J, Part 13, Rolls 10-11/

Orange co., NC--Burwell Benson papers, 1804-1914. /Series J, Part 13, Rolls 11-12/

Orange co., NC--Cameron family papers, 1757-1865. /Series J, Part 1, Rolls 1-69/

Orange co., NC--Matthew S. Davis papers, 1852-1897. /Series J, Part 13, Roll 1/

Orange co., NC--John S. Henderson papers, 1755-1865. /Series J, Part 13, Rolls 20-25/

Orange co., NC--Stephen Moore papers, 1767-1869. /Series J, Part 13, Rolls 9-10/

Orange co., NC--Rufus Reid papers, 1772-1911. /Series J, Part 13, Rolls 37-38/

Orange co., NC--Strudwick family papers, 1701-1826. /Series J, Part 12, Roll 1/

Orange co., NC--Witherspoon & McDowall family papers, 1826-1859. /Series J, Part 13, Roll 11/

Pender co., NC--John Hampden Hill papers, 1875-1880. /Series J, Part 12, Roll 1/

Pender co., NC--Swann family papers, 1784-1865. /Series J, Part 12, Roll 2/

Perquimans co., NC--Skinner family papers, 1705-1900. /Series J, Part 12, Rolls 28-30/

Person co., NC--Cameron family papers--, 1757-1865. /Series J, Part 1, Rolls 1-69/

Person co., NC--Stephen Moore papers, 1767-1869. /Series J, Part 13, Rolls 9-10/

Pitt co., NC--Grimes family papers, 1713-1866. /Series J, Part 12, Rolls 44-50/

Richmond co., NC--Bejamin F. Little papers, 1806-1935. /Series J, Part 13, Rolls 38-39/

Richmond co., NC--Rufus Reid papers, 1772-1911. /Series J, Part 13, Rolls 37-38/

Rockingham co., NC--Mary Jeffreys Bethell diary, 1853-1873. /Series J, Part 13, Roll 12/

Rockingham co., NC--Archibald H. Boyd papers, 1841-1897. /Series F, Part 3, Roll 10/

Rockingham co., NC--John G. Brodnax papers, 1827-1920. /Series J, Part 13, Roll 12/

Rockingham co., NC--Obadiah Fields papers, 1784-1855. /Series F, Part 3, Roll 10/

Rowan co., NC--Beall & Harper family papers, 1830-1914. /Series J, Part 13, Rolls 25-26/

Rowan co., NC--John S. Henderson papers, 1755-1865. /Series J, Part 13, Rolls 20-25/

Rowan co., NC--Macay & McNeely papers, 1746-1918. /Series J, Part 13, Rolls 26-28/

Rowan co., NC--Rufus Reid papers, 1772-1911. /Series J, Part 13, Rolls 37-38/

Rowan co., NC--John Steele papers, 1716-1846. /Series J, Part 13, Rolls 13-19/

Rutherford co., NC--Silas McDowell papers, 1827-1961. /Series J, Part 14, Roll 10/

Stokes co., NC--George Hairston papers, 1779-1950. /Series J, Part 11, Roll 4/

Surry co., NC--Clingman & Puryear family papers, 1810-1940. /Series J, Part 13, Roll 40/

Surry co., NC--Tyre Glen papers, 1806-1882. /Series F, Part 3, Rolls 15-17/

Surry co., NC--Jarratt-Puryear papers, 1807-1881. /Series F, Part 3, Rolls 11-15/

Surry co., NC--Isaac Jarratt papers, 1832-1979. /Series J, Part 13, Roll 40/

Tyrrell co., NC--Pettigrew family papers, 1776-1865. /Series J, Part 2, Rolls 1-29/

Vance co., NC--Burwell family papers, 1750-1943. /Series J, Part 9, Rolls 10-15/

Vance co., NC--William Hargrove papers, 1790-1930. /Series J, Part 13, Roll 5/

Wake co., NC--Cameron family papers, 1757-1865. /Series J, Part 1, Rolls 1-69/

Wake co., NC--Margaret Mordecai Devereux papers, 1837-1856. /Series J, Part 12, Roll 22/

Wake co., NC--Grimes family papers, 1713-1866. /Series J, Part 12, Rolls 44-50/

Wake co., NC--Thos. Devereux Hogg papers, 1829-1910. /Series J, Part 12, Rolls 22-27/

Wake co., NC--Robert A. Jones account book, 1817-1829. /Series J, Part 12, Roll 27/

Warren co., NC--Archibald Davis Alston papers, 1804-1893. /Series J, Part 12, Roll 14/

Warren co., NC--Burgwyn family papers, 1787-1861. /Series J, Part 12, Rolls 18-20/

Warren co., NC--Burwell family papers, 1750-1943. /Series J, Part 9, Rolls 10-15/

Warren co., NC--Matthew S. Davis papers, 1852-1897. /Series J, Part 13, Roll 1/

Warren co., NC--William Eaton papers, 1725-1893. /Series J, Part 13, Roll 1/

Washington co., NC--Pettigrew family papers, 1776-1865. /Series J, Part 2, Rolls 1-29/

Washington co., NC--Wm. Henry Wills papers, 1712-1892. /Series J, Part 12, Rolls 41-43/

Wilkes co., NC--Hamilton Brown papers, 1752-1907. /Series J, Part 14, Rolls 5-8/

Wilkes co., NC--James Gwyn papers, 1653-1887. /Series J, Part 14, Rolls 8 - 9/

Records of the Assistant Commissioner for the State of North Carolina, Bureau of Refugees, Freedmen, and Abandoned Lands, 1865-1870. Washington, DC: National Archives and Records Service, 1972. Microcopy M843. Endorsements Sent. Monthly Reports. Records Relating to Teachers. Reports of Rations Issued and Miscellaneous Ration Reports. Abstracts of Subsistence Reports. Reports on Destitution. Records Relating to Transportation. Case Files. Receipts for Orders. Freedmen's Labor Contracts. Records Relating to Indentures. Reports on Freedmen Available for Work. Miscellaneous Reports. Quartermaster Property Returns. Letters Received. /Microfilm Rolls 3-18, 26-28, 34, 35, 38/

Registers of Signatures of Depositors in Branches of the Freedman's Savings and Trust Company, 1865-1874. Washington, DC: National Archives and Records Service, 1969. Microcopy M816. New Bern. Raleigh. Wilmington. /Microfilm Roll 27/

Registration of Slaves to Work in the Great Dismal Swamp, Gates County, North Carolina, 1847-1861. Cocoa, FL: GenRec Books, 1995. 143p. Index. Map. /GC 975.601 G22f/

Roberson County, NC Record of Marriage and Cohabitation, 1825-1865. Raleigh, NC: North Carolina State Archives, 1966. /Microfilm NC Core Collection–Roberson Co. Roll 51 (c.083-61001)/

Rowan County, NC Record of Cohabitations, 1825-1865. Raleigh, NC: North Carolina State Archives, 19--. /Microfilm NC Core Collection–Rowan Co. Roll 68 (c.085-61001)/

Sensbach, Jon F. ***A Separate Canaan: The Making of an Afro-Moravian World in North Carolina, 1763-1840.*** Chapel Hill, NC: University of North Carolina Press, 1998. 342p. Bibliography. Illustrations. Index. /GC 975.6 Se59s/

Sherrill, Elizabeth Bray. ***Slave Inhabitants in Catawba County, NC, 11 June 1860 - 10 November 1860.*** Sherrills Ford, NC: E. B. Sherrill, 1988. 35p. Index. /GC 975.601 C28s/

Slave Schedules for 1850–North Carolina. Washington, DC: The National Archives, 1964. Microcopy 432. /Microfilm Rolls 650-656/

Slave Schedules for 1860–North Carolina. Washington, DC: The National Archives, 1967. Microcopy 653. /Microfilm Rolls 920-927/

Slavery in Ante-Bellum Southern Industries. Bethesda, MD: University Publications of America, 199-.
North Carolina--Peck, Welford & Company papers, 1834-1844. /Series C, Part 2, Roll 39/
Beaufort co., NC--James Redding Grist business records, 1791-1920. /Series A, Rolls 4-13/
Beaufort co., NC--Richard H. Riddick papers, 1839-1879. /Series A, Rolls 13-14/
Burke co., NC--Waightstill Avery papers, 1777-1866. /Series B, Roll 6/
Burke co., NC--Wm. G. Dickson papers, 1767-1860. /Series B, Rolls 3-4/
Burke co., NC--George Phifer Erwin papers, 1779-1861. /Series B, Rolls 5-6/
Cabarrus co., NC--Bryan & Leventhorpe family papers, 1797-1860. /Series B, Rolls 2-3/
Cumberland co., NC--Tillinghast family papers (Slave Task Book), 1849-1951. /Series A, Roll 4/
Davidson co., NC--Fisher family papers, 1758-1896. /Series B, Rolls 28-38/
Davidson co., NC--Silver Hill Mining company ledger, 1859-1893. /Series B, Roll 21/
Davidson co., NC--Washington Mine account book, 1845-1846. /Series B, Roll 21/
Franklin co., NC--Hawkins family papers, 1738-1865. /Series B, Rolls 8-21/
Lincoln co., NC--Brevard family papers, 1754-1953. /Series B, Rolls 1-2/
Lincoln co., NC--Wm. G. Dickson papers, 1767-1860. /Series B, Rolls 3-4/
Lincoln co., NC--McDowell family papers, 1754-1953. /Series B, Rolls 1-2/
Montgomery co., NC--Fisher family papers, 1758-1896. /Series B, Rolls 28-38/
Rowan co., NC--Bryan & Leventhorpe family papers, 1797-1860. /Series B, Rolls 2-3/
Rowan co., NC--Fisher family papers, 1758-1896. /Series B, Rolls 28-38/
Rowan co., NC--Gold Hill Mining company records, 1850-1872. /Series B, Rolls 6-8/
Rutherford co., NC--Bryan & Leventhorpe papers, 1797-1860. /Series B, Rolls 2-3/
Rutherford co., NC--Gold Hill Mining company records, 1850-1872. /Series B, Rolls 6-8/
Union co., NC--Fisher family papers, 1758-1896. /Series B, Rolls 28-38/
Warren co., NC--Hawkins family papers, 1738-1865. /Series B, Rolls 8-21/
Wilkes co., NC--Bryan family papers, 1797-1860. /Series B, Rolls 2-3/
Wilkes co., NC--Leventhorpe family papers, 1797-1860. /Series B, Rolls 2-3/
Wilkes co., NC--Gold Hill Mining company records, 1850-1872. /Series B, Rolls 6-8/

Stanly County, NC Marriage Register, Colored, 1867-1904; Marriage Register, Colored and White, 1904-1962. Raleigh, NC: North Carolina State Archives, 1968. /Microfilm NC Core Collection–Stanly Co. Roll 19 (c.089-63003)/

Stokes County, NC Cohabitation and Marriage Records–Negro, 1866-1872. Raleigh, NC: North Carolina State Archives, 1971. /Microfilm NC Core Collection–Stokes Co. Roll 47 (c.090-60008)/

Surry County, NC Marriage Register–Negro, 1867-1878. Raleigh, NC: North Carolina State Archives, 1973. /Microfilm NC Core Collection–Surry Co. Roll 40 (c.092-60009)/

Wake County, NC Marriage Register–Colored Females, 1839-1967, Vols. A - Z. Raleigh, NC: North Carolina State Archives, 1971. /Microfilm NC Core Collection–Wake Co. Rolls 86-89/

Wake County, NC Marriage Register–Colored Males, 1839-1967, Vols. A - V. Raleigh, NC: North Carolina State Archives, 1971. /Microfilm NC Core Collection–Wake Co. Rolls 77-80/

Wake County, NC Negro Cohabitations, 1866. Raleigh, NC: North Carolina State Archives, 1972. /Microfilm NC Core Collection–Wake Co. Roll 95 (c.099-60026)/

Watson, C. H. *Colored Charlotte.* Charlotte, NC: A. M. E. Zion Job Print, 1915. /Microfilm LH 154/

White, Barnetta McGhee. *Enslaved Ancestors Abstracted from Deed Books, Granville, North Carolina, Volume 2, 1746-1828.* Durham, NC: B. M. White, 1997. 161p. Bibliography. Index. /GC 975.601 G76w V.2/

NORTH DAKOTA

Newgard, Thomas P., William C. Sherman and John Guerrero. *African-Americans in North Dakota: Sources and Assessments— Personal Accounts and Background Information as Found in Newspapers, Land Records, Interviews and Miscellaneous Documents.* Bismarck, ND: University of Mary Press, 1994. 333p. & 231p. Appendices. Notes. Photographs. /GC 978.4 N451af/

Roper, Stephanie Abbot. *African Americans in North Dakota, 1800-1940.* Grand Forks, ND: University of North Dakota, 1993. 109p. Bibliography. Illustrations. Maps. Tables. /Microfiche/

OHIO

African-American Genealogical Society Cleveland, Ohio. *1995-1996 Members Surname Index.* Cleveland, OH, African-American Genealogical Society Cleveland, Ohio, 1996. 25p. /GC 977.102 C59af 1995-1996/

African-American Genealogical Society Cleveland, Ohio. *1996 Membership List.* Cleveland, OH, African-American Genealogical Society Cleveland, Ohio, 1996. 5p. /GC 977.102 C59afa 1996/

African-American Genealogical Society Cleveland, Ohio. *1998 Members Surname Index.* Cleveland, OH, African-American Genealogical Society Cleveland, Ohio, 1998. 35p. /GC 977.102 C59af 1998/

African-American Genealogical Society Cleveland, Ohio. *Proposed By-Laws.* Cleveland, OH, African-American Genealogical Society Cleveland, Ohio, 1994. 7p. /GC 977.102 C59afb/

Bigglestone, William E. *They Stopped in Ohio: Black Residents and Visitors of the Nineteenth Century.* Oberlin, OH: W. E. Bigglestone, 1981. /GC 977.102 Ob2b/

Dabney, Wendell P. *Cincinnati's Colored Citizens: Historical Sociological and Biographical.* New York: Negro Universities Press, 1970. 404p. Photographs. /GC 977.102 C49da/

Davis, Russell H. *Memorable Negroes in Cleveland's Past.* Cleveland, OH: The Western Reserve Historical Society, 1969. 58p. Illus. /GC 977.102 C59d/

Gerber, David A. *Black Ohio and the Color Line, 1860-1915.* Urbana, IL: University of Illinois Press, 1976. 500p. Index. Notes. /GC 977.1 G31b/

Greene County, Ohio, Clerk of Courts, Emancipation Record, 1805-1844. Columbus, OH: Ohio Historical Society, 1979. /Microfilm OH State Records Roll 4/

Haller, Stephen E. and Robert H. Smith, Jr. *Register of Blacks in the Miami Valley (OH); A Name Abstract (1804-1857).* OH: Wright State University, 1977. 81p. /GC 977.1 H15r/

Kilbourn, John. *Ohio Gazetteer, 1821.* Columbus, OH: P. H. Olmstead, 1821. 204p. Census Reports. /GC 977.1 K55o/

McGee, Betty. *Early Black Settlements in Ohio.* Dayton, OH: MVCGH Conference, 1983. 45 minutes. /Cassette Tape/

McGee, Betty. *Ohio Region Ethnic Groups: Little Publicized Facts on Early Blacks.* Columbus, OH: NGS Conference, 1986. 60 minutes. /Cassette Tape/

Miami County, Ohio, Clerk of Courts, Manumission Record, 1834-1847. Columbus, OH: Ohio Historical Society, 1979. /Microfilm OH State Records Roll 3/

Moody, Minnie Hite. *The Underground Railroad and Other Pieces.* Granville, OH: Granville Historical Society, 1967. 41p. /GC 977.102 G76m/

Nitchman, Paul E. *Blacks in Ohio, 1880.* Decorah, IA: The Anundsen Publishing Company, 1985-87. Index. /GC 977.1 N63b V. 1-10/

Nitchman, Paul E. *Blacks in Ohio, 1880: In The City of Cincinnati.* Decorah, IA: The Anundsen Publishing Company, 1987. 196p. Index. /GC 977.102 C49ni/

The Ohio Black History Guide. Columbus, OH: Ohio Historical Society, 1975. 221p. /GC 016.9771 Oh35/

Rawick, George P. ed., *The American Slave: A Composite Autobiography–Indiana and Ohio Narratives.* Westport, CT: Greenwood Publishing Company, 1977. /GC 977.2 In2455 Sec. 2/

Rawick, George P., ed. *The American Slave: A Composite Autobiography–Ohio....Narratives.* Westport, CT: Greenwood Publishing Company, 1972. /GC 929.11 K136 Sec. 4/

Register of Blacks in Ohio Counties, 1804-1861. Columbus, OH: Ohio Historical Society, 1971. Ross, Clinton, Logan Cos. /Microfilm OH State Records Roll 2/

Snider, Wayne L. *Guernsey County's Black Pioneers, Patriots, and Persons.* Columbus, OH: Ohio Historical Society, 1979. 136p. Index. Notes. Photographs. /GC 977.101 G93sn/

Taylor, Henry Louis, Jr., ed. *Race and the City: Work, Community and Protest in Cincinnati, 1820-1970*. Urbana, IL: University of Illinois Press, 1993. 308p. Index. Notes. /GC 977.102 C49ra/

Thomas, Georgeanne. *Black History in Warren County, Ohio*. S. l.: G. Thomas, 1976. 63p. Bibliography. /GC 977.101 W25t/

Trotter, Joe William, Jr. *River Jordan: African American Urban Life in the Ohio Valley*. Lexington, KY: The University Press of Kentucky, 1998. 200p. Bibliography. Index. Notes. Photographs. Tables. /GC 977 T756r/

Turpin, Joan. *Register of Black, Mulatto and Poor Persons in Four Ohio Counties, 1791-1861*. Bowie, MD: Heritage Books, Inc., 1985. 44p. Index. /GC 977.1 T86r/

Williams, Jacob C., Sr. *Lillie: Black Life in Martins Ferry, Ohio during the 1920s and 1930s*. S. l.: s. n., 1991. 516p. Photographs. /GC 977.101 B41wi/

OKLAHOMA

Baker, T. Lindsay and Julie P. Baker. *The WPA Oklahoma Slave Narratives*. Norman, OK: University of Oklahoma Press, 1996. 543p. Bibliography. Index. /GC 976.6 W919/

Franklin, Jimmie Lewis. *The Blacks in Oklahoma*. Norman, OK: University of Oklahoma Press, 198-. 79p. Bibliography. Photographs. /GC 976.6 F85b/

Rawick, George P., ed. *The American Slave: A Composite Autobiography–Oklahoma and Mississippi Narratives*. Westport, CT: Greenwood Publishing Company, 1972. /GC 976.6 Ok55 Sec. 1/

Rawick, George P., ed. *The American Slave: A Composite Autobiography–Oklahoma Narratives*. Westport, CT: Greenwood Publishing Company, 1977. /GC 976.6 Ok54/

Rawick, George P., ed. *The American Slave: A Composite Autobiography–Oklahoma...Narratives*. Westport, CT: Greenwood Publishing Company, 1979. /GC 929.11 AL113 Sec. 13/

Tolson, Arthur Lincoln. *The Black Oklahomans, A History, 1541-1972*. New Orleans, LA: Edwards Printing Company, 1966. 314p. Bibliography. Index. Notes. /GC 976.6 T587b/

Tolson, Arthur Lincoln. *The Negro in Oklahoma Territory, 1889-1907: A Study in Racial Discrimination*. Norman, OK: The University of Oklahoma, 1966. 188p. Ph.D. dissertation. Bibliography. Notes. /GC 976.6 T587n/

OREGON

McLagan, Elizabeth. *A Peculiar Paradise: A History of Blacks in Oregon, 1788-1940*. Portland, OR: The Georgian Press, 1980. (The Oregon Black History Project) 230p. Index. Bibliography. Photographs. /GC 979.5 M22p/

Rawick, George P., ed. *The American Slave: A Composite Autobiography --Oregon... Narratives*. Westport, CT: Greenwood Publishing Company, 1977. /GC 929.11 Ar486 Sec. 5/

PENNSYLVANIA

African American Genealogy Group of the Afro-American Historical and Cultural Museum Newsletter. Philadelphia, PA: Afro-American Historical and Cultural Museum, v. 1-, 1990-. /Periodical/

The Alleghenian: Newsletter of the Western Pennsylvania African American Historical and Genealogical Society. Pittsburgh, PA: Western Pennsylvania African American Historical and Genealogical Society, v.1-3, 1991-94. /Periodical/

Bell, Raymond M. *Black Persons in Early Washington County, Pennsylvania.* Washington, PA: R. M. Bell, 1978. 8p. /GC 974.801 W27bc/

Bodnar, John E. *Ethnic History in Pennsylvania: A Selected Bibliography.* Harrisburg, PA: Pennsylvania Historical & Museum Commission, 1974. Negro bibliography–p. 27-36. /GC 974.8 B628e/

Bumbrey, Jeffrey Nordlinger. *A Guide to the Microfilm Publication of the Papers of The Pennsylvania Abolition Society at The Historical Society of Pennsylvania.* Philadelphia, PA: Pennsylvania Abolition Society, 1976. 68p. /GC 974.8 B88g/

Dickerson, Dennis C. *Out of the Crucible: Black Steelworkers in Western Pennsylvania, 1875-1980.* Albany, NY: University of New York Press, 1986. 323p. Bibliography. Illustrations. Index. Notes. Photographs. Tables. /GC 974.8 D558o/

Gregg, Robert. *Sparks from the Anvil of Oppression: Philadelphia's African Methodists and Southern Migrants, 1890-1940.* Philadelphia, PA: Temple University Press, 1993. 272p. Index. Notes. Photographs. Tables. /GC 974.802 P53gp/

Hopkins, Leroy T., ed. **"The Negro Entry Book: A Document of Lancaster City's Antebellum Afro-American Community"** in *Journal: A Quarterly Publication of the Lancaster County Historical Society.* Volume 88, no. 4, p.142-180. /Periodical/

Lapsansky, Emma. ***Black Presence in Pennsylvania: "Making it Home."*** University Park, PA: The Pennsylvania Historical Association, 1990. 39p. Bibliography. Photographs. /GC 974.8 L31bl/

Nash, Gary B. and Jean R. Soderlund. ***Freedom by Degrees: Emancipation in Pennsylvania and Its Aftermath.*** New York: Oxford University Press, 1991. 249p. Bibliography. Illustrations. Index. Tables. /GC 974.8 N173f/

Negro Register, 1792-1851, Washington County, Pennsylvania. [Washington County, PA]: s. n., [1974]. 50p. Index. /GC 974.801 W27wan Oversize/

The Pennsylvania Abolition Society papers, 1775-1975. Ann Arbor, MI: Bell and Howell Information and Learning, 1999. 32 rolls. /Microfilm/

Records of Ante-Bellum Southern Plantations from the Revolution through the Civil War. Frederick, MD: University Publications of America, Inc., 198-.
Pennsylvania--Richard Butler papers, 1795-1889. /Series I, Part 5, Rolls 2-3/
Pennsylvania--Capehart family papers, 1782-1983. /Series J, Part 12, Rolls 20-21/
Pennsylvania--Leonidas Chalmers Glenn papers, 1752-1907. /Series J, Part 13, Roll 35/
Pennsylvania--George W. Sargent books, 1840-1900. /Series J, Part 6, Rolls 12-15/
Pennsylvania--John Steele papers, 1716-1846. /Series J, Part 13, Rolls 13-19/
Philadelphia co., PA--Jackson, Riddle, and Company papers, 1835-1839. /Series J, Part 5, Roll 19/

Registers of Signatures of Depositors in Branches of the Freedman's Savings and Trust Company, 1865-1874. Washington, DC: National Archives and Records Service, 1969. Microcopy M816. Philadelphia. /Microfilm Roll 16/

Smedley, R. C. *History of the Underground Railroad in Chester and the Neighboring Counties of Pennsylvania*. Lancaster, PA: Office of the Journal, 1883. 407p. Index. Photographs. /GC 974.8 Sm29h/

Taylor, Frances Cloud. *The Trackless Trail: The Story of the Underground Railroad in Kennett Square, Chester County, Pennsylvania, and the Surrounding Community*. Kennett Square, PA: F. C. Taylor, 1976. 36p. Bibliography. /GC 974.802 K39ta/

Taylor, Frances Cloud. *The Trackless Trail Leads On: An Exploration of Conductors and Their Stations*. Kennett Square, PA: F. C. Taylor, 1995. 82p. Bibliography. /GC 974.802 K39t/

Thompson, Sarah S. *Journey from Jerusalem: An Illustrated Introduction to Erie's African American History, 1795-1995*. Erie, PA: Erie County Historical Society, 1996. 98p. Bibliography. Illustrations. Maps. /GC 974.802 Er4t/

Trotter, Joe William, Jr. and Eric Ledell Smith. *African Americans in Pennsylvania: Shifting Historical Perspectives*. University Park, PA: Pennsylvania State University Press, 1997. 519p. Index. Notes. Photographs. /GC 974.8 Af83/

Winch, Julie. *Philadelphia's Black Elite: Activism, Accommodation, and the Struggle for Autonomy, 1787-1848*. Philadelphia, PA: Temple University Press, 1988. 240p. Bibliography. Index. Notes. /GC 974.802 P53wj/

RHODE ISLAND

Battle, Charles A. *Negroes on the Island of Rhode Island.* Newport, RI: Newport Black Museum, 1971. 39p. /GC 974.501 N47ba/

Census of the Inhabitants of the Colony of Rhode Island and Providence Plantations. Providence, RI: Knowles, Anthony & Company, 1858. 239p. /GC 974.5 R34c/

Chenery, William H. *The Fourteenth Regiment, Rhode Island Heavy Artillery (Colored), In the War to Preserve the Union, 1861-1865.* Providence, RI: Snow & Farnham, 1898. 343p. Illustrations. Index. /GC 973.74 R34ch/

Minority Military Service, Rhode Island, 1775-1783. [Washington, DC], National Society, Daughters of the American Revolution, 1988. 13p. /GC 973.34 R34mi/

Papers of the American Slave Trade. Bethesda, MD: University Publications of America, 1997.
Providence co., RI--James Brown papers, 1723-1824. /Series A, Part 1, Rolls 1-2/
Providence co., RI--Moses Brown papers, 1648-1836. /Series A, Part 1, Rolls 2-19/
Providence co., RI--Obadiah Brown papers, 1719-1776. /Series A, Part 1, Rolls 19-23/
Providence co., RI--Providence Society for Abolishing the Slave Trade minute book, 1789-1827. /Series A, Part 1, Roll 19/

Papers of the American Slave Trade, A Guide to the Microfilm Edition. Bethesda, MD: University Publications of America, 1998. 68p. Subject Index. /GC 974.502 P948gu Pt.1/

Rawick, George P., ed. *The American Slave: A Composite Autobiography–Rhode Island...Narratives.* Westport, CT:

Greenwood Publishing Company, 1979. /GC   929.11   AL113   Sec. 14/

Records of Ante-Bellum Southern Plantations from the Revolution through the Civil War. Frederick, MD: University Publications of America, Inc., 198-
Rhode Island--Arnold family papers, 1758-1915. /Series J, Part 4, Rolls 7-11/
Rhode Island--Screven family papers, 1758-1915. /Series J, Part 4, Rolls 7-11/

Rhode Island Black Heritage Society. *Creative Survival: The Providence Black Community in the 19th Century.* Providence, RI: Rhode Island Black Heritage Society, 198-. 73p. Drawings. Photographs. /GC   974.502   P948cr/

Schipper, Martin P. *A Guide to the Microfilm Edition of Papers of the American Slave Trade: Series A, Selections from the Rhode Island Historical Society.* Bethesda, MD: University Publications of America, 1998. 68p. Index. Maps. /GC   974.502   P948gu/

Stewart, Rowena. *A Heritage Discovered: Blacks in Rhode Island.* Providence, RI: s. n., 19--. 39p. Pictures. Photographs. /GC   974.5   St4h/

Youngken, Richard C. *African Americans in Newport: An Introduction to the Heritage of African Americans in Newport, Rhode Island, 1700-1945.* Newport, RI: The Newport Historical Society, 1998. 85p. Bibliography. Drawings. Maps. Photographs. /GC   974.5   N472y/

SOUTH CAROLINA

And I'm Glad: An Oral History of Edisto Island. Charleston, SC: Tempus, 2000. 192p. Interviews with African Americans. /GC 975.701 C38li/

Ball, Edward. *Slaves in the Family*. New York: Farrar, Straus and Giroux, 1998. 504p. Index. Notes. Photographs. /GC 929.2 B21be/

Ball, Elias. *Elias Ball Papers*. Charleston, SC: South Carolina Historical Society, 1982. Correspondence. Lists. Records. /Microfilm SC Microfiche Fiche 1 - 5/

Begley, Paul R., Alexia J. Helsley, & Steven D. Tuttle. *African American Genealogical Research*. Charleston, SC: South Carolina Department of Archives and History, 1997. 28p. Drawings. /GC 975.7 B39a/

Bellows, Barbara L. *Benevolence Among Slaveholders: Assisting the Poor in Charleston, 1670-1860*. Baton Rouge, LA: Louisiana State University Press, 1993. 217p. Bibliography. Index. Notes. Photographs. /GC 975.702 C38bel/

Brimelow, Judith M. *State Free Negro Capitation Tax Books, Charleston, South Carolina, ca. 1811-1860*. Columbia, SC: Department of Archives and History, 1983. 11p. Guide for SC Archives Microcopy No. 11. /GC 975.702 C38br/

Bryant, Lawrence C. *Negro Lawmakers in the South Carolina Legislature, 1868-1902*. Orangeburg, SC: South Carolina State College, 1968. 141p. /GC 975.7 B84n/

Bryant, Lawrence C. *Negro Legislators in South Carolina, 1865-1894*. Orangeburg, SC: South Carolina State College, 1966. 179p. /GC 975.7 B84na/

Bryant, Lawrence C. *Negro Legislators in South Carolina, 1868-1902*. Orangeburg, SC: South Carolina State College, 1967. 107p. /GC 975.7 B84nb/

Bryant, Lawrence C. *Negro Senators and Representatives in the South Carolina Legislature, 1868-1902*. Orangeburg, SC: South Carolina State College, 1968. 199p. /GC 975.7 B84nc/

Bryant, Lawrence C. *South Carolina Negro Legislators: A Glorious Success*. Orangeburg, SC: South Carolina State College, 1974. 119p. /GC 975.7 B84nd/

Childs, Arney Robinson, ed. *The Private Journal of Henry William Ravenel, 1859-1887*. Columbia, SC: University of South Carolina Press, 1947. 428p. Index. /GC 975.7 R196p/

Church of the Holy Cross, Stateburg. Original Episcopal church records, Sumter County. Black Communicants, 1866, 1870, 1879. Entries Regarding Slave Baptisms and Marriages, 1860s. /Microfiche/

Drago, Edmund L. *Hurrah for Hampton! Black Red Shirts in South Carolina During Reconstruction*. Fayetteville, AR: The University of Arkansas Press, 1998. 158p. Index. Notes. /GC 975.7 D779h/

Dusinberre, William. *Them Dark Days: Slavery in the American Rice Swamps*. New York: Oxford University Press, 1996. 556p. Appendices. Index. Notes. /GC 975.7 D95t/

Easterby, J. H., ed. *The South Carolina Rice Plantation as Revealed in the Papers of Robert F. W. Allston.* Chicago: University of Chicago Press, 1946. 478p. Index. Lists. /GC 929.2 Al585e/

Ferguson, Leland G. *Uncommon Ground: Archaeology and Early African America, 1650-1800.* Washington, DC: Smithsonian Institution Press, 1992. 186p. Bibliography. Illustrations. Index. Maps. /GC 973 F381u/

Gordon, Asa H. *Sketches of Negro Life and History in South Carolina.* Columbia, SC: University of South Carolina Press, 1971. 2nd ed. 337p. Appendix. Index. Notes. /GC 975.7 G653sk/

Harmon, Lillian Marsh. *The Plantation Marshes: The Colony of Edgefield Marshes and the Account of their Lineage.* Edgefield, SC: The Edgefield Advertiser, 1964. /GC 929.2 M3515h/

Helsley, Alexia Jones. *South Carolina's African American Confederate Pensioners, 1923-1925.* Charleston, SC: South Carolina Department of Archives and History, 1998. 140p. Appendices. Index. Photographs. /GC 975.7 H36so/

Holt, Thomas. *Black Over White: Negro Political Leadership in South Carolina during Reconstruction.* Urbana, IL: University of Illinois Press, 1979. Appendices. Bibliography. Index. /GC 975.7 H74b/

In the Shadow of the Big House: Domestic Slaves at Stoney/Baynard Plantation, Hilton Head Island. Columbia, SC: Chicora Foundation, Inc., 1995. 139p. Bibliography. Drawings. Photographs. /GC 975.702 H56a/

Inabinet, Joan. *A Wateree River Plantation Journal: "Rosny," from 1815.* Camden, SC: The Kershaw County Historical Society,

1997. Publication # 8 in the *Preserve* series. 72p. Index. /GC   975.701   K47ij/

James, F. C. ***African Methodism in South Carolina: A Bicentennial Focus***. Tappan, NY: Custombook, Inc., 1987. 532p. Photographs. /GC   975.7   J23a/

Johnson, Michael P. and James L. Roark. ***Black Masters: A Free Family of Color in the Old South***. New York: W. W. Norton & Company, 1984. 422p. Appendix. Index. Notes. /GC   975.702   C38jo/

Johnson, Michael P. and James L. Roark. ***No Chariot Let Down: Charleston's Free People of Color on the Eve of the Civil War***. Chapel Hill, NC: The University of North Carolina Press, 1984. 174p. Bibliography. Index. Letters. /GC   975.702   C38n/

Joyner, Charles. ***Down by the Riverside: A South Carolina Slave Community***. Urbana, IL: University of Illinois Press, 1984. 345p. Index. Notes. /GC   975.7   J85d/

Koger, Larry. ***Black Slaveowners: Free Black Slave Masters in South Carolina, 1790-1860***. Jefferson, NC: McFarland & Company, Inc., 1985. 286p. Appendices. Index. Notes. /GC   975.7   K82b/

Littlefield, Daniel C. ***Rice and Slaves: Ethnicity and the Slave Trade in Colonial South Carolina***. Urbana, IL: University of Illinois Press, 1991. 199p. Bibliography. Index. Maps. Tables. /GC   975.7   L73r/

Mariner's Church, Charleston. Original church records, Charleston County, Marriages of Freedmen, 1867-80. /Microfiche/

Morgan, Philip D. ***Slave Counterpoint: Black Culture in the Eighteenth-Century Chesapeake and Lowcountry***. Chapel Hill,

NC: University of North Carolina Press, 1998. 703p. Illustrations. Index. Notes. /GC 975 M823s/

Olwell, Robert. ***Masters, Slaves, & Subjects: The Culture of Power in the South Carolina Low Country, 1740-1790***. Ithaca, NY: Cornell University Press, 1998. 294p. Bibliography. Illustrations. Index. /GC 975.7 Ol95m/

Pearson, Edward A., ed. ***Designs Against Charleston: The Trial Record of the Denmark Vesey Slave Conspiracy of 1822***. Chapel Hill, NC: The University of North Carolina Press, 1999. 387p. Bibliography. Index. /GC 975.702 C38d/

Plantation Journal, 1834-1851, of Thomas Walter Peyre, 1812-1851. Charleston, SC: South Carolina Historical Society, 1979. /Microfilm SC Microfiche Berkeley Fiche 1/

Powers, Bernard E., Jr. ***Black Charlestonians, A Social History, 1822-1885***. Fayetteville, AR: The University of Arkansas Press, 1994. 377p. Appendix. Bibliography. Illustrations. Index. Notes. Photographs. /GC 975.702 C38po/

Prince William Episcopal Parish Church, McPhersonville. Original church records, Hampton County. Slave Baptismal List, 1837-53. Slave Communicants, 1842. /Microfiche/

Protestant Episcopal Church, Diocese of South Carolina. Original church records. Notes on Confirmation of Blacks. /Microfiche/

Rawick, George P., ed. ***The American Slave: A Composite Autobiography–North Carolina and South Carolina Narratives***. Westport, CT: Greenwood Publishing Company, 1977. /GC 975.6 N8185 Sec. 2/

Rawick, George P., ed. ***The American Slave: A Composite Autobiography–South Carolina Narratives***. Westport, CT: Greenwood Publishing Company, 1972. /GC   975.7   So885   Parts 1-4/

Rawick, George P., ed. ***The American Slave: A Composite Autobiography–South Carolina...Narratives***. Westport, CT: Greenwood Publishing Company, 1979. /GC   929.11   AL113   Sec. 15/

Records of Ante-Bellum Southern Plantations from the Revolution through the Civil War. Frederick, MD: University Publications of America, Inc., 198-.

South Carolina--George Washington Allen papers, 1832-1865. /Series J, Part 7, Rolls 4-5/

South Carolina--Arnold family papers, 1758-1915. /Series J, Part 4, Rolls 7-11/

South Carolina--Iveson Lewis Brookes papers, 1785-1868. /Series J, Part 4, Rolls 37-38/

South Carolina--Hamilton Brown papers, 1752-1907. /Series J, Part 14, Rolls 5-8/

South Carolina--Davidson family papers, 1827-1935. /Series J, Part 13, Rolls 28-34/

South Carolina--James Evans papers, 1826-1927. /Series J, Part 12, Rolls 2-6/

South Carolina--James McKibbin Gage papers, 1835-1876. /Series J, Part 7, Roll 8/

South Carolina--Hughes family papers, 1790-1860. /Series J, Part 6, Rolls 23-24/

South Carolina--Latta family papers, 1799-1878. /Series J, Part 13, Roll 34/

South Carolina--Lipscomb family papers, 1791-1867. /Series J, Part 7, Roll 8/

South Carolina--Benjamin F. Little papers, 1806-1935. /Series J, Part 13, Rolls 38-39/

South Carolina--Pegram-Johnson-McIntosh family papers, 1825-1941. /Series M, Part 5, Rolls 47-48/

South Carolina--John Osbourn diary, 1819-1821. /Series J, Part 13, Roll 34/

South Carolina--Rufus Reid papers, 1772-1911. /Series J, Part 13, Rolls 37-38/

South Carolina--Edmund Ruffin papers, 1794-1865. /Series M, Part 4, Rolls 46-49/

South Carolina--Screven family papers, 1758-1915. /Series J, Part 4, Rolls 7-11/

South Carolina--Absalom Benton Whitaker papers, 1814-1845. /Series J, Part 4, Roll 47/

South Carolina--Wickham family papers, 1766-1945. /Series M, Part 4, Rolls 51-55/

South Carolina --Witherspoon & McDowall papers, 1826-1859. /Series J, Part 13, Roll 11/

Abbeville dist., SC--Colhoun papers, 1774-1961. /Series J, Part 3, Roll 29/

Aiken dist., SC--J. H. Hammond letters, 1831-1845. /Series J, Part 3, Roll 27/

Anderson dist., SC--Ashmore plantation journal, 1853-1859. /Series J, Part 3, Roll 27/

Barnwell dist., SC--Lewis M. Ayer papers, 1771-1865. /Series A, Part 2, Rolls 9-11/

Barnwell dist., SC--James H. Hammond papers, 1774-1887. /Series A, Part 1, Rolls 1-15 & Series F, Part 2, Roll 9/

Barnwell dist., SC--J. H. Hammond letters, 1831-1845. /Series J, Part 3, Roll 27/

Barnwell dist., SC--J. W. Ogilvie account books, 1845-1870. /Series A, Part 2, Rolls 3-4/

Beaufort dist., SC--Thos. A. Coffin papers, 1800-1816. /Series B, Roll 9/

Beaufort dist., SC--Colcock family papers, 1785-1865. /Series H, Rolls 22-23/

Beaufort dist., SC--Louis M. DeSaussure journal, 1835-1865. /Series J, Part 3, Roll 17/

Beaufort dist., SC--Elliott & Gonzales papers, 1701-1866. /Series J, Part 3, Rolls 18-25/

Beaufort dist., SC--John Edwin Fripp papers, 1817-1905. /Series J, Part 3, Roll 25/

Beaufort dist., SC--Greenwood plantation journal, 1858-1864. /Series C, Part 2, Roll 1/

Beaufort dist., SC--Alexander Robert Lawton papers, 1774-1897. /Series J, Part 3, Rolls 26-27/

Beaufort dist., SC--Rockingham plantation journal, 1828-1829. /Series F, Part 2, Roll 8/

Beaufort dist., SC--John Stapleton papers, 1790-1839. /Series A, Part 2, Rolls 6-7/

Berkeley dist., SC--Thomas fam. papers, 1702-1887. /Series A, Part 2, Rolls 5-6/

Camden dist., SC--Boykin family papers, 1748-1860. /Series J, Part 3, Roll 28/

Charleston dist., SC--Ball family papers, 1773-1892. /Series F, Part 2, Rolls 2-4 & Series J, Part 3, Rolls 1-2/

Charleston dist., SC--Saml. Barker papers, 1826-1850. /Series B, Roll 5/

Charleston dist., SC--Cheves family papers, 1814-1919. /Series J, Part 3, Roll 2/

Charleston dist., SC--Colhoun papers, 1774-1961. /Series J, Part 3, Roll 29/
Charleston dist., SC--Stephen Doar papers, 1851-1862. /Series C, Part 2, Roll 1/
Charleston dist., SC--F. H. Elmore papers, 1883-1897. /Series J, Part 3, Roll 29/
Charleston dist., SC--Edw. Frost papers, 1827-1864. /Series C, Part 2, Rolls 1-2/
Charleston dist., SC--Gaillard papers, 1784-1903. /Series B, Rolls 5-7/
Charleston dist., SC--William H. Gilliland papers, 1829-1868. /Series F, Part 1, Roll 8/
Charleston dist., SC--Gourdin papers, 1784-1903. /Series B, Rolls 5-7/
Charleston dist., SC--Grimball family papers, 1683-1916. /Series J, Part 3, Rolls 11-17/
Charleston dist., SC--Horlbeck family inventory book, 1853-1854, 1920. /Series J, Part 3, Roll 2/
Charleston dist., SC--Alfred Huger letterbooks, 1853-1863. /Series F, Part 2, Rolls 7-8/
Charleston dist., SC--Samual Cram Jackson diary, 1832-1833. /Series J, Part 3, Roll 2
Charleston dist., SC--Mitchell King papers, 1801-1876. /Series J, Part 3, Rolls 2-7/
Charleston dist., SC--Thomas Legare receipt book, 1767-1774. /Series J, Part 3, Roll 7
Charleston dist., SC--Manigault papers, 1776-1865. /Series F, Part 2, Rolls 4-6/
Charleston dist., SC--Manigault family papers, 1795-1897. /Series J, Part 3, Roll 17 & Series J, Part 4, Rolls 1-2/
Charleston dist., SC--Arthur Middleton papers, 1803-1938. /Series J, Part 3, Roll 9/
Charleston dist., SC--Nathaniel Russell Middleton papers, 1761-1908. /Series J, Part 3, Rolls 7-9/
Charleston dist., SC--Thomas Middleton plantation book, 1734-1813. /Series J, Part 3, Roll 9/
Charleston dist., SC--J. B. Milliken journals, 1853-1899. /Series B, Roll 8/
Charleston dist., SC--Morris family papers, 1795-1832. /Series J, Part 3, Roll 17/
Charleston dist., SC--Thos. W. Peyre journals, 1834-1859. /Series B. Roll 5/
Charleston dist., SC--Ravenel family papers, 1790-1918. /Series J, Part 3, Roll 9/
Charleston dist., SC--Henry Ravenel papers, 1716-1875. /Series B, Roll 4/
Charleston dist., SC--Thos. P. Ravenel papers, 1728-1950. /Series B, Rolls 1-4/
Charleston dist., SC--Richmond overseer journal, 1859-1860. /Series B, Roll 7/
Charleston dist., SC--Smith letter book, 1771-1784. /Series J, Part 3, Roll 10/
Charleston dist., SC--Wagner family papers, 1914-1919. /Series J, Part 3, Roll 2/
Charleston dist., SC--Alonzo White slave book, 1853-1863. /Series B, Roll 8/

Chesterfield dist., SC--Thomas Steele diary, 1854-1856. /Series J, Part 3, Roll 41/
Claremont dist., SC--Singleton family, 1759-1905. /Series J, Part 3, Rolls 30-41/
Clarendon dist., SC--Singleton family, 1759-1905. /Series J, Part 3, Rolls 30-41/
Colleton dist., SC--Elliott & Gonzales papers, 1701-1866. /Series J, Part 3, Rolls 18-25/
Colleton dist., SC--David Gavin diary, 1855-1874. /Series J, Part 3, Rolls 10-11/
Colleton dist., SC--Glover papers, 1690-1904. / Series A, Part 2, Roll 3 & Series B, Roll 10/
Colleton dist., SC--Grimball family papers, 1683-1916. /Series J, Part 3, Rolls 11-17/
Colleton dist., SC--Heyward family papers, 1708-1866. /Series A, Part 2, Rolls 12-13/
Colleton dist., SC--Manigault family papers, 1795-1832. /Series J, Part 3, Roll 17/
Colleton dist., SC--Morris family papers, 1795-1832. /Series J, Part 3, Roll 17/
Colleton dist., SC--Sanders fam. papers, 1806-1865. /Series F, Part 2, Rolls 6-7/
Colleton dist., SC--Daniel Webb journal, 1817-1850. /Series B, Rolls 9-10/
Darlington dist., SC--Allston correspondence, 1843. /Series J, Part 3, Roll 27/
Darlington dist., SC--Bacot family papers, 1767-1887. /Series J, Part 3, Roll 27/
Darlington dist., SC--Caleb Coker papers, 1856-1861. /Series A, Part 2, Roll 3/
Darlington dist., SC--Thomas C. Law papers, 1798-1879. /Series A, Part 2, Rolls 7-8/
Edgefield dist., SC--Hammond et al papers, 1737-1865. /Series A, Part 2, Rolls 20-24/
Edgefield dist., SC--James T. Ouzts papers, 1856-1876. /Series A, Part 2, Roll 3/
Edgefield dist., SC--John F. Talbert papers, 1838-1866. /Series A, Part 2, Rolls 2-3/
Fairfield dist., SC--Mary Hart Means papers, 1846-1865. /Series A, Part 2, Roll 4/
Fairfield dist., SC--David Milling papers, 1830-1849. /Series A, Part 2, Roll 3/
Fairfield dist., SC--James S. Milling papers, 1852-1883. /Series J, Part 3, Roll 29/
Georgetown dist., SC--Allston correspondence, 1843. /Series J, Part 3, Roll 27/
Georgetown dist., SC--Rev. Alex. Glennie diary, 1832-1859. /Series B, Roll 9/
Georgetown dist., SC--Dr. Andrew Hasell papers, 1830-1842. /Series B, Roll 9/

Georgetown dist., SC--Read-Lance papers, 1677-1865. /Series A, Part 2, Rolls 11-12/

Georgetown dist., SC--Smith letter book, 1771-1784. /Series J, Part 3, Roll 10/

Georgetown dist., SC--Sparkman journal, 1833-1888. /Series J, Part 3, Roll 1/

Georgetown dist., SC--Ben Sparkman plantation journal, 1848, 1853-1859. /Series J, Part 3, Roll 1/

Georgetown dist., SC--James R. Sparkman papers, 1811-1878, 1925. /Series A, Part 2, Roll 6 & Series J, Part 3, Roll 1/

Georgetown dist., SC--John Sparkman papers, 1859-1864. /Series B, Roll 9/

Georgetown dist., SC--Joshua J. Ward journals, 1833-1869. /Series B, Roll 9/

Georgetown dist., SC--Paul D. Weston papers, 1786-1869. /Series B, Rolls 8-9/

Georgetown dist., SC--Francis Withers account book, 1833-1840. /Series J, Part 3, Roll 1/

Horry dist., SC--Daniel W. Jordan papers, 1827-1866. /Series F, Part 2, Rolls 10-16/

Kershaw dist., SC--John M. DeSaussure papers, 1816-1865. /Series A, Part 2, Rolls 8-9/

Kershaw dist., SC--Daniel W. Jordan papers, 1827-1866. /Series F, Part 2, Rolls 10-16/

Orangeburg dist., SC--Michael Gramlin journals, 1839-1858. /Series A, Part 2, Roll 26/

Orangeburg dist., SC--Singleton family, 1759-1905. /Series J, Part 3, Rolls 30-41/

Orangeburg dist., SC--Jas. D. Trezevant recs., 1845-1858. /Series A, Part 2, Roll 3/

Pendleton dist., SC--Colhoun papers, 1774-1961. /Series J, Part 3, Roll 29/

Pendleton dist., SC--John E. Colhoun papers, 1763-1861. /Series A, Part 2, Rolls 13-14/

Richland dist., SC--F. H. Elmore papers, 1883-1897. /Series J, Part 3, Roll 29/

Richland dist., SC--Samual Cram Jackson diary, 1832-1833. /Series J, Part 3, Roll 2

Richland dist., SC--Hampton family papers, 1785-1861. /Series A, Part 2, Rolls 24-26/

Richland dist., SC--Singleton family, 1759-1905. /Series J, Part 3, Rolls 30-41/

Spartanburg dist., SC--Franklin Elmore papers, 1795-1863. /Series C, Part 2, Rolls 2-5/

Spartanburg dist., SC--Franklin H. Elmore papers, 1819-1877. /Series A, Part 2, Roll 26/

Sumter dist., SC--Ashmore plantation journal, 1853-1859. /Series J, Part 3, Roll 27/
Sumter dist., SC--McDonald Furman papers, 1800s. /Series F, Part 2, Roll 9/
Sumter dist., SC--Samuel P. Gaillard journals, 1835-1871. /Series A, Part 2, Rolls 1-2/
Sumter dist., SC--Miller-Furman-Dabbs papers, 1751-1902. /Series A, Part 2, Rolls 14-20/
Sumter dist., SC--Henry L. Pinckney journals, 1850-1869. /Series F, Part 2, Roll 9/
Sumter dist., SC--Singleton family, 1759-1905. /Series J, Part 3, Rolls 30-41/
Union dist., SC--William Sims papers, 1770-1860. /Series F, Part 2, Rolls 9-10/
Union dist., SC--Natalie D. Sumter diary, 1840-1841. /Series A, Part 2, Roll 4/
Williamsburg dist., SC--Sparkman journal, 1833-1888. /Series J, Part 3, Roll 1/
York dist., SC--Franklin H. Elmore papers, 1819-1877. /Series A, Part 2, Roll 26/

Records of the Assistant Commissioner for the State of South Carolina, Bureau of Refugees, Freedmen, and Abandoned Lands, 1865-1870. Washington, DC: National Archives and Records Service, 1972. Microcopy M869. Endorsements sent. Records Relating to the Issuance of Rations. Personnel Rosters. Records Relating to Transportation. Miscellaneous Records. Letters Received. /Microfilm Rolls 3-24, 38-41, 44/

Registers of Signatures of Depositors in Branches of the Freedman's Savings and Trust Company, 1865-1874. Washington, DC: National Archives and Records Service, 1969. Microcopy M816. Beaufort. Charleston. /Microfilm Rolls 25-28/

Rosengarten, Theodore. ***Tombee: Portrait of a Cotton Planter With the Plantation Journal of Thomas B. Chaplin (1822-1890).*** New York: William Morrow and Company, Inc., 1986. 750p. Index. Notes. /GC 975.701 B38r/

St. James, Santee Episcopal Church, McClellanville. Original church records, Charleston County. References to Slave Baptisms and Marriages. /Microfiche/

St. Mark's Protestant Episcopal Church, Charleston. Original church records, Charleston County. Episcopal Church founded by Freedmen in 1865. /Microfiche/

St. Peter's & Christ Episcopal Churches, Charleston. Original church records, Charleston County. Registers for Blacks, including Baptisms (1834-1862) and Marriages (1835-58). /Microfiche/

St. Stephen's Episcopal Chapel, Charleston. Original church records, Charleston County. Baptisms of Blacks, 1872. Marriages for Slaves and Free Blacks, 1822-66. Death and Burial Records, 1822-65 & 1873-78. /Microfilm/

Schwalm, Leslie A. *A Hard Fight for We: Women's Transition from Slavery to Freedom in South Carolina.* Urbana, IL: University of Illinois Press, 1997. 394p. Bibliography. Index. Notes. /GC 975.7 Sch93h/

Slave Schedules for 1850–South Carolina. Washington, DC: The National Archives, 1964. Microcopy 432. /Microfilm Rolls 861-868/

Slave Schedules for 1860–South Carolina. Washington, DC: The National Archives, 1967. Microcopy 653. /Microfilm Rolls 1229-1238/

Slavery in Ante-Bellum Southern Industries. Frederick MD: University Publications of America, 199-.
South Carolina--Brevard family papers, 1754-1953. /Series B, Rolls 1-2/
South Carolina--Cabell family papers, 1774-1941. /Series C, Part 2, Rolls 4-6/
South Carolina--Fisher family papers, 1758-1896. /Series B, Rolls 28-38/
South Carolina--Hawkins family papers, 1738-1865. /Series B, Rolls 8-21/
South Carolina--McDowell family papers, 1754-1953. /Series B, Rolls 1-2/
South Carolina--Peck, Welford & Company papers, 1834-1844. /Series C, Part 2, Roll 39/

South Carolina 1850 Slave Schedules: Federal Census Index. West Jordan, UT: Genealogical Services, 1988. 379p. /GC 975.7 J13soa/

State Free Negro Capitation Tax Books, Charleston, South Carolina, ca. 1811-1860. Columbia, SC: South Carolina Department of Archives and History, 1983. /Microfilm SC State Records (SC-AR-M/11-1 & 2)/

Stevenson, Mary, ed. *The Diary of Clarissa Adger Bowen, Ashtabula Plantation, 1865, The Pendleton Clemson Area, South Carolina*. Pendleton, SC: Historic Restoration, 1973. /GC 975.702 P37s/

Tindall, George Brown. *South Carolina Negroes, 1877-1900*. Columbia, SC: University of South Carolina Press, 1952. 336p. Bibliography. Index. Photographs. /GC 975.7 T492s/

Trinkley, Michael. *Archaeological and Historical Examinations of Three Eighteenth and Nineteenth Century Rice Plantations of the Waccamaw Neck*. Columbia, SC: Chicora Foundation, Inc., 1993. Research Series 31. 229p. Bibliography. Photographs. Tables. /GC 975.7 C433r No. 31/

Trinkley, Michael. *Further Investigation of the Stoney/Baynard Main House, Hilton Head Island, Beaufort County, South Carolina*. Columbia, SC: Chicora Foundation, Inc., 1996. Research Series 47. 60p. Bibliography. Photographs. Tables. /GC 975.7 C433r No. 47/

Trinkley, Michael. *A Historical and Archaeological Evaluation of the Elfe (38BK207) and Sanders (38CH321) Plantations, Berkeley and Charleston Counties, South Carolina*. Columbia, SC: Chicora Foundation, Inc., 1985. 81p. Research Series 5. Bibliography. Maps. Tables. /GC 975.7 C433r No. 5/

Trinkley, Michael. *Plantation Life in the Piedmont: A Preliminary Examination of Rosemont Plantation, Laurens County, South Carolina*. Columbia, SC: Chicora Foundation, Inc., 1992. 75p. Research Series 29. Bibliography. Photographs. Tables. /GC 975.7 C433r No. 29/

Trinkley, Michael and Debi Hacker. *Preliminary Archaeological and Historical Investigations at Old House Plantation, Jasper County, South Carolina*. Columbia, SC: Chicora Foundation, Inc., 1996. 127p. Research Series 49. Bibliography. Drawings. Maps. Photographs. Tables. /GC 975.7 C433r No. 49/

Trinkley, Michael and Natalie Adams. *Archaeological, Historical, and Architectural Survey of the Gibson Plantation Tract, Florence County, South Carolina*. Columbia, SC: Chicora Foundation, Inc., 1992. Research Series 33. 91p. Bibliography. Maps. Photographs. Tables. /GC 975.7 C433r No. 33/

Trinkley, Michael, Debi Hacker, and Natalie Adams. *Broom Hall Plantation: "A Good One and in a Pleasant Neighborhood."* Columbia, SC: Chicora Foundation, Inc., 1995. 328p. Research Series 44. Appendices. Bibliography. Drawings. Maps. Tables. /GC 975.7 C433r No. 44/

Vaughn, Emily E. *Index of Black Churches and Cemeteries in Clarendon County, South Carolina, Headstone Inscriptions*. Buffalo, NY: Research Services & Publishing, 1996. 241p. /GC 975.701 C54v/

Vaughn, Emily E. *Index of Black Churches and Cemeteries in Sumter County, South Carolina, Headstone Inscriptions*. Buffalo, NY: Research Services & Publishing, 1996. 331p. /GC 975.701 Su6va/

Vernon, Amelia Wallace. *African Americans at Mars Bluff, South Carolina*. Baton Rouge, LA: Louisiana State University Press, 1993. 309p. Bibliography. Index. Notes. /GC 975.702 M35v/

Weiner, Marli F. *Mistresses and Slaves: Plantation Women in South Carolina, 1830-80*. Urbana, IL: University of Illinois Press, 1998. 308p. Index. Notes. /GC 975.7 W43m/

Wood, Peter H. *Black Majority: Negroes in Colonial South Carolina From 1670 through the Stono Rebellion*. New York: Alfred A. Knopf, 1974. 346p. Bibliography. Index. /GC 975.7 W85b/

TENNESSEE

Craft, Elizabeth Mathis. *Tennessee DAR Genealogical Records Committee Report, Series 2, Volume 36 -- Steps Along the Way: Ripley High Schools Featuring 1947 Graduates, 264 Jefferson Street, Lauderdale County, Ripley, Tennessee 38063*. TN: Tennessee DAR, 1997. 159p. Index. /GC 976.802 R48te/

Lovett, Bobby L. *The African-American History of Nashville, Tennessee, 1780-1930: Elites and Dilemmas*. Fayetteville, AR: University of Arkansas Press, 1999. 314p. Bibliography. Illustrations. Index. Maps. Notes. Photographs. /GC 976.802 N17l/

Rawick, George P., ed. *The American Slave: A Composite Autobiography–...Tennessee Narratives*. Westport, CT: Greenwood Publishing Company, 1972. /GC 929.11 K136 Sec. 6/

Records of Ante-Bellum Southern Plantations from the Revolution through the Civil War. Frederick, MD: University Publications of America, Inc., 198-.

Tennessee--Walter Alves papers, 1771-1858. /Series J, Part 13, Rolls 10-11/
Tennessee--James Trooper Armstrong papers, 1832-1891. /Series J, Part 6, Roll 29/
Tennessee--Mary Jeffreys Bethell diary, 1853-1873. /Series J, Part 13, Roll 12/
Tennessee--Buchanan & McClellan family papers, 1816-1872. /Series J, Part 7, Roll 8/
Tennessee--William M. Byrd papers, 1832-1914. /Series J, Part 7, Roll 5/
Tennessee--Farish Carter papers, 1794,1806-1868. /Series J, Part 4, Rolls 38-43/
Tennessee--Leonidas Chalmers Glenn papers, 1752-1907. /Series J, Part 13, Roll 35/
Tennessee--Guion family papers, 1789-1927. /Series J, Part 6, Roll 1/
Tennessee--Gustavus A. Henry papers, 1804-1895. /Series J, Part 6, Rolls 18-20/
Tennessee--Chillab Smith Howe papers, 1814-1899. /Series J, Part 6, Rolls 20-23/
Tennessee--Jackson, Riddle, and Company papers, 1835-1839. /Series J, Part 5, Roll 19/
Tennessee--Lewis family papers, 1730-1956. /Series F, Part 12, Rolls 13-14/
Tennessee--Thomas David Smith McDowell papers, 1735-1905. /Series J, Part 12, Rolls 7-12/
Tennessee--Meriwether family papers, 1791-1880s. /Series J, Part 9, Roll 27/
Tennessee--Person family papers, 1739-1907. /Series J, Part 13, Rolls 3-4/
Tennessee--Puryear family papers, 1810-1940. /Series J, Part 13, Roll 40/
Tennessee--Quitman family papers, 1760-1926. /Series J, Part 6, Rolls 5-12/
Tennessee--Rufus Reid papers, 1772-1911. /Series J, Part 13, Rolls 37-38/
Tennessee--Shanks family papers, 1801-1923. /Series J, Part 13, Rolls 4-5/
Tennessee--Thompson family papers, 1809-1924. /Series J, Part 7, Roll 8/
Bedford co., TN--Micahel D. Shoffner papers, 1777-1873. /Series J, Part 8, Roll 19/
Carroll co., TN--Micahel D. Shoffner papers, 1777-1873. /Series J, Part 8, Roll 19/
Cocke co., TN--Elijah Vester papers, 1813-1854. /Series J, Part 8, Roll 20/
Davidson co., TN--Hamilton Brown papers, 1752-1907. /Series J, Part 14, Rolls 5-8/
Davidson co., TN--Harding & Jackson papers, 1819-1895. /Series J, Part 8, Rolls 5-7/
Davidson co., TN--George W. House papers, 1820-1859. /Series J, Part 8, Roll 14/
Davidson co., TN--John Overton papers, 1827-1830. /Series J, Part 8, Roll 19/

Davidson co., TN--Polk, Brown, & Ewell family papers, 1803-1859. /Series J, Part 8, Roll 7/

Davidson co., TN--Paul F. Tavel papers, 1837-1900. /Series J, Part 8, Roll 20/

Hardeman co., TN--John Houston Bills papers, 1843-1871. /Series J, Part 8, Rolls 14 - 18/

Hardeman co., TN--Calvin Jones papers, 1785-1929. /Series J, Part 8, Rolls 1-5/

Haywood co., TN--Harrod C. Anderson papers, 1854-1862, 1886. /Series I, Part 2, Roll 20/

Jefferson co., TN--Hodges family papers, 1788-1889. /Series H, Rolls 25-27/

McNairy co., TN--Elijah Vester papers, 1813-1854. /Series J, Part 8, Roll 20/

Maury co., TN--Hamilton Brown papers, 1752-1907. /Series J, Part 14, Rolls 5-8/

Maury co., TN--Dillion & Polk family papers, 1805-1863. /Series J, Part 8, Roll 14/

Maury co., TN--George Washington Polk papers, 1793-1857. /Series J, Part 8, Rolls 13-14/

Maury co., TN--Polk, Brown, & Ewell family papers, 1803-1859. /Series J, Part 8, Roll 7/

Maury co., TN--Polk & Yeatman family papers--, 1773-1861. /Series J, Part 8, Rolls 8-13/

Stewart co., TN--Paul F. Tavel papers, 1837-1900. /Series J, Part 8, Roll 20/

Sumner co., TN--A. R. Wynne papers, 1818-1866. /Series F, Part 1, Roll 23/

Tipton co., TN--Robert Hall Morrison papers, 1820-1888. /Series J, Part 8, Rolls 18-19/

Records of the Assistant Commissioner for the State of Tennessee, Bureau of Refugees, Freedmen, and Abandoned Lands, 1865-1869 (1870). Washington, DC: National Archives and Records Service, 1976. Microcopy M999. Letters Sent. Press Copies of Telegrams Sent. Endorsements Sent. Registers of Letters Received. School Reports and Related Records. Inspection Reports. Reports of Numbers of Persons Issued Rations. Reports of Freedmen's Homes. Indentures of Apprenticeship. Contracts. Reports Relating to Bounty Claims and Disbursements. Letters Received. /Microfilm Rolls 4-15, 19-25/

Registers of Signatures of Depositors in Branches of the Freedman's Savings and Trust Company, 1865-1874. Washington, DC: National Archives and Records Service, 1969. Microcopy M816. Memphis. Nashville. /Microfilm Rolls 16-17/

Rogers, Louise F. *The Older Black Families of Rogersville, Tennessee*. Rogersville, TN: L. F. Rogers, 1974. 62p. Index. /GC 976.802 R61o/

Slave Schedules for 1850–Tennessee. Washington, DC: The National Archives, 1964. Microcopy 432. /Microfilm Rolls 902-907/

Slave Schedules for 1860–Tennessee. Washington, DC: The National Archives, 1967. Microcopy 653. /Microfilm Rolls 1281-1286/

Slavery in Ante-Bellum Southern Industries. Bethesda, MD: University Publications of America, 199-.
Tennessee--Edward Richard Archer papers, 1861-1863. /Series C, Part 1, Roll 1/
Tennessee--Bryan & Leventhorpe papers, 1797-1860. /Series B, Rolls 2-3/
Tennessee--Hawkins family papers, 1738-1865. /Series B, Rolls 8-21/
Montgomery co., TN--Louisa Furnace Account Books, 1831-1860. /Series B, Rolls 21-22/

Smith, Jonathan K. T. *Public Marriage Records of Black Persons in Madison County, Tennessee, 1868-1888*. Jackson, TN: J. K. T. Smith, 1998. 83p. Index. /GC 976.801 M26smp/

Smith, Jonathan K. T. *Tombstone Inscriptions from Black Cemeteries in Haywood County, Tennessee*. Jackson, TN: J. K. T. Smith, 1998. 114p. Index. Maps. /GC 976.801 H33s/

Smith, Jonathan K. T. *Tombstone Inscriptions from Black Cemeteries in Henderson County, Tennessee*. Jackson, TN: J. K. T. Smith, 1995. 47p. Index. Maps. /GC 976.801 H39sm/

Smith, Jonathan K. T. *Tombstone Inscriptions from Black Cemeteries in Madison County, Tennessee*. Jackson, TN: J. K. T. Smith, 1995. 207p. Index. Maps. /GC 976.801 M26smd/

TEXAS

The Afro-American Texans. San Antonio, TX: University of Texas, 1975. 32p. Illus. Photographs. /GC 976.4 In7af/

Baker, T. Lindsay and Julie P. Baker, eds. *Till Freedom Cried Out: Memories of Texas Slave Life*. College Station, TX: Texas A&M University Press, 1997. 162p. Bibliography. Illustrations. Index. /GC 976.4 T46/

Barr, Alwyn. *Black Texans: A History of Negroes in Texas, 1528-1971*. Austin, TX: Jenkins Publishing Company, 1973. Illustrations. Bibliography. Index. /GC 976.4 B27b/

Beeth, Howard and Cary D. Wintz, eds. *Black Dixie: Afro-Texan History and Culture in Houston*. College Station, TX: Texas A&M University Press, 1992. 294p. Index. Notes. Photographs. /GC 976.402 H81be/

Christian, Garna L. *Black Soldiers in Jim Crow Texas, 1899-1917*. College Station, TX: Texas A&M University Press, 1995. 223p. Bibliography. Index. Notes. /GC 973.001 T31c/

Crouch, Barry A. *The Freedmen's Bureau and Black Texans*. Austin, TX: University of Texas Press, 1992. 187p. Index. Notes. /GC 976.4 C88f/

Dallas, Texas Negro City Directory, 1947-1948. S. l.: s. n., 19--. 356p. /GC 976.402 D16dl/

Govenar, Alan. *Portraits of Community: African American Photography in Texas*. Austin, TX: Texas State Historical Association, 1996. 272p. Appendices. Index. /GC 976.4 G746p/

Rawick, George P., ed. *The American Slave: A Composite Autobiography–Texas Narratives*. Westport, CT: Greenwood Publishing Company, 1972. /GC 976.4 T293 Parts 1-4/

Rawick, George P., ed. *The American Slave: A Composite Autobiography–Texas Narratives*. Westport, CT: Greenwood Publishing Company, 1979. /GC 976.4 T294 Parts 1-9/

Records of Ante-Bellum Southern Plantations from the Revolution through the Civil War. Frederick, MD: University Publications of America, Inc., 198-.

Texas--Archibald Davis Alston papers, 1804-1893. /Series J, Part 12, Roll 14/
Texas--Margaret Butler papers, 1847-1880. /Series I, Part 5, Roll 2/
Texas--Ernest Haywood papers, 1830-1860. /Series J, Part 7, Rolls 12-20/
Texas--Albert Clinton Horton papers, 1850-1881. /Series G, Part 1, Roll 33/
Texas--Quitman family papers, 1760-1926. /Series J, Part 6, Rolls 5-12/
Brazoria co., TX--Perry family papers, 1786-1870. /Series G, Part 1, Rolls 12-31/
Colorado co., TX--Chas. Wm. Tait papers, 1844-1855. /Series G, Part 1, Roll 44/
Falls co., TX--Billingsley family papers, 1838-1866. /Series G, Part 1, Roll 36/
Grimes co., TX--Thomas E. Blackshear papers, 1830-1889. /Series G, Part 1, Roll 44/
Grimes co., TX--Lizzie Scott Nesblett papers, 1849-1865. /Series G, Part 1, Rolls 34-35/
Harrison co., TX--Rebecca M. H. Hagerty papers, 1823-1880. /Series G, Part 1, Roll 42/
Houston co., TX--James M. Hall family papers, 1844-1888. /Series G, Part 1, Roll 33-34/
Marion co., TX--Rebecca M. H. Hagerty papers, 1823-1880. /Series G, Part 1, Roll 42/
Matagorda co., TX--Albert C. Horton papers, 1850-1881. /Series G, Part 1, Roll 33/

Navarro co., TX--Lizzie Scott Nesblett papers, 1849-1865. /Series G, Part 1, Rolls 34-35/

Red River co., TX--Geo. Travis Wright papers, 1824-1868. /Series G, Part 1, Rolls 42-44/

Rusk co., TX--Julien S. Devereux papers, 1787-1865. /Series G. Part 1, Rolls 36-42/

Victoria co., TX--Preston Rose family papers, 1838-1882. /Series G, Part 1, Rolls 31-32/

Wharton co., TX--John P. Bolton papers, 1853-1863. /Series G, Part 1, Roll 33/

Wharton co., TX--Green C. Duncan papers, 1853-1865. /Series G, Part 1, Roll 33/

Wharton co., TX--Albert C. Horton papers, 1850-1881. /Series G, Part 1, Roll 33/

Records of the Assistant Commissioner for the State of Texas, Bureau of Refugees, Freedmen, and Abandoned Lands, 1865-1869. Washington, DC: National Archives and Records Service, 1973. Microcopy M821. Endorsements Sent. Teachers' Letters of Appointment and Other Records Relating to Teachers. Contracts. Record of Schools. Received and Retained Reports Relating to Rations, Lands, and Bureau Personnel. Oaths of Office of Bureau Personnel. Letters and Etc. Received. /Microfilm Rolls 2-18, 29-31/

Richter, William L. *Overreached on All Sides: The Freedmen's Bureau Administrators in Texas, 1865-1868.* College Station, TX: Texas A&M University Press, 1991. 436p. Bibliography. Index. Notes. /GC 976.4 R41o/

Slave Owners of Hunt County, Texas and the Number of Slaves Owned by Each in 1864. Quinlan, TX: The Hunt County Pacer, 1983. 7p. /GC 976.401 H91sl/

Slave Schedules for 1850–Texas. Washington, DC: The National Archives, 1964. Microcopy 432. /Microfilm Rolls 917-918/

Slave Schedules for 1860–Texas. Washington, DC: The National Archives, 1967. Microcopy 653. /Microfilm Rolls 1309-1312/

Slavery in Ante-Bellum Southern Industries. Frederick, MD: University Publications of America, 199-.
Texas--Hawkins family papers, 1738-1865. /Series B, Rolls 8-21/

Smallwood, James M. ***Black Texans During Reconstruction, 1865-1874***. Lubbock, TX: Texas Tech University, 1974. 457p. Bibliography. Notes. /GC 976.4 Sm19b/

Tarrant County Black Historical and Genealogical Society, Inc. Newsletter. Fort Worth, TX: Tarrant County Black Historical and Genealogical Society, Inc., 1982-. /Periodical/

Tyler, Ronnie C. and Lawrence R. Murphy, eds. ***The Slave Narratives of Texas***. Austin, TX: The Encino Press, 1974. 143p. Illustrations. Notes. /GC 976.4 Sl16/

Von der Mehden, Fred R. ***The Ethnic Groups of Houston***. Houston, TX: Rice University, 1984. 240p. Bibliography. /GC 976.402 H81e/

Winegarten, Ruthe. ***Black Texas Women: 150 Years of Trial and Triumph***. Austin, TX: University of Texas Press, 1995. 427p. Appendices. Bibliography. Index. Notes. Photographs. /GC 976.4 W719b/

VERMONT

Minority Military Service, New Hampshire/Vermont, 1775-1783. Washington, DC: National Society Daughters of the American Revolution, 1991. 17p. /GC 973.34 Aalmin/

VIRGINIA

Afro-American Historical Association of Fauquier County, Virginia. Midland, VA: The Association, v.1-, 1992-. /Periodical/

Bassett, John Spencer, ed. *The Westover Journal of John A. Seldon, Esqr., 1858-1862.* Northampton, MA: Department of History of Smith College, 1921. (Volume 5, no. 4 of *Smith College Studies in History.*) /GC 929.2 Se48se/

Bell, John C. *Louisa County Records You Probably Never Saw, of 18th Century Virginia.* Nashville, TN: J. C. Bell, 1983. Louisa County Free Blacks Register, 1816-1817. /GC 975.501 L93be p. 68-90/

Bushman, Katherine G. *The Registers of Free Blacks, 1810-1864, Augusta County, Virginia and Staunton, Virginia.* Verona, VA: Mid-Valley Press, Inc., 1989. 146p. Index. /GC 975.501 Au4reg/

Chester, Thomas Morris. *Black Civil War Correspondent: His Dispatches from the Virginia Front.* Baton Rouge, LA: Louisiana State University Press, 1989. 375p. Index. /GC 973.74 V81che/

Dickerson, Richard B. *Entitled! Free Papers in Appalachia Concerning Antebellum Freeborn Negroes and Emancipated Blacks of Montgomery County, Virginia.* Washington, DC: National Genealogical Society, 1981. 83p. Index. /GC 975.501 M76d/

Duke, Maurice. *Don't Carry Me Back! Narratives by Former Virginia Slaves.* Richmond, VA: Dietz Press, 1995. 180p. Bibliography. Index. Photographs. /GC 975.5 D719/

Engs, Robert Francis. *Freedom's First Generation: Black Hampton, Virginia, 1861-1890.* Philadelphia, PA: University of Pennsylvania Press, 1979. 236p. Bibliography. Index. Photographs. /GC 975.502 H18e/

Fithian, Philip Vickers. *Journal & Letters of Philip Vickers Fithian, 1773-1774: A Plantation Tutor of the Old Dominion.* Williamsburg, VA: Colonial Williamsburg, Inc., 1943. 323p. Index. /GC 929.2 C24527f/

Fitzgerald, Ruth Coder. *A Different Story: A Black History of Fredericksburg, Stafford, and Spotsylvania, Virginia.* S. l.: Unicorn, 1979. 326p. Index. /GC 975.502 F87fi/

Green Jack P., ed. *The Diary of Colonel Landon Carter of Sabine Hall, 1752-1778.* Richmond, VA: Virginia Historical Society, 1965. 2 vols. Index. /GC 929.2 C245cb V. 1-2/

Guild, June Purcell. *Black Laws of Virginia: A Summary of the Legislative Acts of Virginia Concerning Negroes From the Earliest Times to the Present.* New York: Negro University Press, 1969. 249p. Appendices. Index. /GC 975.5 G94b/

Hairston Family Plantation Records. Washington, DC: NSDAR, 1996. Virginia DAR Genealogical Records Committee Report, Ser. 2, Vol. 42. /GC 929.2 H1259v/

Heath, Barbara. *Hidden Lives: The Archaeology of Slave Life at Thomas Jefferson's Poplar Forest.* Charlottesville, VA: University Press of Virginia, 1999. 82p. Bibliography. Drawings. Index. Maps. Notes. Photographs. /GC 975.501 B39he/

Heinegg, Paul. ***Free African Americans of North Carolina and Virginia***. Baltimore, MD: Clearfield Company, Inc., 1994. 699p. /GC 975 H36fa/

Heinegg, Paul. ***Free African Americans of North Carolina and Virginia***. Baltimore, MD: Clearfield Company, Inc., 1997. 3rd edition. 825p. Index. /GC 975 H36faa/

Hodge, Robert A. ***Birth Records, Fredericksburg, Virginia, A-Z, 1900-1940, (Colored)***. Fredericksburg, VA: R. A. Hodge, 1988. 147p. Index. /GC 975.502 F87hon/

Hodge, Robert A. ***Some Pre-1871 Vital Statistics on Colored Persons of Culpeper County, Virginia***. Fredericksburg, VA: R. A. Hodge, 1978. 114p. /GC 975.501 C89so/

Hodges, F. Holly. ***Guide to African-American Manuscripts in the Collection of the Virginia Historical Society***. Richmond, VA: Virginia Historical Society, 1995. 176p. Drawings. Index. /GC 975.5 V819g/

Jackson, Luther Porter. ***Free Negro Labor and Property Holding in Virginia, 1830-1860***. New York: Atheneum, 1969. 270p. Appendix. Bibliography. Index. /GC 975.5 J126f/

Jackson, Luther Porter. ***Negro Office-holders in Virginia, 1865-1895***. Norfolk, VA: Guide Quality Press, 1945. 88p. Photographs. /GC 975.5 J126n/

Jordan, Ervin L., Jr. ***Black Confederates and Afro-Yankees in Civil War Virginia***. Charlottesville, VA: University Press of Virginia, 1995. 447p. Appendices. Bibliography. Index. Notes. /GC 975.5 J76b/

Kambourian, Elizabeth Cann. ***The Freedmen's Bureau in Virginia: Names of Destitute Freedmen Dependent Upon the Government in the Military Districts of Virginia***. Bowie, MD: Heritage Books, Inc., 1997. 205p. Index. /GC 975.5 K128f/

Kerr-Ritchie, Jeffrey R. ***Freedpeople in the Tobacco South, Virginia, 1860-1900***. Chapel Hill, NC: The University Press of North Carolina, 1999. 345p. Appendices. Bibliography. Index. Maps. Notes. /GC 975.5 K468f/

Latimer, Frances Bibbins. ***Instruments of Freedom: Deeds and Wills of Emancipation, Northampton County, Virginia, 1782-1864***. Bowie, MD: Heritage Books, Inc., 1994. 182p. Index. /975.501 N79la/

Madden, T. O., Jr. ***We Were Always Free: The Maddens of Culpeper County, Virginia, A 200-Year Family History***. New York: W. W. Norton & Company, 1992. 218p. Appendices. Index. Notes. Photographs. /GC 929.2 M261m/

McLeRoy, Sherrie S. & William R. ***Strangers in Their Midst: The Free Black Population of Amherst County, Virginia***. Bowie, MD: Heritage Books, Inc., 1993. 224p. Bibliography. Index. Tables. /GC 975.501 Am4ma/

Minchinton, Walter, et al., eds. ***Virginia Slave-Trade Statistics, 1698-1775***. Richmond, VA: Virginia State Library, 1984. 218p. Appendices. Index. /GC 975.5 M66v/

Morgan, Philip D. ***Slave Counterpoint: Black Culture in the Eighteenth-Century Chesapeake and Lowcountry***. Chapel Hill, NC: University of North Carolina Press, 1998. 703p. Illustrations. Index. Notes. /GC 975 M823s/

Norris, Garland C. *Property Tax List of Culpeper County, Virginia and Names of Slaves, 1783*. Raleigh, NC: G. C. Norris, 193-. /GC 975.501 C89n/

Plunkett, Michael. *Afro-American Sources in Virginia: A Guide to Manuscripts*. Charlottesville, VA: University Press of Virginia, 1990. 323p. Index. /GC 975.5 P74a/

Rawick, George P., ed. *The American Slave: A Composite Autobiography–Virginia...Narratives*. Westport, CT: Greenwood Publishing Company, 1972. /GC 929.11 K136 Sec. 5/

Records of Ante-Bellum Southern Plantations from the Revolution through the Civil War. Frederick, MD: University Publications of America, Inc., 198-

Virginia--Simmons Jones Baker papers, 1800-1938. /Series J, Part 12, Roll 17/
Virginia--John Grammar Brodnax papers, 1827-1920. /Series J, Part 13, Roll 12/
Virginia--Hamilton Brown papers, 1752-1907. /Series J, Part 14, Rolls 5-8/
Virginia--Bullock & Hamilton papers, 1757-1971. /Series J, Part 13, Rolls 5-8/
Virginia--Clingman & Puryear family papers, 1810-1940. /Series J, Part 13, Roll 40/
Virginia--Wm. Cuningham & Company papers, 1753-1863. /Series M, Part 2, Rolls 8-9/
Virginia--Dillion & Polk family papers, 1805-1863. /Series J, Part 8, Roll 14/
Virginia--Ferebee, Gregory, & McPherson papers, 1816-1913. /Series J, Part 13, Roll 8/
Virginia--Leonidas Chalmers Glenn papers, 1752-1907. /Series J, Part 13, Roll 35/
Virginia--Jackson family papers, 1784-1880. /Series J, Part 4, Rolls 25-36/
Virginia--Jennings family papers, 1737-1837. /Series M, Part 2, Roll 9/
Virginia--Jerdone family papers, 1736-1918. /Series L, Part 2, Rolls 1-12/
Virginia--Benjamin Franklin Little papers, 1806-1935. /Series J, Part 13, Rolls 38-39/
Virginia--Louis Marshall papers, 1816-1878. /Series J, Part 8, Roll 20/
Virginia--Norton, Chilton, & Dameron papers, 1760-1926. /Series J, Part 6, Rolls 3-5/

Virginia--Person family papers, 1739-1907. /Series J, Part 13, Rolls 3-4/
Virginia--Philip Henry Pitts papers, 1814-1889. /Series J, Part 7, Rolls 6-7/
Virginia--Prince family papers, 1784-1880. /Series J, Part 4, Rolls 25-36/
Virginia--Randolph & Yates family papers, 1815-1865,1952. /Series J, Part 6, Roll 27/
Virginia--Rufus Reid papers, 1772-1911. /Series J, Part 13, Rolls 37-38/
Virginia--Shanks family papers, 1801-1923. /Series J, Part 13, Rolls 4-5/
Virginia--Edmonia Cabell Wilkins papers, 1782-1870. /Series J, Part 12, Rolls 39-41/
Virginia--William Bethell Williamson papers, 1842-1848. /Series J, Part 13, Roll 12/
Virginia--Thomas Yuille papers, 1754-1757. /Series F, Part 3, Roll 29/
Virginia--Southside Virginia family papers, 1748-1918. /Series E, Part 3, Rolls 1-6/
Accomack co., VA--Thos. Baylie Cropper papers, 1832-1879. /Series J, Part 9, Rolls 16-17/
Albemarle co., VA--Charles L. Bankhead papers, 1812-1831. /Series E, Part 1, Roll 18/
Albemarle co., VA--Barbour family papers, 1785-1941. /Series E, Part 2, Rolls 21-24/
Albemarle co., VA--Robert Carter Berkeley diary, 1826. /Series M, Part 4, Roll 6/
Albemarle co., VA--Charles Brown papers, 1792-1888. /Series L, Part 4, Rolls 35-36/
Albemarle co., VA--Cornelius Dabney diary, 1863-1869. /Series J, Part 9, Roll 18/
Albemarle co., VA--Martha Tabb Dyer diaries, 1823-1839. /Series E, Part 1, Roll 39/
Albemarle co., VA--Peachy Ridgway Gilmer papers, 1790-1889. /Series M, Part 4, Roll 12/
Albemarle co., VA--T. L. Jones journal, 1862-1869. /Series J, Part 9, Roll 18/
Albemarle co., VA--Meriwether family papers, 1791-1880s. /Series J, Part 9, Roll 27/
Albemarle co., VA--Louisa H. A. Minor diary, 1858-1866. /Series E, Part 2, Roll 26/
Albemarle co., VA--Randolph family papers, 1820-1864. /Series E, Part 2, Rolls 24-26/
Albemarle co., VA--Thos. Jefferson Randolph papers, 1819-39. /Series M, Part 4, Roll 45/

Albemarle co., VA--Thos. Mann Randolph papers, 1815-1824. /Series M, Part 4, Roll 45/

Albemarle co., VA--George Tucker papers, 1820-1833. /Series E, Part 3, Roll 1/

Amelia co., VA--Cocke family papers, 1770-1860. /Series M, Part 5, Rolls 16-20/

Amelia co., VA--Eggleston family papers, 1777-1899. /Series M, Part 5, Roll 20/

Amelia co., VA--Edmund Ruffin, Jr. plantation diary, 1851-1873. /Series J, Part 9, Roll 28/

Amelia co., VA--Philip Turner Southall account book, 1815-1824. /Series M, Part 5, Roll 48/

Amelia co., VA--Willson family papers, 1781-1838. /Series M, Part 5, Rolls 49-50/

Amherst co., VA--Austin-Twyman papers, 1765-1939. /Series L, Part 4, Rolls 1-35/

Amherst co., VA--Wm. Cabell commonplace books, 1769-1822. /Series M, Part 4, Roll 6/

Amherst co., VA--Minor family papers, 1830-1887. /Series E, Part 1, Roll 36/

Augusta co., VA--Lewis family papers, 1749-1920. /Series M, Part 6, Roll 4/

Augusta co., VA--George N. Thrift papers, 1857-1860. /Series F, Part 3, Roll 35/

Bedford co., VA--John Buford papers, 1804-1898. /Series F, Part 3, Roll 34/

Bedford co., VA--Peachy Ridgway Gilmer papers, 1790-1889. /Series M, Part 4, Roll 12/

Bedford co., VA--John Hook letters & papers, 1774-1808. /Series E, Part 3, Roll 4/

Berkeley co., VA--Battaile Muse papers, 1731-1891. /Series F, Part 3, Rolls 20-29/

Brunswick co., VA--Gilliam family papers, 1794-1865. /Series E, Part 2, Rolls 19-21/

Brunswick co., VA--Tucker family papers, 1814-1835. /Series E, Part 1, Roll 38/

Buckingham co., VA--Austin-Twyman papers, 1765-1939. /Series L, Part 4, Rolls 1-35/

Buckingham co., VA--Bolling family papers, 1748-1956. /Series M, Part 5, Rolls 9-10/

Buckingham co., VA--Linnaeus Bolling diary, 1821-22. /Series M, Part 5, Roll 8/

Buckingham co., VA--Harrison family papers, 1725-1907. /Series M, Part 5, Rolls 28-31/

Buckingham co., VA--Hubard family papers, 1781-1869, 1741-1865. /Series E, Part 1, Rolls 29-34 & Series J, Part 10, Rolls 1-26/

Buckingham co., VA--S. W. Marshall account book, 1855-1857. /Series M, Part 5, Roll 35/

Campbell co., VA--John Davis letters & papers, 1859-1860. /Series E, Part 3, Roll 4/

Campbell co., VA--Ann D. Thompson papers, 1847-1852. /Series E, Part 3, Roll 1/

Caroline co., VA--Berkeley family papers, 1536-1868. /Series E, Part 2, Rolls 1-18/

Caroline co., VA--Woolfolk family papers, 1780-1936. /Series M, Part 3, Rolls 34-36/

Charles City co., VA--Byrd fam. papers, 1757-1867. /Series M, Part 3, Rolls 4-5/

Charles City co., VA--Douthat family papers, 1795-1922. /Series M, Part 3, Rolls 7-9/

Charles City co., VA--Jerdone family papers, 1623-1918. /Series L, Part 2, Rolls 1-12/

Charles City co., VA--Selden family papers, 1811-1868. /Series M, Part 3, Roll 33/

Charles City co., VA--Shirley plantation journal, 1650-1888. /Series C, Part 1, Roll 1 & Series K, Rolls 1-26/

Charles City co., VA--Henry Wills account book, 1782-1795. /Series M, Part 3, Roll 34/

Charlotte co., VA--Claiborne Barksdale account books, 1843-1851. /Series M, Part 5, Roll 1/

Charlotte co., VA--Bruce family papers, 1792-1860 & 1625-1926. /Series C, Part 1, Rolls 7-8 & Series M, Part 5, Rolls 10-14/

Charlotte co., VA--Hannah family papers, 1760-1967. /Series M, Part 5, Rolls 21-28/

Charlotte co., VA--Harris family papers, 1838-1880. /Series E, Part 3, Roll 4/

Charlotte co., VA--Henry family papers, 1763-1920. /Series M, Part 5, Roll 34/

Charlotte co., VA--William Huntington papers, 1808-1856. /Series M, Part 5, Roll 35/

Charlotte co., VA--Jonathan Read account book, 1785-1788. /Series M, Part 5, Roll 48/

Charlotte co., VA--George J. Roberts account book, 1835-1850. /Series M, Part 5, Roll 48/

Charlotte co., VA--Selden family papers, 1811-1868. /Series M, Part 3, Roll 33/

Chesterfield co., VA--Wm. Bolling diary, 1794-95. /Series M, Part 5, Roll 9/

Chesterfield co., VA--Blair Burwell & Co. letterbook, 1834-1840. /Series M, Part 5, Roll 15/

Chesterfield co., VA--Gilliam family papers, 1794-1865. /Series E, Part 2, Rolls 19-21/

Chesterfield co., VA--Harrison family papers, 1768-1908. /Series M, Part 5, Roll 28/

Chesterfield co., VA--Pegram-Johnson-McIntosh family papers, 1825-1941. /Series M, Part 5, Rolls 47-48/

Chesterfield co., VA--Francis G. Ruffin papers, 1802-1860. /Series J, Part 9, Rolls 30-32/

Culpeper co., VA--Hill family papers, 1787-1945. /Series M, Part 4, Rolls 14-17/

Culpeper co., VA--Morton-Halsey family papers, 1822-1865. /Series E, Part 1, Roll 37/

Culpeper co., VA--Battaile Muse papers, 1731-1891. /Series F, Part 3, Rolls 20-29/

Culpeper co., VA--Phillip Slaughter diaries, 1796-1848. /Series E, Part 1, Roll 38/

Cumberland co., VA--Boatwright family papers, 1815-1953. /Series M, Part 5, Roll 8/

Cumberland co., VA--Linnaeus Bolling diary, 1821-22. /Series M, Part 5, Roll 8/

Cumberland co., VA--Eggleston family papers, 1777-1899. /Series M, Part 5, Roll 20/

Cumberland co., VA--Joseph Norton Goodman commonplace book, 1834-1879. /Series M, Part 5, Roll 20/

Cumberland co., VA--Harrison family papers, 1725-1907. /Series M, Part 5, Rolls 28-33/

Cumberland co., VA--Palmore family papers, 1781-1865. /Series E, Part 1, Rolls 35-36/

Dinwiddie co., VA--Gilliam family papers, 1794-1865 & 1851-1876. /Series E, Part 2, Rolls 19-21 & Series F, Part 3, Roll 32/

Dinwiddie co., VA--Francis E. Rives papers, 1817-1848. /Series F, Part 3, Roll 33/

Dinwiddie co., VA--Robert Walker account book, 1794-1830. /Series M, Part 5, Roll 49/

Doddridge co., VA--Geo. N. Thrift papers, 1857-1860. /Series F, Part 3, Roll 35/

Essex co., VA--Landon Carter papers, 1763-1774. /Series M, Part 2, Roll 6/

Essex co., VA--Garnett ledgers, 1794-1851. /Series E, Part 1, Roll 3/

Essex co., VA--James Mercer Garnett papers, 1824-1836. /Series M, Part 3, Roll 18/

Essex co., VA--Hunter family papers, 1766-1918. /Series M, Part 3, Rolls 18-25/
Essex co., VA--Mitchell ledgers, 1794-1851. /Series E, Part 1, Roll 3/
Fairfax co., VA--Custis family papers, 1683-1858. /Series M, Part 2, Rolls 6-8/
Fairfax co., VA--Fairfax family papers, 1756-1787. /Series M, Part 2, Roll 9/
Fairfax co., VA--John Augustine Washington papers, 1824-1860. /Series M, Part 6, Roll 14/
Fauquier co., VA--Clover Hill account book, 1810-1822. /Series M, Part 6, Rolls 1-2/
Fauquier co., VA--Fiery Run Mills account books, 1831-1834. /Series M, Part 6, Roll 2/
Fauquier co., VA--Keith family papers, 1710-1979. /Series M, Part 6, Rolls 3-4/
Fauquier co., VA--Richard Lewis account book, 1859-1862. /Series M, Part 6, Roll 4/
Fauquier co., VA--Millford Mill account book, 1822, 1823-1829, 1834. /Series M, Part 6, Roll 5/
Fauquier co., VA--Battaile Muse papers, 1731-1891. /Series F, Part 3, Rolls 20-29/
Fauquier co., VA--Register of Free Negroes, 1817-1865. /Series M, Part 6, Roll 2/
Fauquier co., VA--Turner family papers, 1740-1927. /Series M, Part 6, Rolls 7-14/
Fauquier co., VA--Thomas Thornton Withers account book, 1844-1862. /Series M, Part 6, Roll 14/
Fluvanna co., VA--Fontaine Humphrey papers, 1819-1831. /Series E, Part 1, Roll 39/
Franklin co., VA--Dickinson family papers, 1818-1860. /Series E, Part 3, Roll 4/
Franklin co., VA--Holland family papers, 1832-1884. /Series E, Part 3, Roll 4/
Franklin co., VA--Bowker Preston papers, 1819-1855. /Series E, Part 3, Roll 3/
Frederick co., VA--Buck family papers, 1822-1888. /Series E, Part 1, Rolls 7-11/
Frederick co., VA--Robert Carter papers, 1772-1794. /Series F, Part 3, Rolls 29-32/
Frederick co., VA--Thomas Massie papers, 1773-1798. /Series M, Part 4, Roll 39/
Frederick co., VA--Battaile Muse papers, 1731-1891. /Series F, Part 3, Rolls 20-29/
Gloucester co., VA--Harrison family papers, 1662-1915. /Series M, Part 3, Rolls 28-32/

Goochland co., VA--William Bolling papers, 1724-1883 & 1794-95,1809, 1827-28, 1836-39, 1840-42. /Series F, Part 3, Rolls 35-37 & Series M, Part 5, Roll 9/

Goochland co., VA--William Bolling slave register, 1752-1890. /Series M, Part 5, Roll 9/

Goochland co., VA--Ann (Powell) Burwell commonplace book, 1746-1839. /Series M, Part 5, Roll 14/

Goochland co., VA--Harrison family papers, 1725-1907. /Series M, Part 5, Rolls 28-33/

Goochland co., VA--John Coles Rutherford diary, 1847. /Series M, Part 4, Roll 49/

Goochland co., VA--Hezekiah Lord Wight papers, 1794-1854. /Series M, Part 4, Roll 59/

Greensville co., VA--Mason family papers, 1789-1965. /Series M, Part 5, Rolls 36-46/

Halifax co., VA--Papers on Slavery, 1801-1859. /Series E, Part 3, Roll 5/

Halifax co., VA--Bailey family papers, 1824-1886. /Series M, Part 5, Roll 1/

Halifax co., VA--William Bailey papers, 1800-1888. /Series E, Part 1, Roll 1/

Halifax co., VA--Barksdale family papers, 1782-1900. /Series E, Part 3, Roll 1-2 & Series F, Part 3, Roll 33/

Halifax co., VA--John Bennett papers, 1827-1880. /Series M, Part 5, Roll 8/

Halifax co., VA--Bruce family papers, 1746-1871 & 1625-1926. /Series E, Part 3, Rolls 7-30 & Series M, Part 5, Rolls 10-14/

Halifax co., VA--Cole family papers, 1859-1861. /Series E. Part 3, Roll 1/

Halifax co., VA--Coleman family papers, 1842-1887. /Series E, Part 3, Roll 1 & Series D, Roll 12/

Halifax co., VA--Dabney Cosby papers, 1830-1854. /Series E, Part 3, Roll 4/

Halifax co., VA--Crenshaw & Miller family papers, 1751-1916. /Series Roll 16/

Halifax co., VA--Hairston & Wilson papers, 1800-1895. /Series J, Part 11, Rolls 1-3/

Halifax co., VA--Howerton family papers, 1817-1858. /Series J, Part 9, Rolls 17-18/

Halifax co., VA--Hubbard family papers, 1811-1868. /Series E. Part 3, Roll 3/

Halifax co., VA--Ragsdale family papers, 1835-1884. /Series M, Part 5, Roll 48/

Halifax co., VA--Richard Randolph papers, 1836-1845. /Series E, Part 3, Roll 3/

Halifax co., VA--Spragins family papers, 1814-1849. /Series E, Part 3, Roll 1/

Halifax co., VA--Watlington family papers, 1803-1814. /Series E. Part 3, Roll 1/

Hanover co., VA--Bassett family papers, 1650-1923. /Series M, Part 3, Rolls 1-4/

Hanover co., VA--Robert Carter Berkeley diary, 1826. /Series M, Part 4, Roll 6/

Hanover co., VA--William Chamberlayne papers, 1766-1831. /Series M, Part 3, Roll 5/
Hanover co., VA--Eliz. E. Cooke diary, 1855-1858. /Series E, Part 1, Roll 39/
Hanover co., VA--Crenshaw & Miller family papers, 1751-1916. /Series Roll 16/
Hanover co., VA--Henry Curtis papers, 1774-1865. /Series M, Part 4, Roll 7/
Hanover co., VA--Dabney fam. papers, 1742-1928. /Series M, Part 4, Rolls 7-12/
Hanover co., VA--Fredericks Hall Plantation books, 1727-1863. /Series J, Part 9, Rolls 6-10/
Hanover co., VA--Harrison family papers, 1662-1915 & 1756-1893. /Series M, Part 3, Rolls 28-32 & Series M, Part 5, Rolls 32-33/
Hanover co., VA--Jerdone fam. papers, 1623-1918. /Series L, Part 2, Rolls 1-12/
Hanover co., VA--Ruffin & Meade papers, 1796-1906. /Series J, Part 9, Rolls 28-30/
Hanover co., VA--Edmund Ruffin papers, 1794-1865. /Series M, Part 4, Rolls 46-49/
Hanover co., VA--Edmund Ruffin, Jr. plantation diary, 1851-1873. /Series J, Part 9, Roll 28/
Hanover co., VA--Francis Gildart Ruffin papers, 1802-1860. /Series J, Part 9, Rolls 30-32/
Hanover co., VA--James Sheppard papers, 1830-1889. /Series F, Part 1, Rolls 22-23/
Hanover co., VA--Wickham family papers, 1754-1977. /Series M, Part 4, Rolls 55-59/
Henrico co., VA--Adams family papers, 1672-1792. /Series M, Part 4, Roll 1/
Henrico co., VA--Thomas Edward Cox books, 1829-1854. /Series J, Part 9, Rolls 15-16/
Henrico co., VA--Gooch family papers, 1812-1961. /Series M, Part 4, Rolls 12-14/
Henrico co., VA--Thos. Mann Randolph papers, 1815-1824. /Series M, Part 4, Roll 45/
Henrico co., VA--William B. Randolph papers, 1696-1884 & 1815-1835. /Series C, Part 1, Rolls 2-7 & Series M, Part 4, Roll 45/
Henrico co., VA--Wm. N. Whiting diary, 1833-1848. /Series M, Part 3, Roll 34/
Henrico co., VA--Wickham family papers, 1766-1945. /Series M, Part 4, Rolls 51-55/
Henry co., VA--Peachy Ridgway Gilmer papers, 1790-1889. /Series M, Part 4, Roll 12/
Henry co., VA--Hairston & Wilson family papers, 1800-1895. /Series J, Part 11, Rolls 1-3/

Henry co., VA--Elizabeth Seawell Hairston papers, 1805-1865. /Series J, Part 11, Roll 1/

Henry co., VA--Peter Wilson Hairston papers, 1773-1877. /Series J, Part 11, Rolls 5-8/

Hopewell, VA--Eppes family muniments, 1806-1948. /Series M, Part 3, Rolls 9-18/

James City co., VA--John Ambler family papers, 1767-1887. /Series E, Part 1, Rolls 5-7/

James City co., VA--Custis fam. papers, 1683-1858. /Series M, Part 2, Rolls 6-8/

James City co., VA--Lee fam. papers, 1638-1867. /Series M, Part 2, Rolls 9-13/

King and Queen co., VA--George E. Grymes journal, 1855-1857. /Series E, Part 1, Roll 38/

King and Queen co., VA--John Walker papers, 1824-1844, ca. 1956. /Series J, Part 9, Rolls 32-33/

King George co., VA--Hooe-Harrison letters, 1832-1836. /Series E, Part 1, Roll 36/

King George co., VA--Tayloe family papers, 1708-1949. /Series E, Part 1, Rolls 3-5 & Series M, Part 1, Rolls 1-57/

King William co., VA--Berkeley family papers, 1536-1868. /Series E, Part 2, Rolls 1-18/

King William co., VA--Charles W. Dabney papers, 1716-1865. /Series J, Part 9, Rolls 1-5/

King William co., VA--Cornelius Dabney diary, 1863-1869. /Series J, Part 9, Roll 18/

King William co., VA--Gwathmey papers, 1790-1982. /Series M, Part 3, Rolls 25- 28/

King William co., VA--Leigh family papers, 1794-1893. /Series M, Part 3, Roll 32/

Lancaster co., VA--Carter family papers, 1651-1861, 1722-1782. /Series M, Part 2, Rolls 1-6 & Series E, Part 1, Rolls 18 & 39/

Loudoun co., VA--Berkeley family papers, 1536-1868. /Series E, Part 2, Rolls 1-18/

Loudoun co., VA--George Carter letterbook, 1807-1819. /Series M, Part 6, Roll 1/

Loudoun co., VA--Robert Carter papers, 1772-1794. /Series F, Part 3, Rolls 29-32/

Loudoun co., VA--William Hill Gray diary, 1846-1880. /Series M, Part 6, Roll 2/

Loudoun co., VA--Battaile Muse papers, 1731-1891. /Series F, Part 3, Rolls 20-29/

Louisa co., VA--Charles W. Dabney papers, 1716-1865. /Series J, Part 9, Rolls 1-5/

Louisa co., VA--Fredericks Hall Plantation books, 1727-1863. /Series J, Part 9, Rolls 6-10/

Louisa co., VA--Jeremiah Collins Harris diary, 1851-1860. /Series M, Part 4, Roll 14/

Louisa co., VA--Holladay family papers, 1728-1968. /Series M, Part 4, Rolls 18-38/

Louisa co., VA--Jerdone family papers, 1623-1918. /Series L, Part 2, Rolls 1 - 12/

Louisa co., VA--Watson family papers, 1750-1866 & 1771-1934. /Series E, Part 1, Rolls 19-29 & Series M, Part 4, Rolls 49-51/

Lunenburg co., VA--William Haynie Hatchett diary, 1853-1855. /Series M, Part 5, Roll 33/

Madison co., VA--Hill family papers, 1787-1945. /Series M, Part 4, Rolls 14-17/

Mecklenburg co., VA--Baskerville family papers, 1747-1928. /Series M, Part 5, Rolls 2-8/

Mecklenburg co., VA--John Bennett papers, 1827-1880. /Series M, Part 5, Roll 8/

Mecklenburg co., VA--Burwell family papers, 1750-1943 & 1813-1928. /Series J, Part 9, Rolls 10-15 & Series M, Part 5, Rolls 15-16/

Mecklenburg co., VA--R. H. Moody papers, 1864-1870. /Series E, Part 3, Roll 3/

Mecklenburg co., VA--E. H. Riggan account book, 1846-1870. /Series J, Part 9, Roll 27/

Mecklenburg co., VA--Skipwith family papers, 1760-1977. /Series L, Part 3, Rolls 1-14/

Mecklenburg co., VA--Tarry family papers, 1765-1915. /Series M, Part 5, Roll 49/

Mecklenburg co., VA--Wimbish family papers, 1838-1913. /Series M, Part 5, Roll 50/

Middlesex co., VA--Berkeley family papers, 1536-1868. /Series E, Part 2, Rolls 1-18/

Middlesex co., VA--Harrison family papers, 1662-1915 & 1768-1908. /Series M, Part 3, Rolls 28-32 & Series M, Part 5, Roll 28/

Middlesex co., VA--Ralph Wormeley letterbook, 1783-1952. /Series M, Part 3, Roll 36/

Nansemond co., VA--John C. Cohoon account book, 1810-1860. /Series E, Part 1, Roll 39/

Nelson co., VA--Wm. Cabell commonplace books, 1769-1822. /Series M, Part 4, Roll 6/
Nelson co., VA--Gordon family papers, 1807-1865. /Series E, Part 1, Rolls 34-35/
Nelson co., VA--Hubard fam. papers, 1781-1869. /Series E, Part 1, Rolls 29-34/
Nelson co., VA--Massie family papers, 1698-1900. /Series M, Part 4, Rolls 39-45/
Nelson co., VA--William Massie family papers, 1747-1882. /Series G, Part 2, Rolls 1-45/
Nelson co., VA--Floyd L. Whitehead papers, 1814-1863, 1830-1886. /Series F, Part 3, Roll 35 & Series J, Part 9, Roll 33/
New Kent co., VA--Bassett fam. papers, 1650-1923. /Series M, Part 3, Rolls 1-4/
New Kent co., VA--William Chamberlayne papers, 1766-1831. /Series M, Part 3, Roll 5/
New Kent co., VA--Custis family papers, 1683-1858. /Series M, Part 2, Rolls 6-8/
New Kent co., VA--Jerdone family papers, 1623-1918. /Series L, Part 2, Rolls 1-12/
New Kent co., VA--William Massie account books, 1748-1749. /Series M, Part 4, Roll 39/
Norfolk co., VA--Wm. N. Whiting diary, 1833-1848. /Series M, Part 3, Roll 34/
Northumberland co., VA--Robert Carter papers, 1772-1794. /Series F, Part 3, Rolls 29-32/
Orange co., VA--Barbour family papers, 1785-1941 & 1741-1890. /Series E, Part 2, Rolls 21-24 & Series M, Part 4, Rolls 1-6/
Orange co., VA--Hawfield Plantation books, 1851-1868. /Series E, Part 1, Roll 39/
Orange co., VA--Horace Dade Taliaferro diary, 1847-1860. /Series M, Part 4, Roll 49/
Orange co., VA--George N. Thrift papers, 1857-1860. /Series F, Part 3, Roll 35/
Patrick co., VA--Elizabeth Seawell Hairston papers, 1805-1865. /Series J, Part 11, Roll 1/
Patrick co., VA--Peter Wilson Hairston papers, 1773-1877. /Series J, Part 11, Rolls 5-8/
Petersburg, VA--Cocke family papers, 1742-1976. /Series M, Part 5, Roll 20/
Petersburg, VA--Ruffin & Meade papers, 1796-1906. /Series J, Part 9, Rolls 28-30/
Petersburg, VA--Danridge Spotswood diary, 1848. /Series M, Part 4, Roll 49/
Petersburg, VA--John Vaughan Willcox accounts, 1828-1833. /Series M, Part 5, Roll 49/
Pittsylvania co., VA--Bruce family papers, 1746-1871. /Series E, Part 3, Rolls 7-30/

Pittsylvania co., VA--H. C. Callaway papers, 1788-1826. /Series E, Part 1, Roll 17/

Pittsylvania co., VA--Crenshaw & Miller family papers, 1751-1916. /Series Roll 16/

Pittsylvania co., VA--Finney family papers, 1849-1876. /Series E, Part 3, Roll 4 & Series F, Part 3, Roll 34/

Pittsylvania co., VA--John Guerrant papers, 1847-1871. /Series E, Part 3, Roll 4/

Pittsylvania co., VA--George Hairston papers, 1779-1950. /Series J, Part 11, Roll 4/

Pittsylvania co., VA--Robert Hairston papers, 1799-1862. /Series J, Part 11, Roll 9/

Pittsylvania co., VA--Daniel Johns papers, 1840-1849. /Series E, Part 3, Roll 3/

Pittsylvania co., VA--Jones family papers, 1826-1863. /Series E, Part 3, Roll 3/

Pittsylvania co., VA--Mitchell family papers, 1834-1875. /Series E, Part 3, Rolls 3 & Series F, Part 3, Roll 34/

Pittsylvania co., VA--Muse family papers, 1864-1877. /Series E, Part 3, Roll 3/

Pittsylvania co., VA--Pocket Plantation papers, 1748-1859. /Series E, Part 1, Rolls 11-16/

Pittsylvania co., VA--Langhorne Scruggs papers, 1840-1901. /Series E, Part 3, Roll 3/

Pittsylvania co., VA--W. E. Sims letters, 1871-1872. /Series E, Part 3, Roll 3/

Pittsylvania co., VA--Wm. Tunstall papers, 1800-1849. /Series E, Part 3, Roll 1/

Pittsylvania co., VA--James Whittle papers, 1837-1884. /Series E, Part 3, Roll 1/

Pittsylvania co., VA--Robt. Wilson account bks., 1799-1822. /Series J, Part 11, Rolls 9-22/

Pittsylvania co., VA--Jos. Wright et al. papers, 1846-1878. /Series E, Part 3, Roll 1/

Powhatan co., VA--Bolling family papers, 1748-1956. /Series M, Part 5, Rolls 9-10/

Prince Edward co., VA--Wm. Bolling diary, 1794-95. /Series M, Part 5, Roll 9/

Prince Edward co., VA--Cocke family papers, 1742-1976. /Series M, Part 5, Roll 20/

Prince Edward co., VA--John Peter Mettauer papers, 1812-1858. /Series M, Part 5, Roll 47/

Prince George co., VA--Friend family papers, 1792-1871. /Series M, Part 3, Roll 18/

Prince George co., VA--Harrison family papers, 1771-1931. /Series M, Part 5, Roll 33/

Prince George co., VA--Ruffin & Meade papers, 1796-1906. /Series J, Part 9, Rolls 28-30/

Prince George co., VA--Edmund Ruffin papers, 1794-1865. /Series M, Part 4, Rolls 46-49/

Prince George co., VA--Edmund Ruffin, Jr. plantation diary, 1851-1873. /Series J, Part 9, Roll 28/

Prince George co., VA--John Vaughan Willcox accounts, 1828-1833. /Series M, Part 5, Roll 49/

Prince William co., VA--Berkeley family papers, 1536-1868. /Series E, Part 2, Rolls 1-18/

Prince William co., VA--Edmund Berkeley accounts, 1848-1860. /Series M, Part 6, Roll 1/

Prince William co., VA--Robert Carter papers, 1772-1794. /Series F, Part 3, Rolls 29-32/

Prince William co., VA--Tayloe family papers, 1708-1861. /Series M, Part 1, Rolls 1-57/

Richmond, VA--American Colonization Society, Virginia Branch minute book, 1823-1859. /Series M, Part 4, Roll 1/

Richmond, VA--Joseph Dickinson papers, 1848-1858. /Series F, Part 3, Roll 35/

Richmond, VA--D. M. Pulliam papers, 1845-1858. /Series F, Part 3, Roll 35/

Richmond, VA--Richmond City Sergeant papers, 1841-51. /Series M, Part 4, Rolls 45-46/

Richmond, VA--Horace Dade Taliaferro diary, 1847-1860. /Series M, Part 4, Roll 49/

Richmond, VA--Watson fam. papers, 1771-1934. /Series M, Part 4, Rolls 49-51/

Richmond co., VA--Carter papers, 1667-1862. /Series L, Part 1, Rolls 1-18/

Richmond co., VA--Landon Carter papers, 1763-1774. /Series M, Part 2, Roll 6/

Richmond co., VA--Robert Carter papers, 1772-1794. /Series F, Part 3, Rolls 29-32/

Richmond co., VA--Tayloe family papers, 1708-1861. /Series M, Part 1, Rolls 1-57/

Roanoke co., VA--Bruce family papers, 1746-1871. /Series E, Part 3, Rolls 7-30/

Roanoke co., VA--Joseph Norton Goodman commonplace book, 1834-1879. /Series M, Part 5, Roll 20/

Rockbridge co., VA--McDowell family papers, 1777-1963, /Series M, Part 6, Rolls 4-5/

Rockbridge co., VA--James McDowell papers, 1767-1858 & 1770-1915. /Series F, Part 3, Rolls 37-38 & Series J, Part 9, Rolls 19-27/

Rockbridge co., VA--Wm. Massie papers, 1747-1865. /Series G, Part 2, Rolls 1-45/

Rockingham co., VA--Lewis family papers, 1749-1920. /Series M, Part 6, Roll 4/

Shenandoah co., VA--John W. Rice account book, 1856-1866. /Series M, Part 6, Roll 6/

Southampton co., VA--Daniel William Cobb diary, 1825, 1842-1872. /Series M, Part 3, Rolls 5-7/

Southampton co., VA--Mason family papers, 1789-1965. /Series M, Part 5, Rolls 36-46/

Southampton co., VA--Elliott Lemuel Story diary, 1838-1876. /Series M, Part 3, Roll 33/

Spotsylvania co., VA--Bassett family papers, 1650-1923. /Series M, Part 3, Rolls 1-4/

Spotsylvania co., VA--Harrison family papers, 1768-1908. /Series M, Part 5, Roll 28/

Spotsylvania co., VA--Holladay family papers, 1728-1968. /Series M, Part 4, Rolls 18-38/

Spotsylvania co., VA--Lewis fam. papers, 1804-1884. /Series M, Part 4, Roll 38/

Spotsylvania co., VA--Llangollen School recs., 1806-1849. /Series M, Part 4, Rolls 38-39/

Spotsylvania co., VA--Spotswood family papers, 1741-1953. /Series M, Part 4, Roll 49/

Stafford co., VA--Henry Fitzhugh papers, 1746-1789. /Series F, Part 3, Roll 29/

Stafford co., VA--Wm. Fitzhugh letterbook, 1679-1699. /Series M, Part 6, Roll 2/

Stafford co., VA--Mercer family papers, 1656-1869. /Series M, Part 2, Rolls 13-15/

Surry co., VA--Gilliam family papers, 1794-1865. /Series E, Part 2, Rolls 19-21/

Sussex co., VA--Gilliam family papers, 1794-1865. /Series E, Part 2, Rolls 19-21/

Westmoreland co., VA--Carter family papers, 1651-1861. /Series M, Part 2, Rolls 1-6/

Westmoreland co., VA--Robert Carter papers, 1772-1794 & 1760-1815. /Series F, Part 3, Rolls 29-32 & Series M, Part 2, Roll 6/

Westmoreland co., VA--Lee family papers, 1638-1867. /Series M, Part 2, Rolls 9-13/

Westmoreland co., VA--Peckatone Plantation papers, 1758-1898. /Series M, Part 2, Rolls 15-17/

York co., VA--Fredericks Hall Plantation books, 1727-1863. /Series J, Part 9, Rolls 6-10/

York co., VA--Jerdone family papers, 1623-1918. /Series L, Part 2, Rolls 1-12/

Records of the Assistant Commissioner for the State of Virginia, Bureau of Refugees, Freedmen, and Abandoned Lands, 1865-1869. Washington, DC: National Archives and Records Service, 1977. Microcopy M1048. Letters and Telegrams Received. Northern Charitable Societies. Federal Agencies. U.S. Army. Records relating to Destitute Freedmen. Narrative Reports of Overseers of the Poor. Lists of Destitute Freedmen. /Microfilm Rolls 7-40, 57, 58/

Records of the Superintendent of Education for the State of Virginia, Bureau of Refugees, Freedmen, and Abandoned Lands, 1865-1870. Washington, DC: National Archives and Records Service, 1977. Microcopy 1053. Teachers' Monthly School Reports. Register of Teachers to Whom Blank Forms and Envelopes Were Sent. /Microfilm Roll 20/

Reese, Margaret C. *Abstracts of Augusta County, Virginia Death Registers, 1853-1896.* Waynesboro, VA: M. C. Reese, 1983. 218p. /GC 975.501 Au4re/

Registers of Free Negroes Commencing September Court 1822, Book No. 2 and Register of Free Blacks 1835, Book No. 3. Fairfax, VA: Office of Comprehensive Planning, History Section, 1977. 292p. Index. /GC 975.501 F16v/

Rozbicki, Micha. *The Complete Colonial Gentleman: Cultural Legitimacy in Plantation America.* Charlottesville, VA: University Press of Virginia, 1998. Bibliography. Illustrations. Index. /GC 975.5 R817c/

Sidbury, James. *Ploughshares into Swords: Race, Rebellion, and Identity in Gabriel's Virginia, 1730–1810.* New York: Cambridge University Press, 1997. 292p. Appendix. Index. Notes. /GC 975.5 Si13p/

Slave Schedules for 1850–Virginia. Washington, DC: National Archives and Records Administration, 1964. Microcopy 432. /Microfilm Rolls 983-993/

Slave Schedules for 1860–Virginia. Washington, DC: National Archives and Records Administration, 1967. Microcopy 653. /Microfilm Rolls 1386-1397/

Slavery in Ante-Bellum Southern Industries. Frederick, MD: University Publications of America, 199-.

Virginia--Preston Davie papers, 1627-1846. /Series B, Part 1, Roll 5/

Virginia--Hawkins family papers, 1738-1865. /Series B, Rolls 8-21/

Alexandria, VA--Walker & McCollam records, 1858-1859. /Series C, Part 2, Roll 42/

Amherst co., VA--Cabell family papers, 1774-1941. /Series C, Part 2, Rolls 4-6/

Appomattox co., VA--Upper Appomattox County papers, 1796-1935. /Series C, Part 2, Rolls 39-42/

Augusta co., VA--Preston family papers, 1727-1896. /Series C, Part 1, Rolls 5-16/

Botetourt co., VA--Francis Thomas Anderson papers, 1828-1915. /Series A, Roll 28/

Botetourt co., VA--Edmundson family papers, 1781-1953. /Series C, Part 2, Rolls 7-11/

Botetourt co., VA--James River Company account book, 1785-1789. /Series C, Part 2, Roll 11/

Botetourt co., VA--Preston family papers, 1727-1896. /Series C, Part 1, Rolls 5-16/

Buckingham co., VA--Alcinda Gold Mining Company, 1839. /Series C, Part 1, Roll 1/

Campbell co., VA--David Ross letterbook, 1812-1813. /Series C, Part 1, Roll 17/

Charlotte co., VA--George J. Roberts account book, 1835-1850. /Series C, Part 2, Roll 39/

Charlotte co., VA--William Joseph Turner account book, 1851-1852. /Series C, Part 2, Roll 39/

Chesterfield co., VA--William Gray papers, 1819-1875. /Series C, Part 2, Rolls 21-36/

Chesterfield co., VA--Jeremiah T. Jones papers, 1841-1878. /Series A, Roll 4/
Chesterfield co., VA--Tompkins family papers, 1792-1869. /Series C, Part 1, Rolls 17-24/
Cumberland co., VA--Upper Appomattox County papers, 1796-1935. /Series C, Part 2, Rolls 39-42/
Dinwiddie co., VA--Peter McEnery papers, 1830-1895. /Series C, Part 2, Rolls 36-38/
Fairfax co., VA--Rosseau account book, 1855-1857. /Series C, Part 2, Roll 39/
Fauquier co., VA--Daniel Anderson account books, 1833-1855. /Series C, Part 2, Roll 20/
Fredericksburg, VA--Peck, Welford & Company papers, 1834-1844. /Series C, Part 2, Roll 39/
Goochland co., VA--Tompkins family papers, 1792-1869. /Series C, Part 1, Rolls 17-24/
Hanover co., VA--Benjamin Brand papers, 1779-1863. /Series C, Part 1, Rolls 1-4/
Hanover co., VA--Bickerton Lyle Winston ledger, 1846-1859. /Series C, Part 1, Roll 26/
King George co., VA--Quesenberry family papers, 1827-1913. /Series C, Part 2, Roll 39/
Lynchburg, VA--Thomas J. Shaw papers, 1818-1914. /Series C, Part 2, Rolls 11-12
Mathews co., VA--James Foster papers, 1796-1832. /Series C, Part 2, Roll 21/
Mathews co., VA--Tompkins family papers, 1792-1877. /Series C, Part 1, Rolls 17-26/
Montgomery co., VA--Edmundson family papers, 1781-1953. /Series C, Part 2, Rolls 7-11/
Montgomery co., VA--James River Company account book, 1785-1789. /Series C, Part 2, Roll 11/
Montgomery co., VA--Preston family papers, 1727-1896. /Series C, Part 1, Rolls 5-16/
Nansemond co., VA--Dismal Swamp Land Company records, 1688-1879. /Series A, Rolls 14-22/
Nansemond co., VA--Andrew Talcott letterbook, 1825-1828. /Series C, Part 2, Roll 12/
Nelson co., VA--Cabell family papers, 1774-1941. /Series C, Part 2, Rolls 4-6/
Norfolk co., VA--Allmand family papers, 1796-1891. /Series C, Part 2, Rolls 19-20/

Norfolk co., VA--Andrew Talcott letterbook, 1825-1828. /Series C, Part 2, Roll 12/
Norfolk co., VA--Frederick Williams papers, 1800-1880. /Series C, Part 2, Roll 42/
Nottoway co., VA--Richard Eggleston Hardaway account book, 1825-1864. /Series C, Part 2, Roll 26/
Orange co., VA--Thomas J. Shaw papers, 1818-1914. /Series C, Part 2, Rolls 11-12/
Page co., VA--George J. Adams papers, 1858-1859. /Series C, Part 1, Roll 1/
Petersburg, VA--Bolling family papers, 1785-1875. /Series C, Part 2, Roll 4/
Petersburg, VA--Peter McEnery papers, 1830-1895. /Series C, Part 2, Rolls 36-38/
Petersburg, VA--Upper Appomattox County papers, 1796-1935. /Series C, Part 2, Rolls 39-42/
Powhatan co., VA--Wm. B. Phillips papers, 1854-1861. /Series C, Part 1, Roll 5/
Prince Edward co., VA--Upper Appomattox County papers, 1796-1935. /Series C, Part 2, Rolls 39-42/
Richmond, VA--Edward R. Archer papers, 1861-1863. /Series C, Part 1, Roll 1/
Richmond, VA--Henry Banks papers, 1781-1817. /Series C, Part 2, Rolls 1-4/
Richmond, VA--Benjamin Brand papers, 1779-1863. /Series C, Part 1, Rolls 1-4/
Richmond, VA--John Gault letter, 1853. /Series C, Part 2, Roll 21/
Richmond, VA--William Gray papers, 1819-1875. /Series C, Part 2, Rolls 21-36/
Richmond, VA--Peter McEnery papers, 1830-1895. /Series C, Part 2, Rolls 36-38/
Richmond, VA--David Ross letterbook, 1812-1813. /Series C, Part 1, Roll 17/
Richmond, VA--Talbott & Brother papers, 1831-1880. /Series C, Part 1, Roll 17/
Richmond, VA--Talcott family papers, 1814-1915. /Series C, Part 2, Rolls 12-19/
Richmond, VA--Tompkins family papers, 1792-1877. /Series C, Part 1, Rolls 17-26/
Rockbridge co., VA--William Weaver papers, 1809-1885 & 1786-1980. /Series A, Rolls 22-28 & Series C, Part 1, Roll 26/
Shenandoah co., VA--Ridwell furnace daybook & account book, 1805-1809 & 1791-1816. /Series B, Rolls 22-27 & Series C, Part 1, Rolls 16-17/
Stafford co., VA--Edrington family papers, 1766-1967. /Series C, Part 2, Rolls 20-21/
Suffolk, VA--Dismal Swamp Land Company records, 1688-1879. /Series A, Rolls 14-22/
Westmoreland co., VA--Quesenberry family papers, 1827-1913. /Series C, Part 2, Roll 39/

Stevenson, Brenda E. *Life in Black and White: Family and Community in the Slave South.* New York: Oxford University Press, 1996. 457p. Appendices. Bibliography. Index. Notes. Photographs. /GC 975.501 L92st/

Takagi, Midori. *"Rearing Wolves to Our Own Destruction:" Slavery in Richmond, Virginia, 1782-1865.* Charlottesville, VA: University Press of Virginia, 1999. 187p. Bibliography. Illustrations. Index. Maps. Notes. /GC 975.502 R41sy/

Tragle, Henry Irving. *The Southampton Slave Revolt of 1831: A Compilation of Source Material.* 489p. Bibliography. Documents. /GC 975.501 So8t/

Virginia Slave-Trade Statistics, 1698-1775. Richmond, VA: The Virginia State Library, 1984. 218p. Appendices. Index. /GC 975.5 M66v/

Walsh, Lorena Seebach. *From Calabar to Carter's Grove: The History of a Virginia Slave Community.* Charlottesville, VA: University Press of Virginia, 1997. Appendices. Bibliography. Drawings. Index. Maps. Notes. Photographs. /GC 975.501 Y82wl/

Weevils in the Wheat: Interviews with Virginia Ex-Slaves. Bloomington, IN: Indiana University Press, 1980. 405p. Index. /GC 975.5 W415/

Wynne, Frances Holloway. *Register of Free Negroes and Also of Dower Slaves, Brunswick County, Virginia, 1803-1850.* Fairfax, VA: F. H. Wynne, 1983. 219p. Index. /GC 975.501 B83w/

WASHINGTON

Mumford, Esther Hall. *Seattle's Black Victorians, 1852-1901*. Seattle, WA: Ananse Press, 1980. 235p. Index. Notes. Photographs. /GC 979.702 Ae18m/

Rawick, George P., ed. *The American Slave: A Composite Autobiography–...Washington Narratives*. Westport, CT: Greenwood Publishing Company, 1977. /GC 929.11 Ar486 Sec. 6/

Rawick, George P., ed. *The American Slave: A Composite Autobiography–...Washington Narratives*. Westport, CT: Greenwood Publishing Company, 1979. /GC 929.11 AL113 Sec. 16/

Taylor, Quintard. *The Forging of a Black Community: Seattle's Central District from 1870 through the Civil Rights Era*. Seattle, WA: University of Washington Press, 1994. 330. Appendices. Bibliography. Index. Notes. Photographs. /GC 979.702 Se18t/

WEST VIRGINIA

Colored Marriage Records, 1909-1937. Wellsburg, WV: Genealogical Society of Salt Lake City, 1971. Index. /Microfilm WV Core Collection Brooke County Roll 3/

Records of Ante-Bellum Southern Plantations from the Revolution through the Civil War. Frederick, MD: University Publications of America, Inc., 198-.
Berkeley co., WV--Battaile Muse papers, 1731-1891. /Series F, Part 3, Rolls 20-29/

Doddridge co., WV--George N. Thrift papers, 1857-1860. /Series F, Part 3, Roll 35/

Jefferson co., WV--Blackford family papers, 1836-1858. /Series M, Part 6, Roll 1/

Jefferson co., WV--Franklin Osburn papers, 1849-1875. /Series M, Part 6, Rolls 5-6/

Trotter, Joe William. *Coal, Class, and Color: Blacks in Southern West Virginia, 1915-32*. Urbana, IL: University of Illinois Press, 1990. 290p. Bibliography. Index. Maps. Photographs /GC 975.4 T756c/

WISCONSIN

Cooper, Zachary. *Black Settlers in Rural Wisconsin*. Madison, WI: State Historical Society of Wisconsin, 1977. 27p. Illus. /GC 977.5 C78b/

Egeness, Herbert. *A History of the Negro Community of Pleasant Ridge, Wisconsin*. Stevens Point, WI: University of Wisconsin, 1968. 29p. Bibliography. Notes. /GC 977.501 Io9e/

BAHAMA ISLANDS

Johnson, Howard. *The Bahamas from Slavery to Servitude, 1783-1933*. Gainesville, FL: University Press of Florida, 1996. 218p. Bibliography. Index. /GC 972.96 J63b/

A Relic of Slavery: Farquharson's Journal for 1831-2. Nassau, Bahamas: The Deans Peggs Research Fund, 1957. (Farquharson's Plantation, Watlings Island) 84p. Maps. /GC 972.96 F23r/

Saunders, Gail. *Bahamian Loyalists and Their Slaves*. Basingstoke, BI: Macmillan Publishers, 1984. 81p. Bibliography. Glossary. Notes. Photographs. /GC 972.96 Sa8b/

CANADA

Bell, Dorothy et al. *Canadian Black Studies Bibliography*. S. l.: s. n., 1971. 111p. /GC 971 C1669/

Black Heritage in Bertie Township, Welland County. St. Catharines, Ontario: Niagara Branch, The Ontario Genealogical Society, 1993. 19p. Index. /GC 971.301 W45bl/

Black Heritage in Grantham Township, Lincoln County. St. Catharines, Ontario: Niagara Branch, The Ontario Genealogical Society, 1993. 9p. Index. /GC 971.301 L63bl/

Clairmont, Donald H. and Dennis W. Magill. *Nova Scotian Blacks: An Historical and Structural Overview*. Halifax, Nova Scotia: Institute of Public Affairs, Dalhousie University, 1970. No. 83. 151p. Bibliography. Notes. /GC 971.6 C527n/

French, Gary E. *Men of Colour: An Historical Account of the Black Settlement on Wilberforce Street and in Oro Township, Simcoe County, Ontario, 1819-1949*. Stroud, Ontario: Kaste Books, 1978. 182p. Bibliography. Index. Maps. /GC 971.301 Si4f/

Grant John N. *Black Nova Scotians*. Halifax, Nova Scotia: Nova Scotia Museum, 1980. 47p. Bibliography. Drawings. /GC 971.6 G76b/

Hornby, Jim. *Black Islanders: Prince Edward Island's Historical Black Community*. Charlottetown, Prince Edward Island: Institute of

Island Studies, 1991. 116p. Bibliography. Drawings. Index. Maps. Notes. Photographs. /GC 971.7 H783b/

McKerrow, Peter Evander. *McKerrow, A Brief History of the Coloured Baptists of Nova Scotia, 1783-1895*. 125p. Bibliography. Index. /GC 971.6 M199b/

Meyler, Peter. *A Stolen Life: Searching for Richard Pierpoint*. Toronto, Ontario: Natural Heritage Books, 1999. 141p. Bibliography. Illustrations. Index. Maps. /GC 971.301 W45me/

Pachai, Bridglal. *People of the Maritimes: Blacks*. Tantallon, Nova Scotia: Four East Publications, 1987. 96p. Bibliography. Drawings. Photographs. /GC 971 P115b/

Perry, Charlotte Bronte. *The Long Road: The History of the Coloured Canadian in Windsor, Canada*. Windsor, Ontario: Sumner Printing and Publishing Company, Ltd., 1969. 2nd ed. 211p. Bibliography. Illustrations. /GC 971.33102 W766p V. 1/

Spray, W. A. *The Blacks in New Brunswick*. Fredericton, N.B.: Brunswick Press, 1972. 72p. Appendices. Notes. /GC 971.5 Sp76b/

Thomson, Colin A. *Blacks in Deep Snow: Black Pioneers in Canada*. Don Mills, Ontario: J. M. Dent & Sons, 1979. 112p. Index. Photographs. /GC 971 T382b/

Walker, James W. St. G. *The Black Loyalists: The Search for a Promised Land in Nova Scotia and Sierra Leone, 1783-1870*. New York: Africana Publishing Company, 1976. 438p. Bibliography. Index. /GC 971.6 W15b/

STOCKHOLDERS
OF THE UNDERGROUND
R. R. COMPANY
Hold on to Your Stock!!

The market has an upward tendency. By the express train which arrived this morning at 3 o'clock, fifteen thousand dollars worth of human merchandise, consisting of twenty-nine able-bodied men and women, fresh and sound, from the Carolina and Kentucky plantations, have arrived safe at the depot on the other side, where all our sympathising colonization friends may have an opportunity of expressing their sympathy by bringing forward donations of ploughs, &c., farming utensils, pick axes and hoes, and not old clothes; as these emigrants all can till the soil. N. B.—Stockholders don't forget the meeting to-day at 2 o'clock at the ferry on the Canada side. All persons desiring to take stock in this prosperous company, be sure to be on hand.

By Order of the
BOARD OF DIRECTORS.

Detroit, April 19, 1853.

(courtesy State Archives of Michigan)

Winks, Robin W. *The Blacks in Canada: A History*. Montreal, Canada: McGill-Queen's University Press, 1997. 546p. Index. Notes. /GC 971 W729b/

CARIBBEAN

Bush, Barbara. *Slave Women in Caribbean Society, 1650-1838*. Bloomington, IN: Indiana University Press, 1990. 190p. Bibliography. Drawings. Index. Maps. Notes /GC 972.9 B96s/

CUBA

Perez, Louis A., Jr., ed. *Slaves, Sugar, & Colonial Society: Travel Accounts of Cuba, 1801-1899*. Wilmington, DE: Scholarly Resources, Inc., 1992. 259p. Bibliography. Index. /GC 972.91 SL1/

GRENADA

Cox, Edward L. *Free Coloreds in the Slave Societies of St. Kitts and Grenada, 1763-1833*. Knoxville, TN: The University of Tennessee Press, 1984. 197p. Bibliography. Index. Notes. /GC 972.973 C83f/

JAMAICA

Higman, B. W. *Montpelier, Jamaica: A Plantation Community in Slavery and Freedom, 1739-1912*. Mona, Jamaica: Press University of the West Indies, 1998. 384p. Bibliography. Illustrations. Index. /GC 972.92 H539m/

Patterson, Orlando. *The Sociology of Slavery: An Analysis of the Origins, Development and Structure of Negro Slave Society in Jamaica*. Jamaica, West Indies: Sangster Book Stores Limited, 1973. 310p. Appendices. Index. Maps. Notes. /GC 972.92 P27s/

Williams, Joseph J. *Whence the "Black Irish" of Jamaica?* New York: Dial Press, 1932. 97p. Bibliography. Index. Photographs. /GC 972.92 W673w/

LIBERIA

Brown, Robert T. *Immigrants to Liberia, 1843 to 1865: An Alphabetical Listing*. Philadelphia, PA: Institute for Liberian Studies, 1980. 65p. /GC 929.19 B81i/

Shick, Tom W. *Emigrants to Liberia, 1820 to 1842*. Newark, DE: University of Delaware, 1971. 111p. /GC 929.19 Sh6e/